THE GRAPHIC DESIGNERS' INDEX 11

RotoVision

CREDITS – COPYRIGHT

DUST JACKET ILLUSTRATION
ILLUSTRATION DE LA JAQUETTE
SCHUTZUMSCHLAGILLUSTRATION
. . . .

Pós Imagen Design
Rue Marquês de Sáo Vicente, 26
Gávea
Rio de Jeneiro
RJ Brazil
Tel/Fax (5521) 239 2131

BOOK DESIGN
DESIGN DU LIVRE
BUCHDESIGN
. . . .

PINEAPPLE DESIGN SA
Rue de la Consolation 56
B-1030 Brussels
Belgium
Tel. +32 (0)2 242 78 20
Fax: +32 (0)2 242 96 40

PUBLISHER
ÉDITEUR
VERLAG
. . . .

ROTOVISION SA
7, rue de Bugnon
CH-1299 Crans
Switzerland
Tel: +41 22 776 0511
Fax: +41 22 776 0889

SALES OFFICE:
Sheridan House
112-116a Western Road
Hove, East Sussex
BN3 1DD
United Kingdom
Tel: +44 (0)1273 727268
Fax: +44 (0)1273 727269

COPYRIGHT
. . . .

© 1997 ROTOVISION SA
ISBN 2-88046-288-6
Printed in Singapore

CONTENT / CONTENU / INHALT

PORTFOLIO PAGE SALES AGENTS

ARGENTINA

DOCUMENTA SRL.
Córdoba 612 entrepiso
1054 Buenos Aires
Tel. +54 1 322-9581
Fax: +54 1 326-9595
Contact: Aquiles Ferrario

AUSTRALIA

MOTIF VISION
69 Alder Way
Duncraig
WA 6023
Tel. 09-387 7798
Mobile: 041 211 4221
Contact: Peter Pendrill

AUSTRIA

INSIDER
MODELLAGENTUR
Semperstrasse 31-15
1180 Vienna
Tel. 1-479 66 22
Fax: 1-479 66 22 74
Contact: Marina Baumann

BELGIUM

SEDIP
Rue Vanderkindere 318
1180 Bruxelles
Tel. +32 2-343 44 99
Fax: +32 2-343 79 51
Contact: Mrs E. Wibaut

BRAZIL

CASA ONO COMÉRCIO E
IMPORTAÇÃO LTDA.
Rua Fernão Dias 492 - Pinheiros
São Paulo SP - CEP 05427
Tel. +55 11-813 6522
Fax: +55 11-212 6488
Contact: Hirokazu Taguchi

CHILE

BOOKMAN
Pedro de Valdivia 1781
Local 176
Santiago
Tel. +56 2-204 5172/274 9108
Fax: +56 2-204 5172
Contact:
Christian and Mirko Bulat

COLOMBIA

Carrera 63A - Nro. 60-56
Santafé de Bogota
Tel. +571 231 2314
Celular: 57 93 228 0068
Contact: Pilar Gaitan Sandoval

COSTA RICA

HEVIN PUBLIC SA
Pavas del Cementerio 100
Sur 250 Oeste, Casa 31
1200 San José
Tel. +506 231 6921
Fax: +506 231 6921
Contact: Henry Vindas Calderón

ECUADOR

LIBRI MUNDI
Juan León Mera 851
PO Box 17-01-3029
Quito
Tel. +593 2 521 606 / 544 185 /
234 791 / 529 587
Fax: +593 2 504 209
Contact:
Marcela Garcia Grosse-Luemern

FRANCE

Paris:

MM EDITIONS
31-35, rue Gambetta
F-92150 Suresnes
Tel. +33 1 41 18 86 18
Fax: +33 1 45 06 29 81
Contact: Louis Vaudeville

North-East France:

SEDIP
53, rue Jules-Ferry
F-59310 Orchies
Tel. +33 (3) 20 64 87 29
Contact: Françoise Lalanne

North-West France:

MAT CONSEIL
"Fayel"
F-35320 La Couyère
Tel. +33 (2) 99 43 19 84
Fax: +33 (2) 99 44 23 36
Contact: Graham Keysell

GREECE

STUDIO CLIP
121th Anexartisias Str.
16451 Argyroupolis, Athens
Tel. +301 996 1342/995 5374
Fax: +301 993 3334
Contact: Joanna Papadopoulou

HONG KONG

MANIFEST MARKETING LTD
16A Hollywood Centre
79-91 Queens Road West
Tel. 2915 2157
Fax: 2975 4374
Mobile: 9481 5586
bvd@hk.super.net.
Contact: Bryan VanDale

INDIA

MAGNUM BOOKS
Suite 9, "Ajanta" Chheda Nagar
Bombay-400 089
Tel. 555 26 60
Fax: 91-22-5563953
Contact: K.S. Ganesh

INDONESIA

PT GRAFINDO INTER PRIMA
32 Kwitang Road
PO Box 4215
Jakarta
Tel, 62 21 390 1613
Fax: 62 21 310 7886
Contact: Wani Kusmulyana

JAPAN

AGOSTO INC.
7F Shine Building
4-4 Kojimachi - Chiyoda-ku
Tokyo 102
Tel. 03-3262 4595
Fax: 03-3262 9463

KOREA

AHN GRAPHICS LTD
260-88 Songbuk 2-Dong
Songbuk-gu
Seoul 136-012
Tel. 02-743 80 65 / 6.
02-763 23 20
Fax: 02-743 33 52

MALAYSIA

FLO ENTERPRISES
SDN.BHD.
24 Lorong PJS 1/2A
Taman Perangsang
Batu 6, Jalan Kelang Lama
46000 Petaling Jaya
Selangor Darul Ehsan
Tel. 60 3793 3118
Fax: 60 3793 1066
Contact: Johnny Leong

MEXICO

INTERBOOKS
Juan Escutia #42
Locales E, F y G
Col. Condesa
06140 México DF
Tel. +52 5-553 1845 / 553 1402
Fax: +52 5-553 1244
Contact: María Elena Trujillo

SOMOHANO EDICIONES SA
Tenancingo #9
Col. Condesa
06140 México DF
Tel. +52 5-211 7697 / 553 3873
Fax: +52 5-212 1581
Contact: Andrea Trujillo

PHILIPPINES

MARKETING HORIZONS
Room 202 Veca Building
Pasong Tamo cor. Estrella Streets
Makati City
Metro Manilla
Tel. 63 2890 7612
Fax: 63 2890 7637
Contact: Betty B. Bravo

PORTUGAL

DESTARTE
Rua Santo António da Glória, 90
1200 Lisboa
Tel. +351 1 347 9164/347 0199
Fax: + 351 1 347 5811
Contact: Jorge Linhares

SCANDINAVIA

BOE MEDIA
Stockholmsvägen 33-35
181 33 Lidingö
Sweden
Tel. 08-767 00 15
Fax: 08-767 00 14
Contact: Barbro Olson-Ehn

SINGAPORE

*PAGE ONE - THE
DESIGNERS BOOKSHOP PTE
LTD*
Blk 4 Pasir Panjang Road
08-33 Alexandra Distripark
0511 Singapore
Tel. 65 273 0128
Fax: 65 273 0042
Contact: Mark Tan

SOUTH AFRICA

*TRUDY DICKENS
ASSOCIATION
OF MARKETEERS*
P.O. Box 98853
Sloane Park
2152 Johannesburg
Tel. 011-462 2380/706 1633
Fax: 011-706 4151
Mobile: 083-250 8635

SPAIN

INDEX BOOK SL
Consell de Cent 160 - Local 3
08015 Barcelona
Tel. +34 (3) 454 5547
Fax: +34 (3) 454 8438
indexbook@interfad.es
Contact: Sylvie Estrada

SWITZERLAND

T-CASE AG
Zollikerstrasse 19
CH-8008 Zürich
Tel./Fax: +41 1 383 4680
Contact: Katja Carazzi

TAIWAN

TANG YUNG CO.
8F-2 No. 291 Sec 2
Fu Hsing S. Road
Taipei
Tel. 886 2708 9572
Fax: 886 2703 1642
Contact: Danny Chao

UNITED KINGDOM

*INDEPENDENT SPIRIT
BUSINESS*
2nd Floor - 22 Greek Street
Soho
London W1V 5LF
Tel. (0) 171 287 4908
Fax: (0) 171 439 0559
Mobile: 0973 553082
Contact: Jonathan Roberts

URUGUAY

GRAFFITI
Convención 1366 - Local 8
CP 11100 Montevideo
Tel. +598 2-922 976
Fax: +598 2-922 976
Contact: Carlos Mañosa

VENEZUELA

*CONTEMPORÁNEA DE
EDICIONES*
Av. La Salle Cruce con Lima
Edificio Irbia - Urb. Los Caobos
1050 Caracas
Tel. +58 2-793 7591 / 793 0396
Fax: +58 2-793 6566
Contact: Luis Fernando Ramirez

REGIONAL OFFICES:
ASEAN COUNTRIES

PROVISION
1 Selegie Road N°. 08-23
Paradiz Center
Singapore 188306
Tel. 334 77 20
Fax: 334 77 21
Contact: Alice Goh

SOUTH AMERICA

*DELEGACIÓN AMÉRICA
LATINA*
Alsina 120
5147 Argüello
Córdoba
Argentina
Tel. & Fax: +54 543 20925
Contact: Alejandro Christe

GEOGRAPHICAL ALPHA INDEX

GEOGRAPHICAL ALPHA INDEX

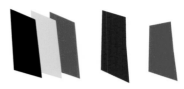

ARGENTINA
ARGENTINE
ARGENTINIEN

AUSTRALIA
AUSTRALIE
AUSTRALIA

BELGIUM/FRANCE
BELGIQUE/FRANCE
BELGIEN/FRANKREICH

BRAZIL
BRÉSIL
BRASILIEN

C H I L E   F R A N C E
C H I L I   F R A N C E
C H I L E   F R A N K R E I C H

FOBBIA DESIGNS   **32**

Isidora Goyenechea 3346
Santiago
Tel. +56 2 334 5337
Fax: +56 2 233 4779

(B3 + H2)   **154-155**

102, rue du Château
F-92100 Boulogne
Tel. +33 1 46 03 86 20
Fax: +33 1 46 05 84 31

Kantstrasse 23a
D-66111 Saarbrücken
Germany
Tel. +49 681 936 57 12
Fax: +49 681 936 57 11

ALLIANCE DESIGN   **148-149**

17, rue des Dames-Augustines
F-92200 Neuilly-sur-Seine
Tel. +33 1 41 05 73 00
Fax: +33 1 41 05 08 40

ANTARCTIQUE   **150-153**

88, boulevard de la Villette
F-75019 Paris
Tel. +33 1 44 52 52 80
Fax: +33 1 44 52 52 81

BCR   **156-157**

11-15, rue de la Rochefoucauld
F-92100 Boulogne
Tel. +33 1 48 25 95 83
Fax: +33 1 48 25 95 81

BLACK & GOLD   **158-159**

16-18, rue Quincampoix
F-75004 Paris
Tel. +33 1 48 04 33 78
Fax: +33 1 42 71 04 28

CALYPSO   **162-165**

151, rue de Billancourt
F-92100 Billancourt
Tel. +33 1 46 04 03 03
Fax: +33 1 46 04 82 64

CARRÉ NOIR   **166-167**

Square Monceau
82, boulevard des Batignolles
F-75850 Paris Cedex 17
Tel. +33 1 42 94 02 27
Fax: +33 1 42 94 06 78

CB'A   **168-169 & 240-241**

94, avenue de Villiers
F-75017 Paris
Tel. +33 1 40 54 09 00
Fax: +33 1 47 64 95 75

C'CAPITAL   **160-161**

5, passage Thiéré
F-75011 Paris
Tel. +33 1 57 00 80 00
Fax: +33 1 47 00 83 30

COCKPIT DESIGN   **170-171**

64, rue Tiquetonne
F-75002 Paris
Tel. +33 1 40 13 04 94
Fax: +33 1 40 13 07 94

DEMONIAK   **144-145**

96, rue du Faubourg-Poissonnière
F-75010 Paris
Tel. +33 1 49 70 06 06
Fax: +33 1 42 85 47 83

DESGRIPPES GOBÉ
& ASSOCIATES   **172-173**

18 bis, av. de la Motte-Picquet
F-75007 Paris
Tel. +33 1 44 18 44 18
Fax: +33 1 45 51 96 60

DESIGN BOARD   **174-177**
& 248-249

19, rue de la Dhuis
F-75020 Paris
Tel. +33 1 40 30 47 47
Fax: +33 1 40 31 03 15

Avenue Georges Lecointe, 50
B-1180 Bruxelles
Tel. +32 2 375 39 62
Fax: +32 2 375 50 48

DESIGN STRATEGY   **178-179**

41, rue Camille-Pelletan
F-92300 Levallois-Perret
Tel. +33 1 41 40 00 00
Fax: +33 1 41 40 00 01

DIALOG   **180-181**

171, quai de Valmy
F-75010 Paris
Tel. +33 1 42 05 60 60
Fax: +33 1 46 07 65 88

DIDIER SACO   **182-183**

10, rue des Jeûneurs
F-75002 Paris
Tel. +33 1 40 26 96 26
Fax: +33 1 40 26 95 26

DIEDRE DESIGN   **242-243**

89, rue Damrémont
F-75018 Paris
Tel. +33 1 42 62 51 46
Fax: +33 1 42 54 94 06

DRAGON ROUGE   **184-185**
& 250-251

32, rue Pagès, BP 83
F-92153 Suresnes Cedex
Tel. +33 1 46 97 50 00/50 62
Fax: +33 1 47 72 05 03/
46 97 50 81

EKONOS ET ASSOCIÉS   **186-187**

3, rue des Quatre-Cheminées
F-92100 Boulogne
Tel. +33 1 46 20 24 24
Fax: +33 1 46 20 01 28

EPOUDRY GUISLAIN
DESIGN   **188-189**

23, rue d'Alésia
F-75014 Paris
Tel. +33 1 45 43 05 03
Fax: +33 1 45 43 06 01

EPSIGN   **190-193**

2, rue des Tennerolles
F-92210 Saint-Cloud
Tel. +33 1 46 02 00 33
Fax: +33 1 46 02 57 23

EURO RSCG DESIGN   **194-195**

84, rue de Villiers
F-92683 Levallois-Perret Cedex
Tel. +33 1 41 34 43 60
Fax: +33 1 41 34 44 47

F R A N C E
F R A N C E
F R A N K R E I C H

EXTRÊME   196-197

127-129, rue du Mont-Cenis
F-75018 Paris
Tel. +33 1 49 25 80 50
Fax: +33 1 49 25 84 63

GBGM   252-253

28, rue Broca
F-75005 Paris
Tel. +33 1 44 08 60 61
Fax: +33 1 44 08 60 89

GRIFFE   198-199

2, rue Maurice-Hartmann
F-92137 Issy-les-Moulineaux
Tel. +33 1 40 95 27 10
Fax: +33 1 40 95 74 07

IDENTITÉS   200-201

218, boulevard Jean-Jaurès
F-92514 Boulogne Cedex
Tel. +33 1 47 61 62 80
Fax: +33 1 47 61 62 81

IG DESIGN   202-203

3 bis, rue de l'Éperon
F-75006 Paris
Tel. +33 1 44 07 24 00
Fax: +33 1 44 07 30 54

LA COMPAGNIE DESIGN   204-205

Immeuble Atria
2, rue du Centre
F-93885 Noisy-le-Grand
Tel. +33 1 43 05 00 11
Fax: +33 1 43 05 51 15

LOGIC DESIGN   206-209

140, rue Galliéni
F-92100 Boulogne
Tel. +33 1 46 04 88 04
Fax: +33 1 46 04 88 06

LONSDALE DESIGN   210-211

10, rue Jacques-Bingen
F-75017 Paris
Tel. +33 1 40 53 02 02
Fax: +33 1 40 53 02 01

MBD DESIGN   212-213

11, rue Victor-Hugo
F-93177 Bagnolet Cedex
Tel. +33 1 48 57 30 00
Fax: +33 1 48 57 41 31

MEDIA PACK   214-215

97, rue Racine
F-69100 Villeurbanne
Tel. +33 4 78 85 36 13
Fax: +33 4 78 85 35 79

ZI du Plateau
529, rue du Marché-Rollay
F-94500 Champigny sur Marne
Tel. +33 1 45 16 17 17
Fax: +33 1 45 16 35 99

MENU & ASSOCIÉS   216-217

83-87, rue de Paris
F-92100 Boulogne-Billancourt
Tel. +33 1 46 99 67 57
Fax: +33 1 48 25 93 33

MICHEL BLANC SA   244-245

1, rue d'Anjou
F-92602 Asnières
Tel. +33 1 47 90 66 87
Fax: +33 1 47 33 49 07

OVA'O   218-219

261, rue Saint-Honoré
F-75001 Paris
Tel. +33 1 40 15 97 97
Fax: +33 1 40 15 97 22

PARIS VENISE DESIGN   222-223

4 bis, rue Descombes
F-75017 Paris
Tel. +33 1 40 53 85 85
Fax: +33 1 40 53 85 84

PDA   254-255

European Packaging Design
Association
82, boulevard des Batignolles
F-75850 Paris
Tel. +33 1 42 94 02 27
Fax: +33 1 42 94 06 78

POINT MIRE   224-225

11, rue Moreau-Vauthier
F-92100 Boulogne
Tel. +33 1 46 99 18 40
Fax: +33 1 46 99 00 01

P'RÉFÉRENCE   220-221

45, rue des Apennins
F-75017 Paris
Tel. +33 1 44 85 86 00
Fax: +33 1 44 85 86 44

PUBLICIS DESIGN   226-227

25, rue Plumet
F-75015 Paris
Tel. +33 1 47 34 48 18
Fax: +33 1 47 83 51 99

RAISON PURE
INTERNATIONAL   228-229

38, rue Lantiez
F-75017 Paris
Tel. +33 1 42 63 45 45
Fax: +33 1 42 28 18 60

STYLE MARQUE   230-231

10, rue des Moulins
F-75001 Paris
Tel. +33 1 42 96 16 78
Fax: +33 1 42 60 17 10

TEAM CRÉATIF   232-233

89, rue de Miromesnil
F-75008 Paris
Tel. +33 1 42 89 90 00
Fax: +33 1 42 89 90 01

TONNERRE DE BREST !   234-235

35, rue de la Fédération
F-93100 Montreuil
Tel. +33 1 49 88 10 80
Fax: +33 1 49 88 11 43

TRAPÈZE   236-237

12, rue des Pyramides
F-75001 Paris
Tel. +33 1 42 60 73 73
Fax: +33 1 42 60 63 73

H E L L A S
RÉPUBLIQUE HELLÉNIQUE
Ä G Ä I S

**ELENI ADRIANI
ZERVOU   123**

*34 Griva Street
G-15232 Athens
Tel. +30 1 68 12 193
Fax: +30 1 68 59 663*

**STUDIO IMAGE
& GRAPHICS LTD   122**

*George Nikolaidis
36 Filevetou Street
G-17672 Athens
Tel. +30 1 95 97 480
Fax: +30 1 93 29 929*

DELEMA/TBWA   126-127

*Ioulia Papamichael
36 Grivas Dighenis Avenue
1674 Nicosia
Cyprus
Tel. +357 2 459 562
Fax: +357 2 458 136
e+mail: delema@spidernet.com.cy*

**THOMPSON
COMMUNICATIONS   124-125**

*10th Gr. Afxentiou Avenue
PO Box 291
Larnaca
Cyprus
Tel. +357 4 629 257
Fax: +357 4 627 279*

I N D O N E S I A
I N D O N É S I E
I N D O N E S I E N

GELSONS'S TRIJAYA UTAMA   96

*Jeferey Manza
JL. Prapanca Raya No. 108
12150 Jakarta
Tel. +62 21 723 6773
Fax: +62 21 721 0344*

PT. ADWITIYA ALEMBANA   94

*Riswanto Ramelan
Gedung Fortune 3
JL. Ampera Raya #37
12560 Jakarta
Tel. +62 21 789 2154
Fax: +62 21 789 2157*

PT. WADHIA BALA   95

*Ronald Pakpahan
JL. Radio IV / 18
12130 Jakarta
Tel. +62 21 721 1084
Fax: +62 21 725 0349*

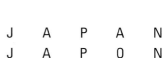

J A P A N
J A P O N
J A P A N

AGOSTO INC.   75

*Shine Bldg 7F, 4-4 Kojimachi
Chiyoda-ku
J-102 Tokyo
Tel. +81 3 3262 4595
Fax: +81 3 3262 9463*

CREATIVE SANO JAPAN   70-71

*3-17 Kandajinbo-cho
Chiyoda-ku
J-101 Tokyo
Tel. +81 3 5276 2841/2842
Fax: +81 3 5276 2843*

NAYUTA CO. LTD.   67

*Ichiteru Bld. 3-1-3 Misaki-cho
Chiyoda-ku
J-101 Tokyo
Tel. +81 3 3222 0701
Fax: +81 3 3222 1955*

OSHIMA JIMUSHO   74

*7-11-11 4F, Tsukiji
Chuo-ku
J-104 Tokyo
Tel. +81 3 3541 7977
Fax: +81 3 3541 7074*

T & R INC   68-69

*Fukumatsu Bld. 8 & 9F, 7-1
Sumiyoshi-cho
Shinjuku-ku
J-162 Tokyo
Tel. +81 3 3226 8021
Fax: +81 3 3226 7854*

T-BREAK INC   72-73

*Green Terrace Tomigaya 102
2-13-11 Tomigaya, Shibuya-ku
J-151 Tokyo
Tel. +81 3 3466 4476
Fax: +81 3 3466 4477*

M A L A Y S I A
M A L A I S I E
M A L A Y S I A

**CAUSE-COLYBRAND
CONSULTING SDN. BHD.   80**

*Nor Raphil Abdul Rahan
Suite 15-01 15th Floor IGB Plaza
Jalan Kampar off Jalan
Tun Razak
50400 Kuala Lumpur
Tel. +60 3 443 7873
Fax: +60 3 443 2027*

**FIXGO ADVERTISING
(M) SDN. BHD.   79**

*Allan Tan
28 Jalan SS 19/1D
Subang Jaya
47500 Petaling Jaya
Tel. +60 3 733 6596
Fax: +60 3 733 1857*

**MUSTAFA ZAHIDIN
GROUP   78**

*Muhammad Farid Abdullah
93c Jalan SS 21/60 Damansara
Utama
47400 Petaling Jaya
Tel. +60 3 719 1004
Fax: +60 3 719 1005*

M E X I C O
M E X I Q U E
M E X I K O

AGUILERA AGUILAR, MIGUEL ANGEL 38

Sor Juana Ines de la Cruz 15
Dept 4
Santa Mariá la Ribera
06400 México DF
Tel. +52 5 547 3918
Fax: +52 5 547 0119

AGUILERA ARTE GRAFICO 49

Halcones #112
Col. Lomas de Guadalupe
01720 México DF
Tel. +52 5 635 2457
Fax: +52 5 635 2474

ALTA RESOLUCIÓN GRÁFICA DE MÉXICO SA CV 37

Francisco Petrarca 336/302
Polanco
11570 México DF
Tel. +52 5 203 2011/284 1584
Fax: +52 5 254 3536

ARMO DISEÑO SA DE CV 36

Necaxa 165
Col Portales
03300 México DF
Tel. +52 5 539 8825
Fax: +52 5 609 0043

ARQUITECTURA TERRENAL SA DE CV 51

Arq. Gerardo Mejia Salgado
Juan Aldama No. 400 sur
San Mateo Oxtotitlan
Toluca, Edo Méx
Tel. +52 721 78 00 78
Fax: +52 721 78 00 78

ARTE-2 TECNODISEÑO Y COMUNICACIÓN 48

V. Río Becerra 26-1
Col. San Pedro de los Pinos
03800 México DF
Tel. +52 5 271 4465
Fax: +52 5 271 0362

COLOR TECNIC LAB SA DE CV 45

Sergio Montes Resendiz -
Luiggi Curiel
Garrido 276
Colonia Tepeyac Insurgentes
07020 México DF
Tel. +52 5 577 4132
Fax: + 52 5 781 8412

DIRECT MARKETING GROUP 44

Grupo Imagen
Vasco de Quiroga 1800, 1er Piso
Colonia Santa Fé
01210 México DF
Tel. +52 5 257 1600/257 0030
Fax: +52 5 257 0460

DISEÑO INTEGRAL DIFUSION SA DE CV 34

Tlacoquemetatl 123-6o piso
Col. del Valle
03100 México DF
Tel. +52 5 575 3806
Fax: +52 5 575 7671

ESTAFETA MEXICANA SA DE CV 35

Praga No. 31 1er
Col Juarez
06600 México DF
Tel. +52 5 208 9105/325 9157
Fax: +52 5 208 9118

GRUPO MH DISEÑO COMUNICACIÓN 47

Diagonal de Patriotismo 1
06170 México DF
Tel. +52 5 273 9292
Fax: +52 5 277 9702

INDUSTRIARTE 39

Lazaro Cardenas #15
Col. El Mirador,
54080 México DF
Tel. +52 5 736 0441
Fax: +52 5 786 0427

LA MAQUINA DE GUTENBERG SA DE CV 41

Francisco Mazquez Garcia
Jalapa 87
Valle Ceylan
54150 Estado de México
Tel. +52 5 389 8190/391 6705
Fax: +52 5 391 6705

MACIAS PICHARDO, ENRIQUE 50

Cuernavaca 114 - 401
Col. Condesa
06140 México DF
Tel. +52 5 553 0102
Fax: +52 5 553 9040

MUCHO RUIDO 42

Ricardo Calderón - Arturo Perez
Ríos V,
Plazuela de Reyes 123
Los Reyes Coyoacan
03100 México DF
Tel. +52 5 617 7314/619 3000

RUIZ GONZÁLEZ, JORGE LUIZ 40

Esbozo Estudio SA de CV
Atlanta 134-201
Col. Cd de Los Deportes
03870 México DF
Tel./Fax: +52 5 563 9514

SALAMANDRA DISEÑADORES 43

Yolanda Ramirez - Mario Lazo
Darwin 18, 1° Piso,
Col Anzures
11590 México DF
Tel. +52 5 254 5551
Fax: +52 5 533 0130

TOLONE, DIANA GARCIA BELLO DE 52

Tolone & Asociados
Ac. Fuentes Brotantes No. 35
Fracc. Vista del Valle
Naucalpan
53290 México
Tel. +52 5 364 1309
Fax: +52 5 364 1100

UNI CONSULTORES EN DISEÑO S.C. 46

Pisa No. 10, Atizapán
Edo. de México
54500 México DF
Tel. +52 5 308 2592/808 0554

N O R W A Y
N O R V È G E
N O R W E G E N

P H I L I P P I N E S
P H I L I P P I N E S
P H I L I P P I N E N

P O R T U G A L
P O R T U G A L
P O R T U G A L

S I N G A P O R E
S I N G A P O U R
S I N G A P U R

NORWAY

**BRUNO OLDANI
AS DESIGNSTUDIO   280-285**

*Bygdøy allé 28 B
N-0265 Oslo
Tel. +47 22 55 01 26
Fax: +47 22 56 02 01*

DÉVILLE DESIGN AS   286-287

*Parkveien 62A
N-0254 Oslo
Tel. +47 22 12 82 50
Fax: +47 22 55 18 20*

PHILIPPINES

CREATIVE RESPONSE   118

*Irene Silos
2411 Cityland 10, Tower 11
6817 H.V. Dela Costa Street
Salcedo Village
1227 Makati City
Tel. (632) 893 7662
Fax: (632) 893 7851*

**GRAPHIC ATELIER (MANILA),
INC.   114-115**

*Margarita Delgado-Guingona
6th Floor, Salamin Building
197 Salcedo Street
1200 Makati
Metro Manila
Tel. (632) 818 5634/37/38
Fax: (632) 818 5624*

**MEGA PACIFIC GRAPHIC
DESIGN, INC.   119**

*Marvi Yap
18th Floor, Strata 100 Bldg.
Emerald Avenue, Ortigas Center
1605 Pasig City
Tel. (632) 633 3884/631 4730
633 4879/633 8792/633 4787
633 4786/631 2859/633 4785
Fax: (632) 631 2862*

**UNA GRAPHICA MANILA,
INC.   116-117**

*Gina Ysip-Manalang
W-1203 B Philippine Stock
Exchange Center
Exchange Road, Ortiga Center
Pasig City
Metro Manila
Tel. (direct line): (632) 633 6365
Tel. (632) 635 6349
635 6350/635 6634
Fax: (632) 633 6365*

PORTUGAL

**AFINAL DESIGN & PUBLICATION
LDA   303**

*Rua Candido
de Figueiredo, 78-2° Dto.
P-1500 Lisboa
Tel. +351 1 774 3916
Fax: +351 1 778 8281*

ANTERO FERREIRA   294-295

*Rua de Roriz 203
P-4100 Porto
Tel. +351 2 610 4657
Fax: +351 2 610 4757*

**ANTONIO QUEIROZ
DESIGN   300-301**

*Av. Comendador Ferreira
de Matos 68-2° Fte.
P-4450 Matosinhos
Tel. +351 2 938 352 5139
Fax: +351 2 938 35 31*

ATELIER DO SUL   302

*Esplanada de Santa Maria
P-8100 Boliqueime
Tel. +35 1 89 366 123
Fax: +35 1 89 366 439*

**CAIXA ALTA DESENHO
GRAFICO   298-299**

*R Américo Durão, Lote 14-A 1°
P-1900 Lisboa
Tel. +351 1 849 90 70
Fax: +351 1 847 23 90*

HOMO HABILIS   292-293

*Rua da Meditação, 48-3°
P-4150 Porto
Tel. +351 2 600 64 16
Fax: +351 2 600 64 16*

MACHADO, JOÃO   296-297

*Rua Padre Xavier Countinho 125
P-4150 Porto
Tel. +351 2 610 37 72
Fax: +351 2 610 37 72*

**JONES & JONES
(COMMUNIQUÉ)   290-291**

*Rua Nova 3 Loja B
P-8100 Boliqueime*

SINGAPORE

**AC GRAPHICS WORKSHOP
PTE LTD   88**

*Alan Chew
28 Kallang Place #03-15
1233 Singapore
Tel. +65 294 4688
Fax: +65 294 6162*

**CRUNCH
COMMUNICATIONS   82-83**

*K.H. Simm
213 Henderson Rd
#03-11 Henderson Ind Park
159553 Singapore
Tel. +65 272 3222
Fax: +65 272 8522*

IMMORTAL DESIGN   84-85

*Saxone Woon
10 Jiak Chuan Road
089264 Singapore
Tel. +65 227 9406
Fax: +65 227 7026*

LANCER DESIGN PTE LTD   86-87

*Mark Phooi
2 IMM Bldg
Jurong East St. 21 #05-26
609601 Singapore
Tel. +65 562 4756
Fax: +65 567 7688*

SOUTH AFRICA
AFRIQUE DU SUD
SÜDAFRIKA

SPAIN
ESPAGNE
SPANIEN

EMS   61

PO Box 650831
Benmore
SA-2010 Sandton
Tel. 011 883 3513
Fax: 011 883 1781

**IMAGINATION
CORPORATION   58-59**

PO Box 4919
Rivonia
SA-2128 Sandton
Tel. 011 8073470
Fax: 011 8073225

ORANGE MARKETING   64

PO Box 10056
Caledon Square
SA-7905 Cape Town
Tel. 021 4616173
Fax: 011 4616174

**PATON TUPPER ASSOCIATES -
NATAL (PTY) LTD   62-63**

Po Box 433
SA-4000 Durban
Tel. 031 207 3121

THE GRAPHIC SHACK   60

PO Box 16379
Vlaeberg
SA-8018 Cape Town
Tel. 021 238 6088

**ACCIÓN COMPAÑÍA DE SERVICIOS
DE PUBLICIDAD SL   354-355**

c/Doctor Domack 3, 20 Pta. 8
E-46006 Valencia
Tel. +34 6 334 1077
Fax: +34 6 334 1091

ALCOGRAF SL   356-357

Ctra de Ayora S/N
E-02640 Almansa (Albacete)
Tel. +34 67 340 611
Fax: +34 67 340 344

ALTO CONTRASTE SL   324-325

Cochabamba 24
E-28016 Madrid
Tel./Fax: +34 1 458 8892

**ANTONIO LAX DISEÑADOR
SL   330-331**

Castelló 38 4°D
E-28001 Madrid
Tel. +34 1 435 7138
Fax: +34 1 435 3597

ARKÉ 144 SL   332-333

Glorieta de Bilbao No. 5, 4° Izda
E-28004 Madrid
Tel. +34 1 447 6878
Fax: +34 1 447 6768

**ARTECHE,
MARIO GAZTELU-ITURRI   313**

Luchana 4-3° Dpto 1
E-48008 Bilbao
Tel./Fax: +34 3 416 6057

**ASOCIACIÓN DE DISEÑADORES
DE LA COMUNIDAD
VALENCIANA   345**

S. Vicente 35, 4A
E-46002 Valencia
Tel. +34 6 351 0028
Fax: +34 6 394 0842

BORRON S.COOP   334-335

Moratin 52-4
E-28014 Madrid
Tel. +34 1 429 2426
Fax: +34 1 429 7595

**CABODEVILLA
ASOCIADOS SL   316-317**

Avenida Carlos III, 11 2° dcha
E-31002 Pamplona
Tel. +34 48 22 05 43
Fax: +34 48 22 02 10

**CELMA & DURAN
ASSOCIATS   388**

Ramon Turro No. 101 2° 2a
E-08005 Barcelona
Tel. +34 3 300 9184
Tel. +34 3 300 3728

**CLAM SERVICIOS
INTEGRALES SL   322-323**

c/Londres 17
Bajo Izquierda
E-28028 Madrid
Tel. +34 1 356 0137
Fax: +34 1 356 0137

CONCEPTE I FORMA SL   348-349

Plaza del angel, 2 pta. 6
E-46450 Benifaió (Valencia)
Tel. +34 6 178 1671
Fax: +34 6 179 4713

COSMIC   378-379

Arbau 153 5°A
E-08036 Barcelona
Tel. +34 3 410 9988
Tel. +34 3 410 6602

COTA CERO SCV   350-351

Calle San Fernando 55
Enlo Izqda.
E-03001 Alicante
Tel. +34 6 520 7237
Fax: +34 6 520 6254

CUSTOM GRAPHICS SL   336-337

Nuñez de Balboa 49, 6 pta 63
E-28001 Madrid
Tel. +34 1 578 3047
Fax: +34 1 578 2832

DAVID RUIZ & COMPANY   366-367

Enric Granadou 135 2° 1°
E-08008 Barcelona
Tel. +34 3 218 1115
Fax: +34 3 416 0183

DI 7   340-341

Antoni Torrandell 17
Binissalem, Palma
E-07350 Mallorca, Islas Baleares
Tel. +34 71 37 03 48

DIGRAF   338

Costa Rica 13 1° A3
E-28016 Madrid
Tel. +34 1 345 1576
Fax: +34 1 345 1044

DOBLE SENTIDO   308-309

Lehendakari Aguirre 133
E-48015 Bilbao
Tel. +34 4 476 1161
Fax: +34 4 476 0394

E DE P   360

Folgueroles, 15 Bajos 2a
E-08022 Barcelona
Tel. +34 3 212 4563
Fax: +34 3 418 2648

**EDIZIO GRAFIKOA
ZUBIAURRE   312**

Santa Klara 40 3°
E-20870 Elgoibar-Gipúzkoa
Tel. +34 43 74 44 44
Fax: +34 43 74 44 44

EIDOLOGIC   376-377

República Argentina 28 Pai Esc.
Isquierda
E-08023 Barcelona
Tel. +34 3 434 0974

EQUIPO GUÍA   352-353

Avenida de Alcoy n° 3
E-03560 Campello (Alicante)
Tel. +34 6 563 4625
Fax: +34 6 563 6373

ERIC MILET GRAPHIC DESIGN   339

Gran Via, 68 3°G
E-28013 Madrid
Tel. +34 1 559 7277
Fax: +34 1 548 0117

S P A I N
E S P A G N E
S P A N I E N

ESPLUGA, DAVID   370-371

Enric Granados, 135 Atico 1a
E-08008 Barcelona
Tel. +34 3 218 7408
Fax: +34 3 218 9971

ESTILOGRAFICO, S. COOP   318-319

Santa Ines 8 (Jardines Argatxa)
E-20600 Eibar
Tel. +34 43 10 00 38
Fax: +34 43 10 67 60

ESTUDIO FEELING SL   362-363

Troneta 20 2°
E-03203 Elche (Alicante)
Tel. +34 6 542 4826
Fax: +34 6 545 9044

FERNÁNDEZ, PACO   326-327

General Palanca 42, Atico.
E-28045 Madrid
Tel. +34 1 528 1207

HORIXE SL   321

Manuel Iribarre 12 - 14 Lonja
E-31008 Pamplona
Tel. +34 48 17 27 09
Fax: +34 48 17 17 24

ILUNE DISEÑO   310-311

Marcelo Celayeta 75 Ofic. 10
E-31014 Pamplona
Tel. +34 48 14 39 80
Fax: +34 48 14 39 80

K J PACKAGING SL   358-359

Plaza Ramon Contreras
Mongrell, 8
E-46019 Valencia
Tel. +34 6 365 5678
Fax: +34 6 365 5701

L & A DISEÑO   320

Virgen de Begona 10
E-48006 Bilbao
Tel. +34 4 479 0429
Fax: +34 4 412 9066

**MARTÍN & GUTIERREZ
SCP   374-375**

Plaza Colon 24 1° 1°
E-08002 Barcelona
Tel. +34 3 301 5659
Fax: +34 3 301 5283

MIX TECNOLOGIES SL   342-343

Miguel Santanoreu, 4 2° 1
E-07006 Palma de Mallorca
Islas Baleares
Tel. +34 71 770 710

**NACHO LAVERNIA Y ASOCIADOS
DISEÑO INDUSTRIAL Y GRAFICO
SL   346-347**

Justicia No,1 Entresuelo 2°
E-46003 Valencia
Tel. +34 6 352 2422
Fax: +34 6 352 4855

NEXT   372-373

Passeig de Gracia 62, 3° 2a
E-08007 Barcelona
Tel. +34 3 487 2269
Fax: +34 3 487 2184

NUÑEZ, PATI   368-369

Sant Agustí No. 5 4° 1a
E-08012 Barcelona
Tel. +34 3 415 2577
Fax: +34 3 415 0248

ONNO COMUNICACION SL   381

Sant Antoni Maria Claret 24 2°
E-08037 Barcelona
Tel. +34 3 459 3538
Fax: +34 3 459 3341

PEDRAGOSA, JUAN   384-385

Cartagena 245 3° B
E-08025 Barcelona
Tel. +34 3 450 1953
Fax: +34 3 348 0119

**SERVICIOS SISTEMAS GRAFICOS
SA   382-383**

Ballester 27-29 entlo 1a
E-08023 Barcelona
Tel. +34 3 418 7462
Fax: +34 3 418 2797

SIDE-ART   380

Sant Antoni Maria Claret 24 2°
E-08037 Barcelona
Tel. +34 3 459 3538
Fax: +34 3 459 3341

SORMEN CREATIVOS SA   314-315

Andalucia 2, bajo
E-01003 Vitoria Gasteiz
Tel. +34 45 27 01 55
Fax: +34 45 27 01 55

SPARRING PARTNERS   386-387

Muntaner 472, entlo 4a
E-08006 Barcelona
Tel. +34 3 202 1020
Fax: +34 3 201 3655

**STUDIO GRAFICO PUBLIBI
SL   306-307**

P. Zumaburu 14 bajo
E-20160 Lasarte Gipúzkoa
Tel. +34 43 360 206/7
Fax: +34 43 360 205

TEIGA, XOSÉ   344

Joaquin Costa 24, 3°
E-36001 Pontevedra
Tel. +34 08 087 132

TRAPPING SL   328-329

Calle Zurbano 261° Dcha
E-28010 Madrid
Tel. +34 1 310 1030
Fax: +34 1 310 1030

VECTOR GRAPHIC   361

Rambla Cataluyna No. 120 entlo
E-08008 Barcelona
Tel. +34 3 415 9110
Fax: +34 3 237 8265

ZONA DE COMUNICACIO   364-365

Gran Via de los Corts Catalanes
640 1° 1a
E-08007 Barcelona
Tel. +34 3 412 3567
Fax: +34 3 412 7106

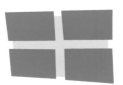

S W E D E N
S U È D E
S C H W E D E N

**DETONATOR DESIGN
GROUP   268-269**

Slipg. 3
S-117 39 Stockholm
Tel. +46 8 629 55 33

F PLUS +   270-271

Själagårdsg. 8a
S-111 31 Stockholm
Tel. +46 8 21 31 31

GHETTO DESIGN   266-267

Svartensg. 4
S-116 20 Stockholm
Tel. +46 644 44 04 702

**GULD & GRÖNA
SKOGAR   276-277**

Munkbro 9
S-111 28 Stockholm
Tel. +46 8 23 03 75

OMNIBUS TYPOGRAFI   274-275

Box 135
S-135 23 Tyresö
Tel. +46 742 83 36

P. GRÖN DESIGN   264-265

Rättviksvägen 24, Box 17
S-790 20 Grycksbo
Tel. +46 23 400 06

SANDLER MÄRGEL   272-273

Rädmansgatan 57
S-113 60 Stockholm
Tel. +46 8 30 30 58

SLITZ   261

Åsvägen 7
S-171 37 Solna
Tel. +46 8 240 240

STUDIO BUBBLAN   262-263

7:e Villag 28
S-502 44 Borås
Tel. +46 33 41 44 41

T A I W A N
T A Ï W A N
T A I W A N

UNITED KINGDOM
GRANDE-BRETAGNE
GROSSBRITANNIEN

V E N E Z U E L A
V É N É Z U É L A
V E N E Z U E L A

ARTONE PHOTO & DESIGN
ASSOCIATES LTD   99

4F No 5 Alley 6
Lane 222
Tun Hua N. Rd
Taipei
Tel. +886 02 712 3722
Fax: +886 02 712 0728

E. BA & TAN ADVERTISING CO.
LTD   100-101

no 7-1 Lane 146 Sec 1
Hsin Sheng S. Rd
Taipei
Tel. +886 02 394 273
Fax: +886 02 394 2743

GREEN FINGERS DESIGN
CO.   102-105

Jack S.H. Yang
no 151-15 Sec 5
Minsheng East Rd
Taipei
Tel. +886 02 761 7927
Fax: +886 02 761 7925

TANG YUNG CO LTD   108-109

8F-2 No 291 Sec 2
Fu Hsing S Rd
Taipei
Tel. +886 02 708 909
Fax: +886 02 703 1642

T TWO PHOTOGRAPHY
& DESIGN FIRM   111

1F No 33 Sec 2
Keelung Rd
Taipei
Tel. +886 02 377 324
Fax: +886 02 377 0149

VIVID ADVERTISING CO.
LTD   106-107

6F-1 No 6 Chin Hwa Street
Hsin Chu City
Tel. +886 03 531 7423
Fax: +886 03 712 7420

ART 2 GO   130-131

7 Barton Road
London W14 9HB
Tel. 0171 386 7316

COLE, NICHOLAS   132

Link House
2 Norfolk Square
Brighton
East Sussex BN1 2PB
Tel. 01273 730072
Fax: 01273 730002

CREMADES GOMEZ Y ASOCIADOS
CA   54-55

Edificio Torre Humboldt, Piso 17,
Ofc.17-12
Avenida Rio Caura, Urb. Parque
Hunboldt
1080 Caracas
Tel. +58 2 976 1140/976 2403/
976 4837/976 6237
Fax: +58 2 976 2165

ARGENTINA
ARGENTINE
ARGENTINIEN

▼

FERRARI CHIAPPA SRL

Hipólito Yrigoyen 2411
7600. Mar del Plata
República Argentina
Telefax 54. 23. 92-1498

ferrari
chiappa

Alejandro ESTEVEZ
Socio gerente
Director de cuentas

Leandro CHIAPPA
Socio gerente
Director de arte

Guillermo VIERA CHAVARRI
Director de arte

Mario GEMIN
Director de arte asociado

Pablo ALAGUIBE
Redactor

Raúl POLLINI
Director de fotografía

Silvina SANCHIS
Directora de marketing

FILOSOFIA DE LA EMPRESA

Primero: La comunicación como un plano de gestión integral, articulada y permanente. Sea cual fuere el nivel de complejidad de la empresa o institución.

Segundo: Un acuerdo entre cliente y agencia. Se establece una base desde donde partirán todos los mensajes, conformando un sistema de identidad coherente.

Luego la acción. La absoluta obligación de proponer lo inesperado, superador, efectivo. En un contexto que no suele dar segundas oportunidades, golpes únicos. Toda inversión debe dar resultados. Todo imprevisto debe resolverse. Respuestas creativas coordinadas en una estrategia global

AREAS DE ESPECIALIZACION

Imagen corporativa, packaging, folletería, diseño editorial. Stand y punto de venta, producto. Desarrollo de estrategia creativa. Redacción. Planificación de medios. Acciones en vía pública y punto de venta.

PRINCIPALES CLIENTES

Arellano / Mateyko (Producciones)
Amanecer S.A (Industria láctea)
Arre Beef S.A. (Frigorífico)
Correo Argentino (en Mar del Plata)
Fazio S.A. (Audio Video Hogar)
Gris (Museum Shop)
La Primera Alborada (Capitalización y ahorro)
Los Vasquitos (Haras y stud)
Mar del Plata Aquarium (Oceanario)
Midachi (Trio cómico)
Murhuen Producciones (Espectáculos)
Seba S.A. (Concesionario oficial Volkswagen)
Teach (Instituto de informática para niños)
Teatro Auditorium (Mar del Plata)
Tio Curzio (Eventos especiales)
Torres de Manantiales (Hotel)
Villa Victoria Ocampo (Mar del Plata)

FACTURACION

En el período comprendido entre enero y diciembre de 1995: u$s 1.107.000.-

PREMIOS

Estrella de Mar 1995 a la mejor imagen gráfica. Para el espectáculo Romeo y Julieta

FECHA DE CREACION

28 de agosto de 1989

LA PRIMERA ALBORADA
Identidad corporativa

CORREO ARGENTINO
Símbolo para el servicio
de venta de estampillas y
retiro de correspondencia
a domicilio

FRIGORIFICO ARRE BEEF
Identidad corporativa

TOP BEEF
Envases de hamburguesas
cuatro variedades

TEATRO AUDITORIUM
Programas mensuales
año 1995 y 1996

Colombo
DISEÑO
TALLER DE COMUNICACION E IMAGEN

Management

Carlos Alberto Colombo
Director Creativo

María Laura Ferreyra
Asistente de Cuentas

Mercedes Argimón
Secretaria Administrativa

Bettina Ospital
Conrado Pirosanto
Juan Martín Colombo
Diseñadores Gráficos

Lavalle 166 5º piso B
Capital Federal, Buenos Aires.
C.P: 1047. ARGENTINA
Tel/fax: (54-1) 312-0650
(54-1) 311-4257
(54-1) 446-4322

PRINCIPIOS

Nuestra tarea está concebida para responder a un concepto integral de comunicación, donde todas las variables - publicidad, promoción, marketing directo, packaging, señalética - se unen para que la organización comunique un mensaje único y propio.

A través de la excelencia creativa en el diseño y la producción, los distintos mensajes gráficos que generamos confluyen en los objetivos y estrategias de marketing de nuestros clientes.

CALIDAD TOTAL

La calidad es un concepto que se extiende más allá de nuestros trabajos. Así abarca:

El servicio, con un trato de persona a persona con nuestros clientes.

La respuesta, acordes a las velocidades de las decisiones actuales.

El compromiso con el cliente y sus expectativas.

La búsqueda permanente de nuevas soluciones para los mismos problemas.

SERVICIOS

Desarrollo de identidad corporativa.
Diseño de packaging.
Publicidad gráfica: afiches, folletos, catálogos, desarrollo de promociones y material P.O.P.
Ilustraciones y fotografía publicitaria e industrial por digitación computada.
Desarrollo de embalajes.
Fotocromía.
Impresiones: cromolitografía, offset, huecograbado y flexografía.

CLIENTES PRINCIPALES

Nestlé Argentina S.A., Arcor S.A.I.C., Parker Pen Argentina S.A.,
Esnaola e Hijos S.A., Peñaflor S.A., Johnson & Johnson de Argentina S.A., G & M S.A., Banco Transandino S.A., Revear S.A.

EQUIPO

Contamos con cuatro centros de diseño y edición Apple Macintosh de última generación tanto en hard como software y una impresora láser color de alta definición.

PRINCIPLES

We have conceived our task in response to the need of an integral communication concept where all variables - advertising, publicity, direct marketing. packaging, signal systems - work as a whole leading to a unique and appropriate message from the organization.

Through the outstanding creative performance in design and production, the different graphic messages that we produce, converge on our client's marketing target and strategies.

TOTAL QUALITY

Quality is a concept that involves every aspect of our work.
Thus including:
The service, with a personal treatment with our clients.
The timely answer required for present decision makings.
Full commitment with the client and his espectations.
The constant search for solutions to the same problems.

SERVICES

Corporative indentity development.
Packaging design.
Graphic advertising: posters, leaflets, catalogues, publicity development, and P.O.P. material.
Advertising and Industrial illustrations and photography, with digital image.
Packaging development.
Photochromy.
Printing: chromolithography, offset, photogravure and flexography.

MAIN CLIENTS

Nestle Argentina S.A., Arcor S.A.I.C., Parker Pen Argentina S.A., Esnaola e Hijos S.A.,
Peñaflor S.A., Johnson & Johnson de Argentina S.A., G & M S.A., Banco Transandino S.A., Revear S.A.

EQUIPO

Four Apple Macintosh last generation desing and edition centers with the latest hardware and software systems, and laser color high definition printer.

DISEÑO
TALLER DE COMUNICACION E IMAGEN

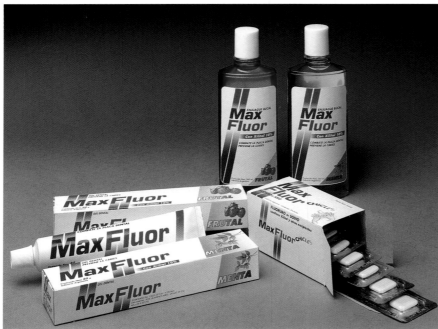

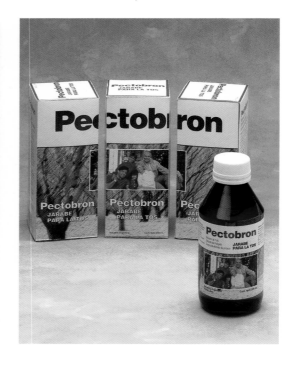

LUIS MARIA DUBOIS

▼ ▼ ▼ ▼ ▼ ▼ ▼ ▼ ▼ ▼ ▼ ▼ ▼ ▼

Capdevila 3233 PB "3"
1431 Buenos Aires
Argentina
Tel: +54 1 543 7881

B R A Z I L

B R É S I L

B R A S I L I E N

▼

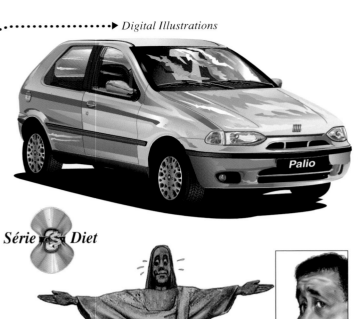

Digital Illustrations

Série Diet

PETRO METAL

GRUPO DE DANÇA DC

GUTE'S
ecological ride

TOP Tennis
OPEN DE SQUASH

DE 02 A 11 DE JUNHO
LOCAL: TOP TENNIS

ORGANIZA O:
TOP TENNIS

IQUE PROMOÇÕES LTDA

Rua Santa Luzia, 799/502
Centro - Rio de Janeiro - Brazil
CEP 20030-040
Tel. & Fax: 55 21 252 1972 - 262 0487 - 253 9764
Celular: 55 21 984 8996

● Digital Illustrations ● Design
● Corporate Identity and Logotypes ● Brochures
● Record Covers ● Posters

● Editorial Illustrations ● Caricatures ● Cartoons
● 3 D Caricatures ● Comics and
Character development to advertising editorial

IQUE PROMOÇÕES LTDA

Rua Vice Governador Rubens Berardo, 65
Bloco 02 - Apto 303 - Gávea
CEP: 22430-070 - Rio de Janeiro - Brasil
Tel.& Fax: 55 21 512 3116
Celular: 55 21 984 8996

●Digital Illustrations ● Design
●Corporate Identity and Logotypes ● Brochures
●Record Covers ● Posters

●Editorial Illustrations ● Caricatures ● Cartoons
● 3 D Caricatures ● Comics and
Character development to advertising editorial

1

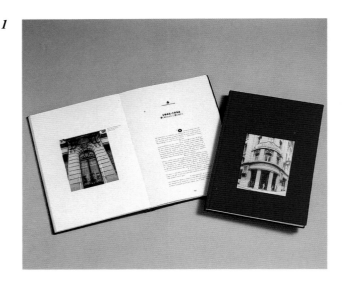

3

2

5

4

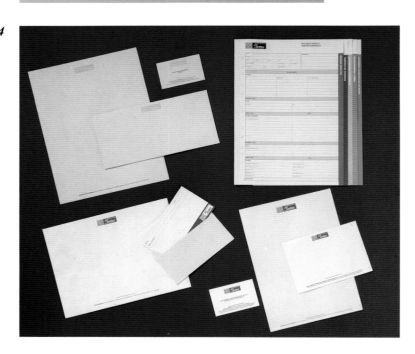

TRIO

▾ ▾ ▾ ▾ ▾ ▾ ▾ ▾ ▾ ▾ ▾ ▾ ▾

Projeto Gráfico
Rua Arnaldo Quintela, 106 22280-070 Rio de Janeiro RJ Brazil
Tels. (021) 542 4948 / 542 4339 Fax: (021) 542 1913

1-Livro comemorativo do Primeiro Centenário da Sul América Seguros; 2-Mala direta, display e láminas dobráveis (origami), para o restaurante japonês Kotobuki Lake; 3-Catálogo com mostruário de couros para e Pelle; 4-Logotipo e impressos diversos para o Hospital Pró-Cardíaco; 5-Marcas para C&M Promoções Culturais, VCF Representações e para o Restaurante Happy Ours.

KAZUKO SUZUKI SATO

▼ ▼ ▼ ▼ ▼ ▼ ▼ ▼ ▼ ▼ ▼ ▼ ▼

K.S. Design
Praça Generoso Marques, 102
Galeria Heisler, Conj. 123
Cep. 80020-250
Curitiba-Parana
Brazil
Tel: (041) 233-0905
Fax: (041) 233-0905

Product Design
Visual Communication

Package Design
Environmental Design

INNOVADESIGN

▼ ▼ ▼ ▼ ▼ ▼ ▼ ▼ ▼ ▼ ▼ ▼ ▼ ▼

PRAIA DO FLAMENGO, 66/B/1204, 1205, 1206
CEP 22.228-900 - FLAMENGO - RIO DE JANEIRO - RJ - BRAZIL
TEL./FAX: 55.21.205-0443
http://www.innovadesign.com.br

Design

Propaganda

Suporte de Marketing

Design

Advertising

Marketing Support

C H I L E

C H I L I

C H I L E

▼

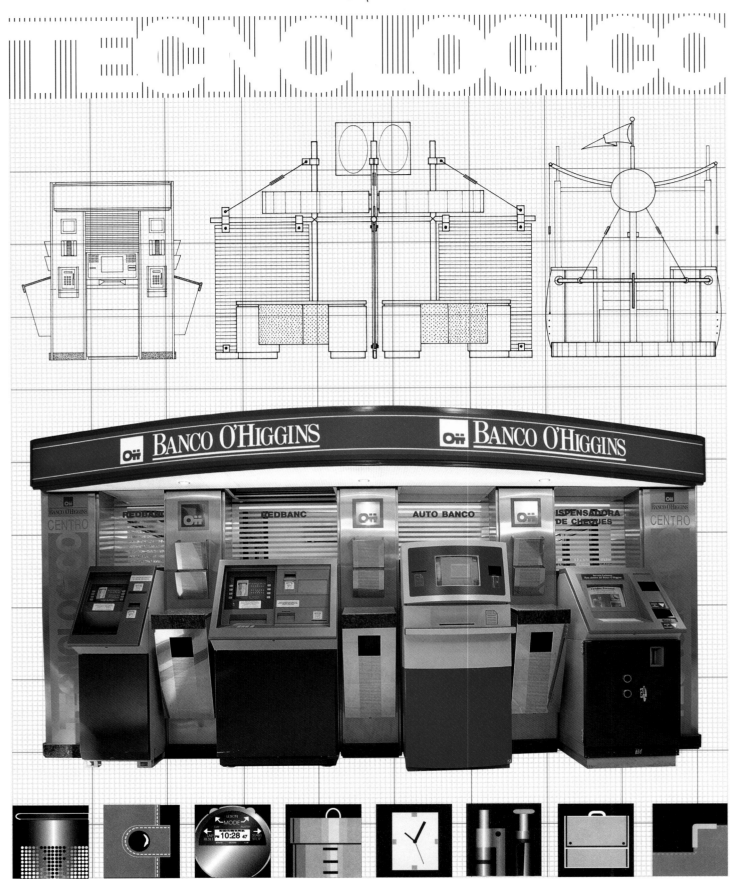

CENTRO DE DISEÑO E INTERIORISMO

REALIZACIONES AL FIN DEL SIGLO

M E X I C O

M E X I Q U E

M E X I K O

▼

SERVICIOS DE
MERCADOTECNIA
una división del Grupo Estafeta

Praga #31- 1er piso Col. Júarez,
C.P. 06600 México, D.F.
Tel: 325 91 03 /325 91 37 Fax: 208 91 88

Lic. Diego Ortiz-Monasterio / Director

campaña otoño 1995 / **Estafeta**

campaña otoño 1996 / **Estafeta**

Planes de Mercadotecnia

Programas de usuario frecuente

Mercadotecnia uno a uno

Publicidad y Comunicación

Líder de Mensajería y Paquetería

EDGARDO LÓPEZ GARCÍA, FEDERICO CASTELLANOS VAN RHIJN
▼ ▼ ▼ ▼ ▼ ▼ ▼ ▼ ▼ ▼ ▼ ▼ ▼ ▼ ▼

ARMO DISEÑO, S.A. DE C.V.
Necaxa 165
Col. Portales
C.P. 03300 México D.F.
Tel: (525) 539 8825
Fax: (525) 609 0043
armodi@.data.net.mx

Empresa especializada en diseño
y producción de promoción en sitio, displays,
punto de venta y señalización

Designers and Manufacturers of High
Quality Point of Purchase display, in store
media, interactive kiosks and signposting

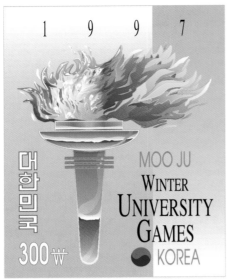

1 9 9 7

MOO JU

WINTER UNIVERSITY GAMES

300 ₩

KOREA

PARTICIPACION ● FERNANDO RONCES R.

versión con protección

TERNO
PUBLICIDAD S.A. DE C.V.

JORGE ◆ MIGUEL ANGEL ◆ CARLOS
AGUILERA AGUILAR

SOR JUANA INES DE LA CRUZ No.15-4
SANTA MARÍA LA RIBERA, MÉXICO, D.F., 06400
TEL. 547 3918   FAX 547 0119
LDCALÍZADOB   227.7979   PIN 625.2683

Arte Objeto Méxicano
Creativos en Diseño Gráfico
Etiqueta, Identidad Corporativa

Mexican Objet Art
Creatives in Graphic Design
Labels, Corporate Identity

ALEJANDRO GARCIA
ESPINDOLA

Diseñador Gráfico.
Especialista en diseño de imagen. Inicia su actividad profesional en 1989. Actualmente colabora en el departamento de Diseño de Exposiciones y Display con clientes como: American Express, Brother Int., Vitro Envases, Gillette, Apple Comp., Apasco, etc. Forma parte de Industriarte como asesor gráfico y es socio desde 1995.

MONICA ROSAS REYES

Licenciada en Diseño de la Comunicación Gráfica (UAM Azc.) con Maestría en Artes Visuales (ENAP) en la Academia de San Carlos. Ha participado en exposiciones nacionales e internacionales siendo seleccionadas para exposición varias de sus piezas. Perteneció al Taller de Producción de Maris Bustamante, con clientes como: TV Azteca, Cía. de Teatro de Jesusa Rodríguez, Astrid Haddad, DDF, etc. Profesora de la Universidad Mesoamericana en la ciudad de Oaxaca. Es directora de industriarte desde 1994.

industriarte
ASESORES EN DISEÑO

Retorno 27 No. 13
Col. Avante, Coyoacán
C.P. 04460 Cd. de México
Tels: 544 2702/362 0545/516 5363

EXPOSICIONES
Y DISPLAY

MEDICOS RESIDENTES

ESTUDIO 3
DISEÑO GRAFICO
E INDUSTRIAL

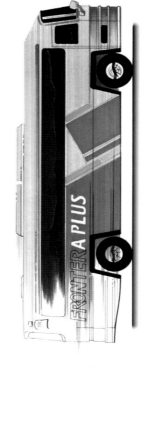

FRONTERA PLUS

Ejecutivo

© DINA Int.

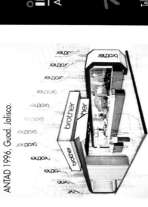

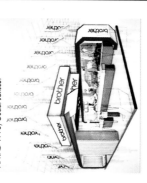

ANTAD 1996, Guad. Jalisco.

La Diana Casadera
1993

16 de septiembre, México

La Diana Casadera
1993

Primera
Bienal
Internacional
Juguete Arte-
Objeto
1995-1996

JORGE LUIS RUIZ GONZÁLEZ

▼ ▼ ▼ ▼ ▼ ▼ ▼ ▼ ▼ ▼ ▼ ▼ ▼ ▼

ESBOZO ESTUDIO S.A. DE C.V.
Atlanta 134-201
Col.Cd.de los Deportes
03870 Mexico D.F.
Tel y Fax: (5) 563 9514

Director de arte diseño gráfico,
portadas de discos, retoque,
caligrafia, arte digital,
manipulación de imagenes,
caricatura,
ilustración y diseño de moda

AGENT:
Adrian Carranza V
484 2 Ave. 8E New York
NY. 10016
Tel & Fax: (212) 725 1296

La Máquina de Gutenberg

Diseño Gráfico • Diseño Industrial • Fotografía • Empaque • Impresión

México

91(5) 391 6705 / 389 8190   aracelir@mpsnet.com.mx

Xtabentún

Cliente: Licores Argáez S.A. de C.V.
Diseño y producción de botella y empaque,
cambio de imágen gráfica.

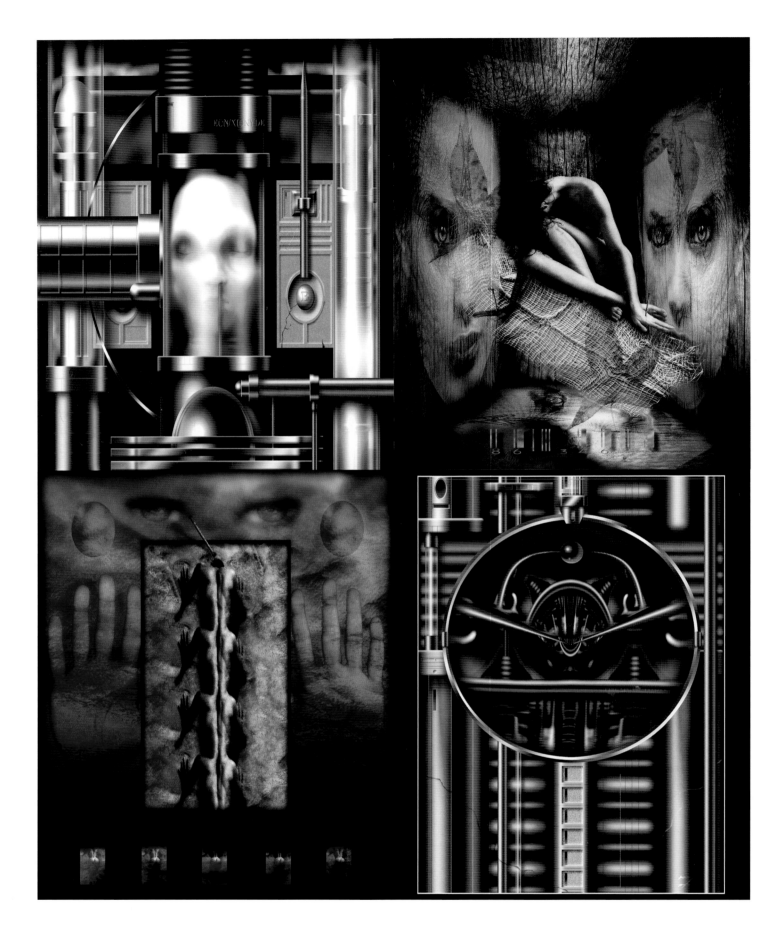

MUCHO RUIDO
▼ ▼ ▼ ▼ ▼ ▼ ▼ ▼ ▼ ▼ ▼ ▼ ▼ ▼ ▼

RICARDO CALDERON - ARTURO PEREZ RIOS V.
PLAZUELA DE LOS REYES 123
LOS REYES COYOACAN
03100 MEXICO DF
Tel: 617 73 14 619 3000

YOLANDA RAMIREZ/MARIO LAZO

▼ ▼ ▼ ▼ ▼ ▼ ▼ ▼ ▼ ▼ ▼ ▼ ▼ ▼

IDENTIDAD CORPORATIVA

DISEÑO EDITORIAL

SEÑALIZACION

DISEÑO AMBIENTAL

SALAMANDRA
DISEÑADORES S.C.

DARWIN 18-1, COL. ANZURES

C.P. 11590 MEXICO D. F.

254 3981/4048 Y 254 5551 (FAX)

salamadi@infosel.net.mx.

PROYECTO: "Posters y Flyers" American Express Travelers Cheques
CLIENTE: Banco Inverlat.
Retoque Digital* cheque sobre toalla, Preprensa e Impresión.

PROYECTO: Album y estampas "LO MAS PRENDIDO DE LOONEY TUNES"
CLIENTE: Dinamics
Manejo de Licencia, Diseño integral de la promoción*, Retoque Digital*, Preprensa e Impresión.
MR y © 1996 Warner Bros.

PROYECTO: Anuncio para revista de "Piano Disc".
CLIENTE: Veerkamp
Dirección Fotográfica*, Diseño*, Retoque Digital* y Preprensa.

PROYECTO: Album y estampas "EL GRAN ESCAPE".
CLIENTE: Dinamics.
Manejo de licencia, Diseño integral de la promoción*, Retoque Digital *, Preprensa e Impresión
MR y © 1995 Warner Bros

PROYECTO: Album y estampas "AVENTURAS EN EL TIEMPO".
CLIENTE: Fideicomiso CPW México.
Diseño integral de la promoción*, Retoque Digital *, Preprensa e Impresión.
MR y © 1996 Société des Produits Nestlé S.A.

*Dirección Creativa Norma Lazcano M. / Jorge Jaimes H.

e-mail
dmgjjh@mpsnet.com.mx

GRUPO IMAGEN

Direct Marketing Group S.A. de C.V.
Av. Vasco de Quiroga #1800 1er. piso
Col. Sta. Fé México D.F. 01210
Tels.: 257-1600 257-0030
Fax: 257-0460

- Diseño
- Retoque Digital
- Animación 3D
- Manejo de Licencias
- Promociones
- Correo Directo
- Preprensa
- Impresión
- Acabados

SERGIO MONTES *PHOTOGRAPHY*
LUIGGI CURIEL *DESIGN*

▼ ▼ ▼ ▼ ▼ ▼ ▼ ▼ ▼ ▼ ▼ ▼ ▼ ▼ ▼ ▼ ▼

Garrido No. 276, Col. Tepeyac Insurgentes
México 07020, D.F.
Tels. (525)577-4132 & (525)781-8412

Gral. Vicente Guerrero No. 38, La Herradura
Naucalpan 53840, México
Tel. (525)295-2424

email: lcuriel@infosel.net.mx

Portadas de
libros técnicos para
el programa EBC
Conalep / Banco Mundial

Estampilla Postal
XIV Maratón
Internacional de la
Ciudad de México
SEPOMEX

Estampilla Postal / Centenario del cine en México
Servicio Postal Mexicano (SEPOMEX)

Estampilla Postal / Día internacional
para la preservación de la capa de ozono
SEPOMEX

Estampilla Postal / La ciencia desde México
SEPOMEX

Estampilla Postal
Centenario del natalicio de David Alfaro Siqueiros
SEPOMEX

LAS BUENAS IDEAS SE PREMIAN

6o. CONCURSO NACIONAL DE DISEÑO Y ELABORACION DE MATERIALES DIDACTICOS

Material Escrito ◆ Material Audiovisual
Prototipos Didácticos ◆ Software Educativo
Junio de 1995

Informes e inscripciones en los planteles o representaciones y en las Oficinas
Nacionales del Conalep, en la Dirección de Materiales y Prototipos Didácticos,
o al teléfono 91(72) 71-0800 exts. 2486 y 2495, Fax 91(72) 71-0488

conalep *Colegio Nacional de Educación Profesional Técnica*

Cartel y trípticos para el 6o. Concurso nacional de diseño
Colegio Nacional de Educación Profesional Técnica (Conalep)

Portadas de libros
técnicos para el programa
de coediciones Conalep

¡Las buenas ideas se premian!

Diamond Tours, S.A. Panamá

Total Trade Co. Panamá

UNI/Consultores en Diseño, S.C.
DISEÑO INDUSTRIAL ◆ DISEÑO GRÁFICO

César Fernández de la Reguera Martín
Patricia Mitre Martínez
Tel. 308 25 92 / 808 05 54 BIP 6299800 clave 43665
Apartado Postal 161, Colonia Boulevares, Estado de México C.P. 53140

UNI/CONSULTORES EN DISEÑO, S.C. ◆

grupo
MH
Diseño & Comunicación

Diagonal Patriotismo 1 1er. piso
Col. Hipódromo Condesa
México, D.F. C.P. 06170
Tel. 273 9292 / 227 4700 al 09
Fax 277 9702

ARTE-2
tecnodiseño y comunicación

V. Río Becerra 26-1
03800 D.F. México
Tel. (52 5) 271-44-65
Fax (52 5) 271-03-62
E-mail arte@data.net.mx

COMPANY PROFILE

Arte-2 is a young firm, founded in 1991, that offers integrated solutions for all kinds of graphic communication needs through a large variety of services, that cover all stages of the graphic material production. From the creation of the original concept, to the final product.

In Arte-2, we strongly belive that our work deals with the transmission of concepts through visual communication. That is why our goal is to provide our clients, by closely working with them, with powerful and aesthetic designs that are also effective for their marketing strategies.

Since its foundation, Arte-2, has been improving the quallity of its work, not only by constantly applying the leading technology to the graphic production, but also by offering the best service to its customers. Today, because of this philosophy, Arte-2 has become a steady and well positioned company.

If you want to catch up with what Arte-2 is doing right now, you can visit it's web page, which will probably be in the internet by the time this book is published.
The address is not defined yet, but you'll find a link from the R&R design page at:
http://www.rrdesign.com

1. Notice and diploma for a paint contest for children

2. Stationary of the corporate identity designed for an ice company

3. Poster and brochure for a movie

4. Catalog for a cloth factory

5. Group of materials created for a locomotives maintenance company

6. Package design

7. Halloween game

8. Package designs for a video collection for children

9. Package designs for a video collection for children

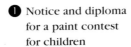

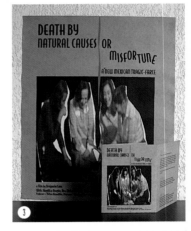

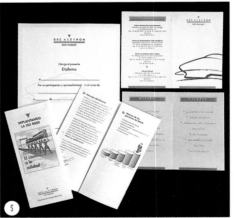

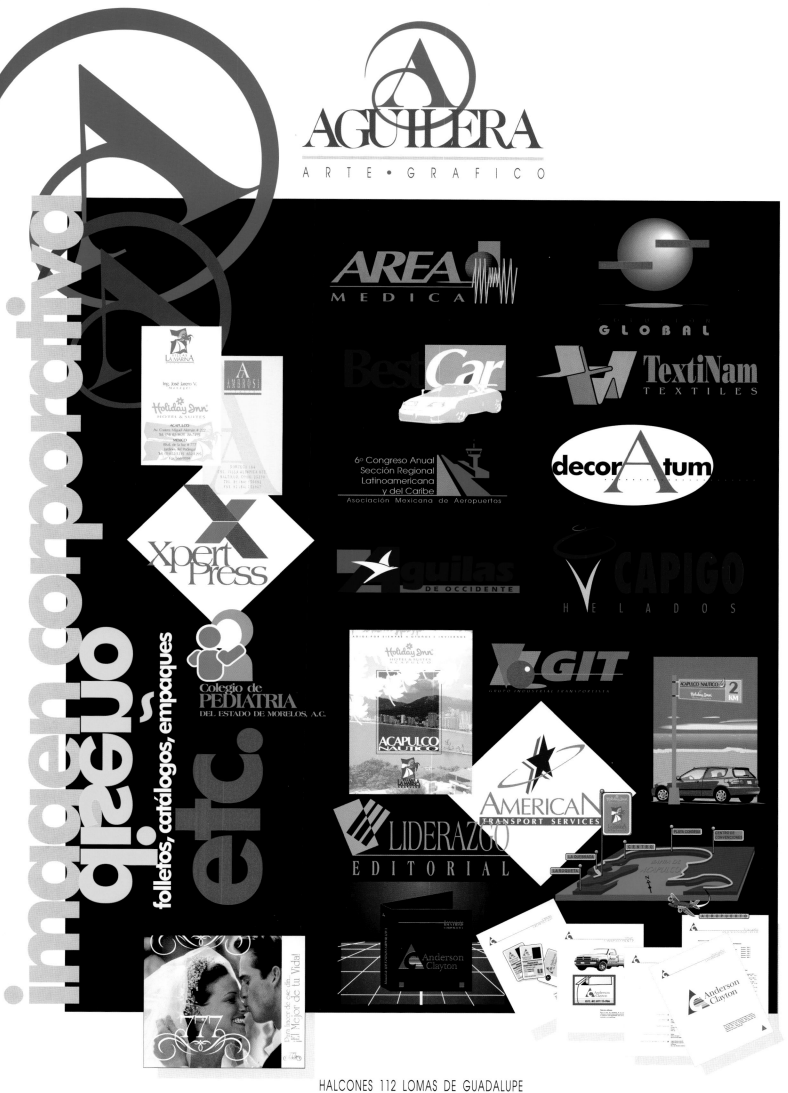

HALCONES 112 LOMAS DE GUADALUPE
MEXICO 01720, D.F.
MEXICO CITY
TEL/FAX 91 (5) 635.2457 635.2474
At´n. Lic. Augusto Aguilera E.

ENRIQUE MACIAS

▼ ▼ ▼ ▼ ▼ ▼ ▼ ▼ ▼ ▼ ▼ ▼ ▼ ▼

Cuernavaca # 114-401
06140 México, D.F.
Tel: (525) 553-0102
Fax: (525) 553-9040

Especialidades en: Alimentos, Gente,"Still Life"
Efectos especiales e Imagen Digital.

ARQ. GERARDO MEJIA SALGADO

▼ ▼ ▼ ▼ ▼ ▼ ▼ ▼ ▼ ▼ ▼ ▼ ▼ ▼

ARQUITECTURA TERRENAL S.A. DE C.V.
Juan Aldama No. 400 sur
San Mateo Oxtotitlan
Toluca, Edo. México
Tel. & Fax: (072) 78 00 78

Arquitectura y Diseño de Interiores

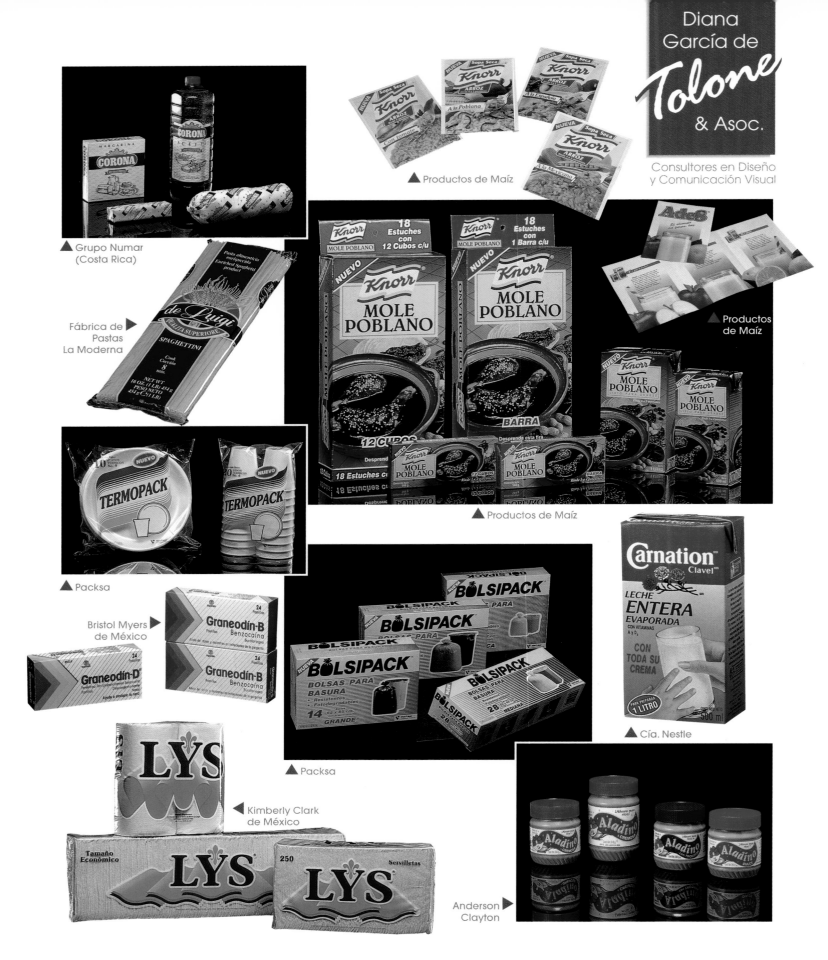

Diana
García de
Tolone
& Asoc.

Consultores en Diseño
y Comunicación Visual

▲ Grupo Numar
(Costa Rica)

◀ Fábrica de
Pastas
La Moderna

▲ Productos de Maíz

▲ Productos
de Maíz

▲ Productos de Maíz

▲ Packsa

Bristol Myers ▶
de México

▲ Packsa

▲ Cía. Nestle

◀ Kimberly Clark
de México

Anderson ▶
Clayton

DIANA GARCIA DE TOLONE
▼ ▼ ▼ ▼ ▼ ▼ ▼ ▼ ▼ ▼ ▼ ▼ ▼

Ac. Fuentes Brotantes 35 • Fracc. Vista del Valle
Naucalpan Edo. de Méx. • C.P. 53290
Tel./Fax: 364-11-99 • Tel. 364-13-09

• Diseño Gráfico/Estructural de Empaques
• Diseño Editorial (Folletos y Catálogos)
• Identidad Corporativa

Graphic/Structural Packaging Design •
Editorial Desing •
Corporate Identity •

VENEZUELAN

VÉNÉZUÉLA

VENEZUELA

▼

CREMADES

GOMEZ

& ASOCIADOS C.A.

ESTANDARIZACION
Y COMUNICACION

PINCO
SUPER
PROTECTOR
Barniz para Madera

COMUNICACION GRAFICA
& PROCESOS

Nestlé CRUNCH®

AV. RIO CAURA, TORRE HUMBOLDT, PLANTA ALTA, OFC.PA-09
URB. PARQUE HUMBOLDT, CARACAS 1080 - VENEZUELA.
TELF.: (582) 976.11.40 - 976.24.03
976.48.37 - 976.62.37 - FAX: (582) 976.21.65

BEST PRINT
BP
BEST PRINT

FOTOGRAFIA

EMPAQUES

AV. RIO CAURA, TORRE HUMBOLDT, PLANTA ALTA, OFC.PA-09
URB. PARQUE HUMBOLDT, CARACAS 1080 - VENEZUELA.
TELF.: (582) 976.11.40 - 976.24.03
976.48.37 - 976.62.37 - FAX: (582) 976.21.65

COMUNICACION GRAFICA
& PROCESOS

DISEñO GRAFICO

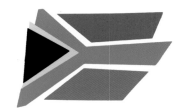

SOUTH AFRICA
▼ ▼ ▼ ▼
AFRIQUE DU SUD
▼ ▼ ▼ ▼
SÜDAFRIKA

▼

IMAGINATION CORPORATION

IMAGINATION CORPORATION

COMPANY PROFILE

The Imagination Corporation is dedicated to the total concept of design - the structuring of visual or formal elements so that the whole is greater than the sum of the parts. The medium is indeed immaterial, it is the visual expression of our clients identities that predominates.

It is our responsibility to use the most appropriate media to underpin this expression and to differentiate our clients within their respective markets.

To this end, our range of disciplines extend from identity development through literature design, package design, and environmental design to multimedia design.

Although it only one measure of success, Imagination Corporation has already won over 20 local and international design awards. The Imagination Corporation is a member of the Jupiter Group whose range of skills extend throughout the communications mix and include three advertising agencies, market research, training and companies specialising in the development of new electronic media. The Imagination Corporation does not live by trends or fads. We believe in expressing the message through the idioms found in our own experiences and the environments in which our messages will be read.

PO Box 4919, Rivonia, 2128
Telephone - (011) 807 3470
Facsimile - (011) 807 3225
Internet - imagine@is.co.za

KEY PERSONNEL

BILLY DE KLERK
Managing Director

HEATHER GOMES
Design Director

LEE SELSICK
Design Director

CORE BUSINESS

CORPORATE IDENTITY
LITERATURE DESIGN
INTERACTIVE DESIGN
PACKAGE DESIGN
MULTIMEDIA
ENVIRONMENTAL DESIGN

CLIENT - ASSOCIATION OF MARKETERS
ITEMS - THE 19TH ANNUAL LOERIE AWARDS CAMPAIGN

CLIENT - FXI
ITEM - ANNUAL REPORT

CLIENT - JOHANNESBURG ART GALLERY
ITEM - POSTER

CLIENT - BURHOSE
ITEM - NUDES PACK

CLIENT - RUSTLERS VALLEY
ITEM - EASTER FESTIVAL POSTER

CLIENT - PENNY BLACK
ITEM - CORPORATE IDENTITY

CLIENT - FACTS & FICTION
ITEM - LOGO

CLIENT - ONLINE
ITEM - LOGO

CLIENT - ABRO LUNTZ
ITEM - LOGO

CLIENT - DEPT OF ARTS, CULTURE, SCIENCE & TECHNOLOGY
ITEM - LOGO

CLIENT - SILICON GRAPHICS
ITEM - SILICON SAFARI LOGO

CLIENT - PICK 'N PAY
ITEM - 30 YEARS LOGO

CLIENT - MEDIAVENTURES INTERNATIONAL
ITEM - LOGO

Everybody's cup of tea

GRAPHIC DESIGN • 3D GRAPHICS • 3 D ANIMATION • ILLUSTRATION • MULTIMEDIA PRESENTATION
WEB DESIGNING • ADVERTISING • MEDIA PLANNING • MEDIA PLACEMENT

THE GRAPHIC SHACK cc

S3, 155 LOOP STREET, CAPE TOWN 8000, SOUTH AFRICA
P O BOX 16379 VLAEBERG 8018, SOUTH AFRICA
TELEPHONE: 27 21 236088 • FAX: 27 21 234480 • E-MAIL: GSHACK@KINGSLEY.CO.ZA

EMS

DESIGN
effective marketing services

integrity

Effective Marketing Services is a strategic design consultancy specialising in the disciplines of graphic, product, environmental and digital design.

EMS is the design division of Saatchi & Saatchi Advertising South Africa, with the resources and infrastructure to support a variety of design projects ranging from corporate identity development through to digital multimedia.

Saatchi & Saatchi Centre
70 Grayston Drive – Sandton
Johannesburg – South Africa
e-mail address ems@icon.co.za
Tel (2711) 883-3513
Fax (2711) 883-1781

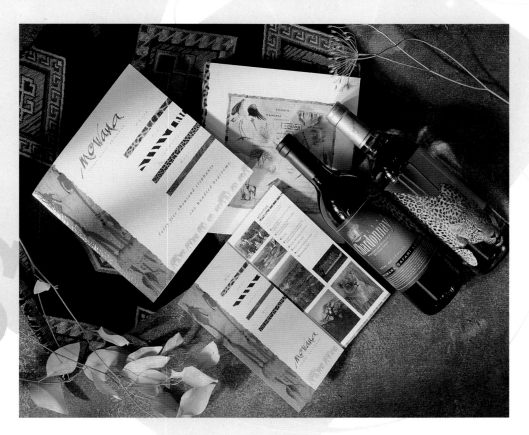

PATON TUPPER
A S S O C I A T E S

G R A P H I C   D E S I G N   A N D   M A R K E T I N G   C O M M U N I C A T I O N S

542 RIDGE ROAD DURBAN 4001 PO BOX 433 DURBAN 4000 TEL (031) 2073121 FAX (031) 287226 e-mail paton.tupper@owlco.co.za

Who? We're an agency with a reputation for providing clients with unparalleled creativity, service and professionalism.

What? We have a long list of satisfied clients for whom we've produced successful projects including corporate identity development,

sales promotion campaigns, packaging designs, advertising campaigns and marketing strategies.

Why? Because we're among the best! Here are a few examples of the kind of work we do for our clients.

CLIENT: R J REYNOLDS – SALES PROMOTION

CLIENT: GLODINA HOLDINGS – ANNUAL REPORT

LOGO DESIGNS

CLIENT: ILLOVO – LEAFLET

CLIENT: CGP
TRADE PRESENTER

CLIENT: NATIONAL BRANDS – PACKAGING

CLIENT: SPAR HOUSE BRANDS – PACKAGING

CLIENT: G M PHARMACEUTICALS – PACKAGING

CLIENT: CGP
TRADE PRESENTER

CLIENT: THE HOME OF
THE FISHERMAN
PACKAGING

CLIENT: RAWDONS HOTEL
PACKAGING

Client: Hyperama - Item - Popcorn Packaging

Client: Truworths - Item - Credit drive promotion

Client: SodaStream - Item - Promotion

Client: Fresta Holdings - Item - Monteverde Packaging

Client: Dairybelle - Item - Corporate Brochure

Client: Truworths - Item - 'Made in the world' Truworths charge cards

Client: Orange - Item - Party invite

Client: Truworths - Item - 'Made in the world' launch travel competition

All it takes to start the creative juices of Orange flowing - is a challenge.

At Orange we are a group of enthusiastic, uncommonly talented creative dynamos - not to mention dedicated professionals. We have produced some of the most exciting, vital...and...well, downright dynamic design solutions around.

We at Orange like to maintain a close working relationship with our clients to ensure that their products get the best. And that we achieve, if not exceed, our clients' marketing goals. No matter how great or small.

This personalised touch shows in our client portfolio which includes Truworths 'Made in the World', Hyperama and OK house brand packaging projects, Dairybelle Corporate brochures and ads and Cadbury's moulded range packaging, to mention just a few of our segments.

So if you want to turn your blue chip Orange. Give us a call. And let's get some creative juices flowing.

ORANGE

MARKETING (Pty) Ltd.

P.O. BOX 10056, CALEDON SQUARE 7905.
FIRST FLOOR, 72 BARRACK STREET,
CAPE TOWN 8001.
TEL: (2721) 461-6173 FAX: (2721) 461-6174
107 DUNOTTAR STREET, SYDENHAM,
JOHANNESBURG 2012.
TEL: (2711) 640-6894 FAX: (2711) 640-7392
E-MAIL: orange@dockside.co.za

JAPAN
JAPON
JAPAN

▼

NAYUTA CO.,LTD

▽▽▽ ▽ ▽ ▽ ▽ ▽ ▽ ▽

TOSHIYUKI FUNATSU
Ikki Bldg.
3-1-3 Misaki-cho
Chiyoda-ku
Tokyo 101 JAPAN
Tel: (03) 3222-0701
Fax: (03) 3222-1955
nayuta@po.iijnet.or.jp

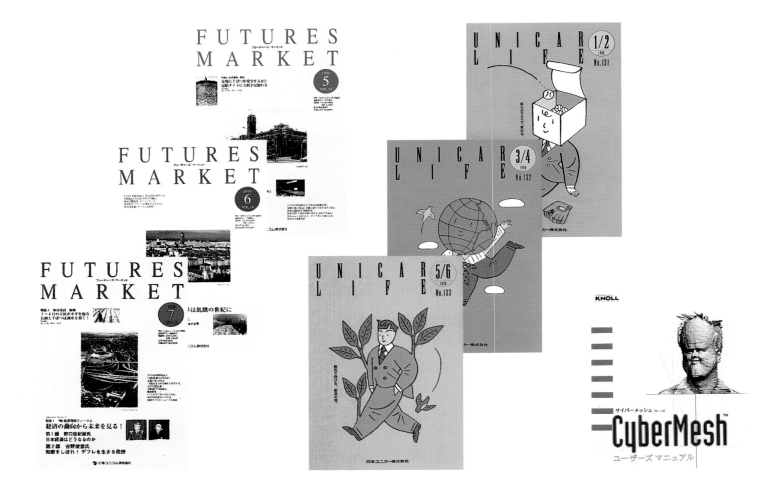

T&R Inc.

Fukumatsu Bld.8 & 9F
Sumiyoshi-cho 7-1
Shinjuku-ku, Tokyo, Japan
Tel. (03)3226-8021 Fax: (03)3226-7854
E.Mail tandr@po.iijnet.or.jp

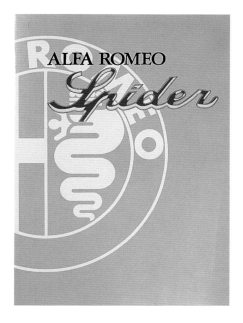

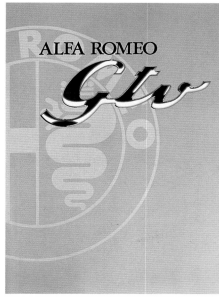

T&R Inc.

▼ ▼ ▼ ▼ ▼ ▼ ▼ ▼ ▼ ▼

Fukumatsu Bld.8 & 9F
Sumiyoshi-cho 7-1
Shinjuku-ku, Tokyo, Japan
Tel. (03)3226-8021 Fax: (03)3226-7854
E.Mail tandr@po.iijnet.or.jp

CREATIVE•SANO•JAPAN

▼ ▼ ▼ ▼ ▼ ▼ ▼ ▼ ▼ ▼ ▼ ▼

Miwa Building 301
3-17 Kandajinbo-cho
Chiyoda-ku
Tokyo 101 Japan
Tel. (03)-5276-2841, 2842
Fax. (03)-5276-2843

ネクスター GOLF Lesson Comic

CREATIVE・SANO・JAPAN

Miwa Building 301
3-17 Kandajinbo-cho
Chiyoda-ku
Tokyo 101 Japan
Tel. (03) 5276-2841,2842
Fax. (03) 5276-2843

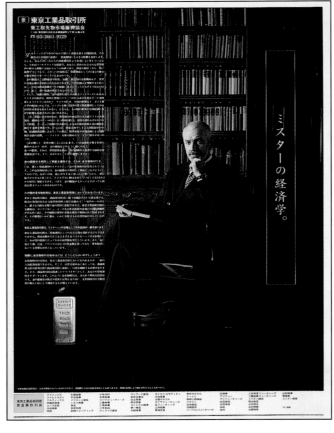

T-BREAK, INC.
▼ ▼ ▼ ▼ ▼ ▼ ▼ ▼ ▼ ▼ ▼ ▼ ▼ ▼ ▼ ▼

TAKAHIRO EGUCHI
Green terrace Tomigaya 102
2-13-11 Tomigaya
Shibuya-ku
Tokyo 151 Japan
Tel: (03) 3466-4476
Fax: (03) 3466-4477

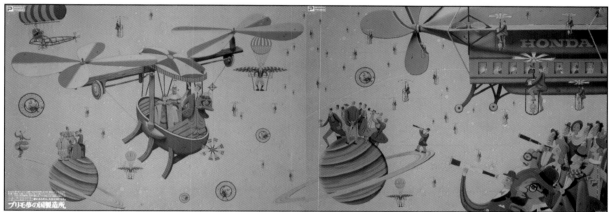

T-BREAK, INC.

▼ ▼ ▼ ▼ ▼ ▼ ▼ ▼ ▼ ▼ ▼ ▼ ▼

TAKAHIRO EGUCHI
Green terrace Tomigaya 102
2-13-11 Tomigaya
Shibuya-ku
Tokyo 151 Japan
Tel: (03) 3466-4476
Fax: (03) 3466-4477

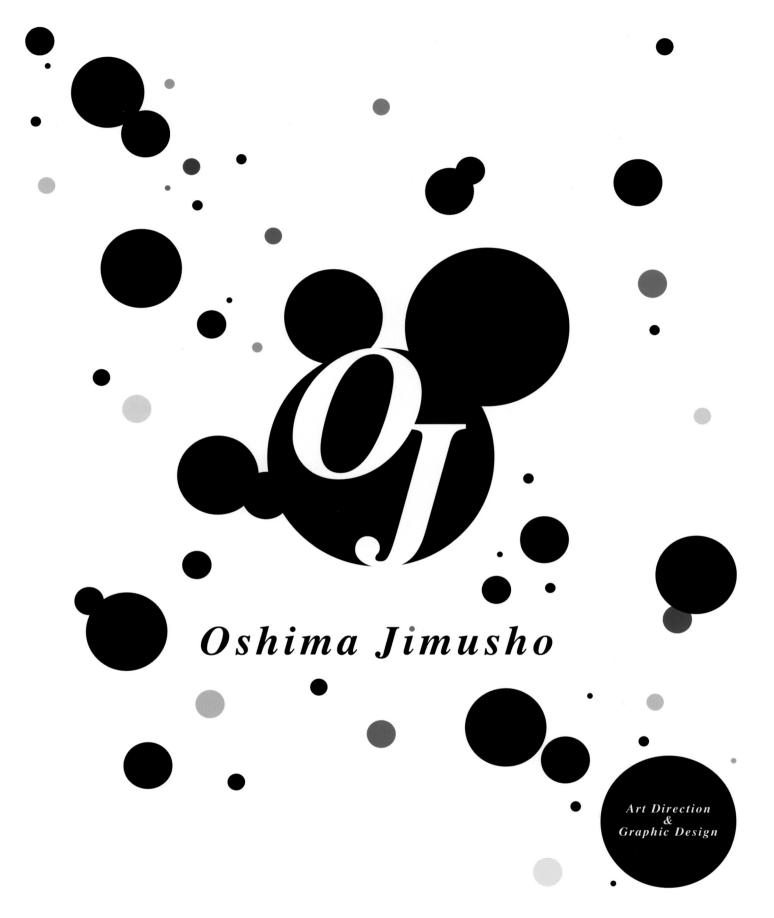

Oshima Jimusho

Art Direction
&
Graphic Design

Oshima Jimusho
▼ ▼ ▼ ▼ ▼ ▼ ▼ ▼ ▼ ▼

7-11-11-4F Tsukiji
Chuo-ku
Tokyo 104 - Japan
Tel.(03)3541-7977
Fax.(03)3541-7074

AGOSTO, INC.

▼ ▼ ▼ ▼ ▼ ▼ ▼ ▼ ▼ ▼ ▼ ▼

7F Shine Building, 4-4 Kojimachi
Chiyoda-ku, Tokyo 102 Japan
Tel: 03-3262-4595 Fax: 03-3262-9463
E-MAIL: agosto@po.iijnet.or.jp

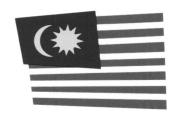

M A L A Y S I A

▼ ▼ ▼ ▼

M A L A I S I E

▼ ▼ ▼ ▼

M A L A Y S I A

▼

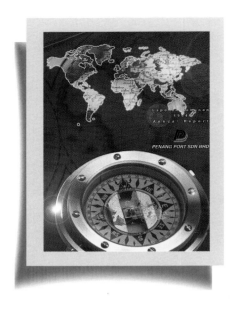

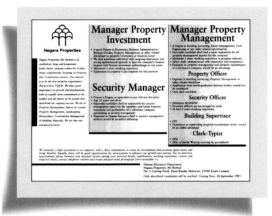

MUSTAFA ZAHIDIN GROUP

**Mustafa Zahidin & Associates
Sdn Bhd**

(240009 K)

93C, Jalan SS21/60
Damansara Utama
47400 Petaling Jaya
Selangor Darul Ehsan
Tel: 603 - 7191004
Fax: 603 - 7191005

**Mustafa Zahidin (Penang)
Sdn Bhd**

(375050 H)

264-B, 2nd Floor
Victoria Street
10300 Penang
Malaysia
Tel: 604 - 2617226
Fax: 604 - 2614826

**Mustafa Zahidin (Johore)
Sdn Bhd**

(400001 X)

44B, Jalan Padi Satu
Bandar Baru UDA
81200 Johor Bahru
Johor, Malaysia
Tel: 607 - 2352787/2353787
Fax: 607 - 2354787

Muzacomm Sdn Bhd

(332926 H)

94C, Jalan SS21/62
Damansara Utama
47400 Petaling Jaya
Selangor Darul Ehsan
Tel: 603 - 7190099
Fax: 603 - 7190066

JUST WHAT IS IT THAT MAKES GENTING HIGHLANDS THE PREFERRED DESTINATION FOR CONVENTIONS?

It could be the cool and refreshing mountain air that makes us so inviting. Or the many conference rooms in our 5 hotels that can cater for meetings of all sizes. Maybe it's because we provide complete state-of-the-art facilities and expertise to ensure your event is a definite success. Then again, it could be the luxurious accommodation and friendly service. But more than that, Genting Highlands Resort is FUN! You'll find two exciting Theme Parks, an 18-hole course and international performances so you'll never feel bored in between conventions.

Genting Highlands Resort

For more information,
Please fax your business card to Ms Valerie at 03-261 6611 (Fax) or call us at Resorts World Bhd at 03-2622666 (Tel)
Penang: 04-227 6284 Ipoh: 05-549 7988 Johor Bahru: 07-334 4555

Genting Highlands Resort - Magazine Ad

Casino de Genting
CNY Greeting Card

Your Magical Gateway

HIGHLANDER Kids Club
Logo Design

Glenmarie Golf &
Country Club Invitation

Caelygirl Undergarments

EON Calendar

Proton Pert - Magazine Ad

FGA Premium

Follow Me Packaging Design

CFGA

FIXGO ADVERTISING (M) SDN BHD
(Incorporated in Malaysia under Company No.:34768-K)
28, JALAN SS19/1D SUBANG JAYA, 47500 PETALING JAYA,
SELANGOR, MALAYSIA.**TEL:**03-733 6596 **FAX:**03-733 1857.
E-Mail: fixgo@sj28fga.po.my

CAUSE-COLYBRAND CONSULTING

Cause-Colybrand Consulting Sdn Bhd (362388-A)
Suite 15-01, 15th Floor, IGB Plaza, Jalan Kampar
Off Jalan Tun Razak, 50450 Kuala Lumpur, Malaysia

tel (603) 443 7873 fax (603) 443 2027
e-mail info@colybrn.po.my

COLOUR SEPARATION BY

PIONEER GRAPHIC SCANNING
28-38 Jalan 5526/11, 47301 Petaling Jaya, Malaysia. tel (603) 703 9322 fax (603) 703 5411

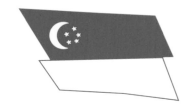

S I N G A P O R E
▼ ▼ ▼ ▼
S I N G A P O U R
▼ ▼ ▼ ▼
S I N G A P U R

▼

IMMORTAL

10 JIAK CHUAN ROAD

FACSIMILE 65 227 7026

REPUBLIC OF SINGAPORE

TELEPHONE 65 227 9406

E-MAIL immortal@singnet.com.sg

IMMORTAL
The Design Station Private Limited
*is a multi-disciplinary design consultancy
established in 1990 that specialises in
Corporate Identity, Brand Identity and
Packaging, Print, and Environmental
Graphics.*

IMMORTAL
Marketing Communications Pte Ltd
*is an integrated marketing communications
company that provides strategic business
development and planning expertise.*

I-DESIGN & MARKETING
Sdn Bhd
*is incorporated to provide consultancy
service in design and marketing
communications for Malaysia.*

*Block C6-1, First Floor
Jalan Selaman 1, Dataran Palma
68000 Ampang, Selangor, Malaysia
Facsimile 603 470 2427
Telephone 603 470 2428*

Clockwise from top right

Kim Eng Holdings, Singapore
  *Corporate Identity on Stationery
  Annual Reports*

Hotel Sedona Bintan Lagoon, Indonesia
  *F & B Menus
  Guest Collateral*

Pulai Springs Resort, Malaysia
  *Signage System
  F & B Menus
  F & B Identities*

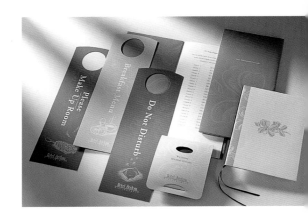

RAFFLES TOWN CLUB
SINGAPORE

Clockwise from top left

Raffles Town Club, Singapore
  Visual Identity

Khong Guan Biscuit, Singapore
  Premium Biscuit Assortment Packaging

Danone Asia, Indonesia
  Tuc Biscuit Packaging
  Prince Sandwich Biscuit Packaging

Chain Suppliers, Singapore
  Softex Personal Care Products Packaging

Asiatic Union Perdana, Indonesia
  ABC Selera Warisan
  Instant Noodle Packaging

Malaysia Dairy Industries, Singapore
  Marigold Asian Drinks Packaging

CRUNCH COMMUNICATIONS

Design
Advertising
Corporate identity
Packaging Design
Brochure Design
Annual Report
Digital Imaging

Photo Imaging

Here, at Crunch, we provide a wide range of services in design and advertising in both the Chinese and English languages. Our resident team of talents consists of specialists in visual communications and creative design which can help you become perceptibly different from your competitors.

Illustrated here are projects ranging from Corporate Identity programmes to property marketing brochures, company profiles to advertising collaterals. If we may be of any service to you, please do not hesitate to call **2728 322** and ask for **Sim**.

We are always at your service.

Magazine ad

Tian Ping Villa | Leaflet

MPH | Christmas Catalogue '96

If you can envision a grand classic hotel here,
the opportunity to realise it is now.

Press Ad

Keppel Bank | Priority Centre Corporate Identity

Sony Midi-Hifi | Point of Purchase

Lunar New Year Card

Ngee Ann City | Marketing Brochure and Video

CRUNCH COMMUNICATIONS
Blk 213 Henderson Road #03-11
Henderson Industrial Park
Singapore 159553
Tel: 2728 322 Fax: 2728 522
Email: crunch@pacific.net.sg

ANNUAL REPORT

BROCHURE

Ministry Of Health
Singapore

Civil Aviation Authority
of Singapore

Singapore Changi Airport
Terminal 1&2 brochures

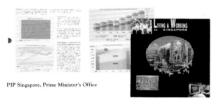

Singapore College Of Insurance

Guthrie GTS Limited

PIP Singapore, Prime Minister's Office

Singapore Manufacturers Association

NOL Annual Report

Social Integration Management Services, Prime Minister's Office

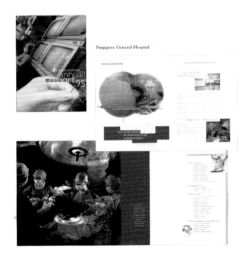

Singapore General Hospital

CHIO LIM STONE FOREST

Singapore Foreign Exchange Market Committee

Port Of Singapore Authority

LANCER GROUP

Lancer Design is a young & progressive design agency with a six-year track record. It has an open management system which adapts to today's fast-paced business environment.

It is constantly upgrading its overall business performance and is guided by a simple business theory of the 3 'Es' i.e. **Effectiveness, Efficiency & Economy**

Clients have benefited from our operational efficiency through lower cost, quicker turnaround and effective design communications.

Members of Lancer Group
- Lancer Design Pte Ltd
- Lancer Communications
- Focal D'zign Pte Ltd

Group Strength
25 staffs

IDENTITY

NEWSLETTER

MARKETING
INSTITUTE OF
SINGAPORE

MDIS
MANAGEMENT DEVELOPMENT INSTITUTE OF SINGAPORE

NYP
Nanyang
Polytechnic

BS
FORMWORK

family's bank

Thomson Television

Changi Sailing Club

Tru-Marine Pte Ltd

Matsushita Technology (S) Pte Ltd

EXCELLENCE
Esmarco Pte Ltd

Singapore Institute
of Purchasing &
Materials Management

Motorola Pagers

COPPER
Asia Pacific Breweries (S) Pte Ltd

Picture of Health

Admiralty Resort & Country Club

MINISTRY OF HEALTH
SINGAPORE

Manufacturers digest
Singapore Confederation
of Industries

S.C.I
Singapore College of Insurance

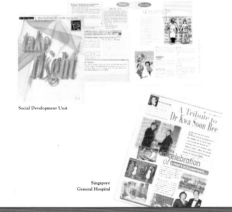
Social Development Unit

A Tribute to
Dr Kwa Soon Bee
Singapore
General Hospital

Areas of Expertise

- Creative Design Concept and Development ● Editorial/Copywriting
- Computer Graphic Imaging/Illustration ● Photography & Art Direction
- Marketing Management Consultancy ● Advertising ● Direct Mail
- Product Launch/Promotional Campaign ● Packaging Design

Key Personnel

- Mark Phooi   Creative Director
- Tony Chan   Art Director
- Max Chia   Business Development Manager
- Jessica Hong Operations Manager

Principal Clients

- Asia Pacific Breweries Ltd ● Comfort Group Ltd ● Singapore General Hospital
- Guthrie GTS Limited ● Transmarco Data Systems ● Singapore Swimming Club
- Pulai Springs Country Club ● Changi Sailing Club ● Prime Minister's Office
- Singapore Foreign Exchange ● Social Development Unit ● National Heritage Boards
- Ministry of Information & The Arts ● Civil Aviation Authority of Singapore
- Urban Development Board (URA) ● Ministry of Health

LANCER
LANCER GROUP

No. 2 IMM Building Jurong East St 21 #05-26
S'pore (609601) Tel: (65) 562 4756 Fax: (65) 567 7688
E-mail: lancomms@singnet.com.sg

A Celebration of Life in Work

[**AC GRAPHIC WORKSHOP PTE LTD**]   *28 Kallang Place #03-15 Singapore 339158 Tel: (65) 2944688 Fax: (65) 2946162*

A U S T R A L I A

A U S T R A L I E

A U S T R A L I A

▼

COCKBURN
CORPORATION LIMITED

DUXTON

QUATTRO

Corporate Identity

Packaging

Signage

TurnerDesign

61 King Street Perth 6000 Western Australia • Tel (619) 321 3811 Fax (619) 321 1936

JET VISUAL

Brand Management

Corporate Identity

Corporate Design

Packaging Design

Promotion

Signage

160 Beaufort Street Perth Western Australia 6000

Telephone 09 227 1995 Facsimile 09 328 3037

Website http://www.jetvisual.com.au

INDONESIA
INDONÉSIE
INDONESIEN

▼

RESEARCH ● PROMOTION PLAN ● GRAPHIC DESIGN ● PHOTOGRAPHY

Originality
Creativity
_____ +

PT. WADHIA BALA Jl. Radio IV/18, Jakarta 12130, Indonesia. Phone (62 - 21) 721-1084 (Hunting) Fax. (62 - 21) 725-0349

GRAPHIC DESIGN
AUDIO VISUAL
PRODUCTION

Adwitiya design

EXHIBITION
DESIGN AND CONSTRUCTION

[there is a possibility you like all our designs]

name •
position •
company •
address •
T •
F •

stamp(s)

Want information about
☐ corporate identity
☐ brochures
☐ annual reports
☐ packaging
☐ logo's
☐ exhibition
☐ audiovisual
☐

Adwitiya design
Gedung Fortune 3
Jl. Ampera Raya 37
Jakarta 12560
INDONESIA

GRHA
ADHIKA
FORTUNE

PT ADWITIYA ALEMBANA
Gedung
building
Fortune
3

Jalan
street
Ampera
Raya No. 37

Jakarta
12560
INDONESIA

T [62 21]
7892154
7892155
7892156

F [62 21]
7892157

T A I W A N

T A Ï W A N

T A I W A N

▼

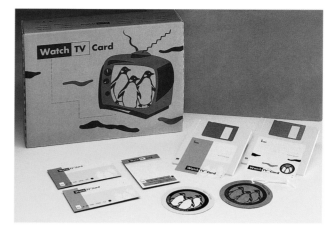

Designer, Lillian Wang
Photographer, Alian Chen
Copywriter, Solsem Su

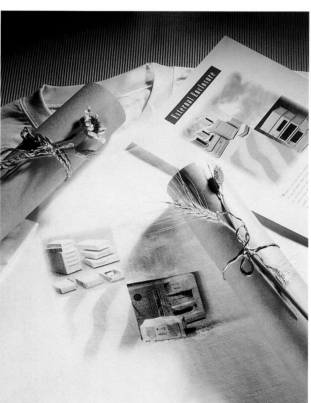

T Two Photography & Design Firm

tel: 377 3240 • 377 3291
fax: 377 0149
add: 1 FL, NO.33, Keelung Rd., Sec.2,
Taipei,Taiwan,R.O.C.

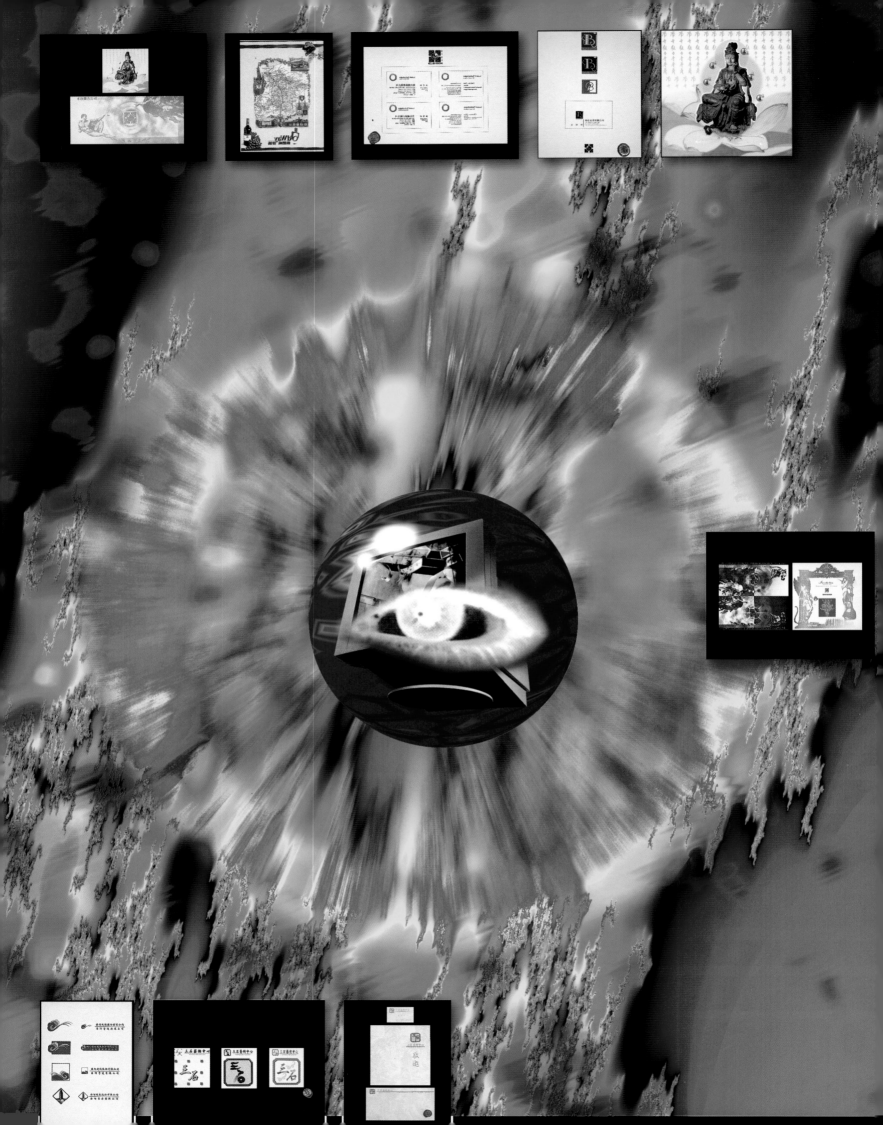

VIVID..YOUR KEY TO SPLENDID ARTISTRY

VIVID

TANTALIZES

YOUR
Senses

VIVID IMAGINATION
AMAZING FANTASY
INNOVATIVE CREATIONS
FASCINATING DESIGNS
PICTURESQUE PRODUCTIONS

V
I
V
I

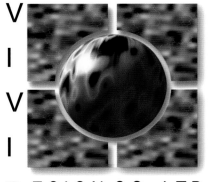

DESIGN CO., LTD.

VIVID DESIGN CO.,LTD. VI

CORPORATE IDENTITY PROGRAMMES
ADVERTISING DESIGN
EDITORIAL DESIGN
CORPORATE PROFILES
PACKAGING DESIGN
PRINT DESIGN
ANNUAL REPORTS
LOGO DESIGN
CALENDAR
POSTERS
HOMEPAGE DESIGN
DISPLAY DESIGN

 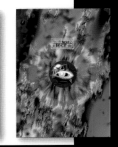

NO.6,6F-1,Chin Hwa ST.
HSINCHU CITY 300
TAIWAN, R.O.C.
TEL:886-35-317423
FAX:886-35-317420

AD:LU CHEN MU
DESIGNER:ANDY

The Miracle Of VIVID Makes You More Competitive

The Miracle Of VIVID Makes You More Competitive

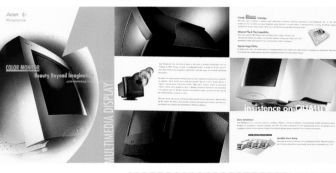

DIGI AM

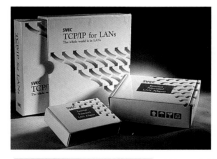

Artone design   4F, NO. 5, LONQ 6, LANE 222, TUN-HWA N. RD., TAIPEI, TAIWAN TEL:886-2-7123722 FAX:886-2-7120728

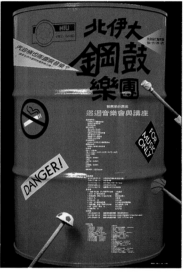

GREEN FINGERS DESIGN COMPANY
綠手指文化事業有限公司

▼ ▼ ▼ ▼ ▼ ▼ ▼ ▼ ▼ ▼ ▼ ▼ ▼ ▼

DESIGNER
JACK S.H. YANG/ 楊勝雄
NO.151-15, Sec.5
Minsheng East Rd.,
Taipei, Taiwan, R.O.C.
Tel: (02)761-7927, 761-7928
Fax: (02)761-7925

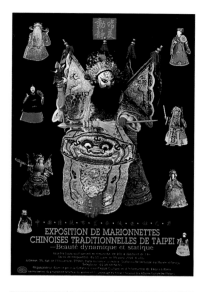

THE NIGHT OF
CHINESE FOLK ARTS
中国民俗の夜

GREEN FINGERS DESIGN COMPANY
綠手指文化事業有限公司
▼ ▼ ▼ ▼ ▼ ▼ ▼ ▼ ▼ ▼
DESIGNER
JACK S.H. YANG/ 楊勝雄
NO.151-15, Sec.5
Minsheng East Rd.,
Taipei, Taiwan, R.O.C.
Tel: (02)761-7927, 761-7928
Fax: (02)761-7925

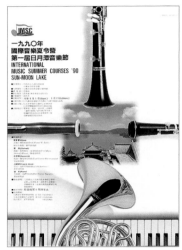

GREEN FINGERS DESIGN COMPANY
綠手指文化事業有限公司
▼ ▼ ▼ ▼ ▼ ▼ ▼ ▼ ▼ ▼ ▼ ▼
DESIGNER
JACK S.H. YANG/ 楊勝雄
NO.151-15, Sec.5
Minsheng East Rd.,
Taipei, Taiwan, R.O.C.
Tel: (02)761-7927, 761-7928
Fax: (02)761-7925

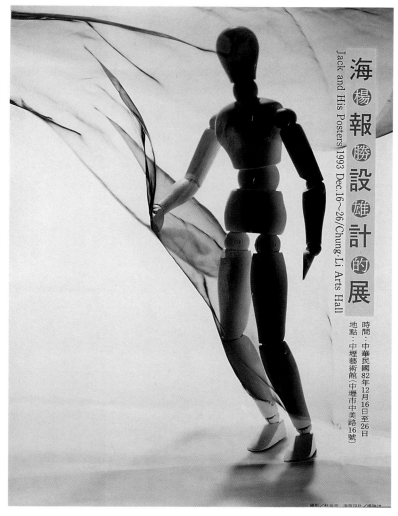

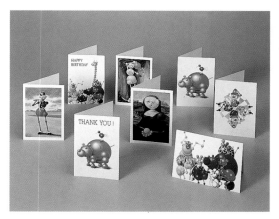

GREEN FINGERS DESIGN COMPANY

綠手指文化事業有限公司

▼ ▼ ▼ ▼ ▼ ▼ ▼ ▼ ▼ ▼

DESIGNER

JACK S.H. YANG/ 楊勝雄

NO.151-15, Sec.5

Minsheng East Rd.,

Taipei, Taiwan, R.O.C.

Tel: (02)761-7927, 761-7928

Fax: (02)761-7925

DISCOVERO

E.BA&TAN

E.BA&TAN ADVERTISIN CO.,LTD.

CORPORATE IDENTITY
ILLUSTRATION
GRAPHIC DESIGN
PACKAGING
GIFT & STATIONERIES
PHOTOGRAPHY
MARKETING AND VISUAL COMMUNICATIONS

Director/Producer
YOKEN WU
Producer/Design
E.BA JEW

意博恩騰廣告有限公司

台灣省 台北市 新生南路 一段一四六巷七之一號
NO 7-1 ALLEY 146 SEC 1 HSIN SHEN S.RD.TAIPEI TAIWAN R.O.C.
TEL:(8862) 394-2733 FAX:(8862) 394-2743

企業識別體系規劃設計/插畫噴修/包裝設計/禮品規畫設計/電腦影像處理/市場行銷規畫/印刷物品製作發包

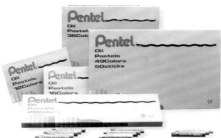

     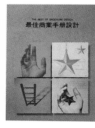  

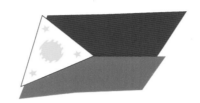

PHILIPPINES

PHILIPPINES

PHILIPPINEN

▼

" _very simple_

ideas

lie within the

reach

only of complex

minds. "

--- Rémy de Gourmont

CREATIVE △ RESPONSE

Los Angeles ■
249 N. Brand St.
Suite 312 Glendale
CA 91203
Phone (818) 247-1399
Fax (818) 247-1376
E-mail cresponse@earthlink.net

Manila ■
2411 Cityland 10, Tower II
6817 H.V. dela Costa St.
Salcedo Village, Makati City 1227
Philippines
Phone (632) 893-7662
Fax (632) 893-7851
E-mail creative@skyinet.net

una
GRAFIKA MANILA INC.

Creativity that transcends Formula.

Graphic Design

Advertising

Digital Imaging

Audio Visual Presentations

Special Events

Exhibit Design

Product Launching

Packaging

Corporate Identity

CREATIV

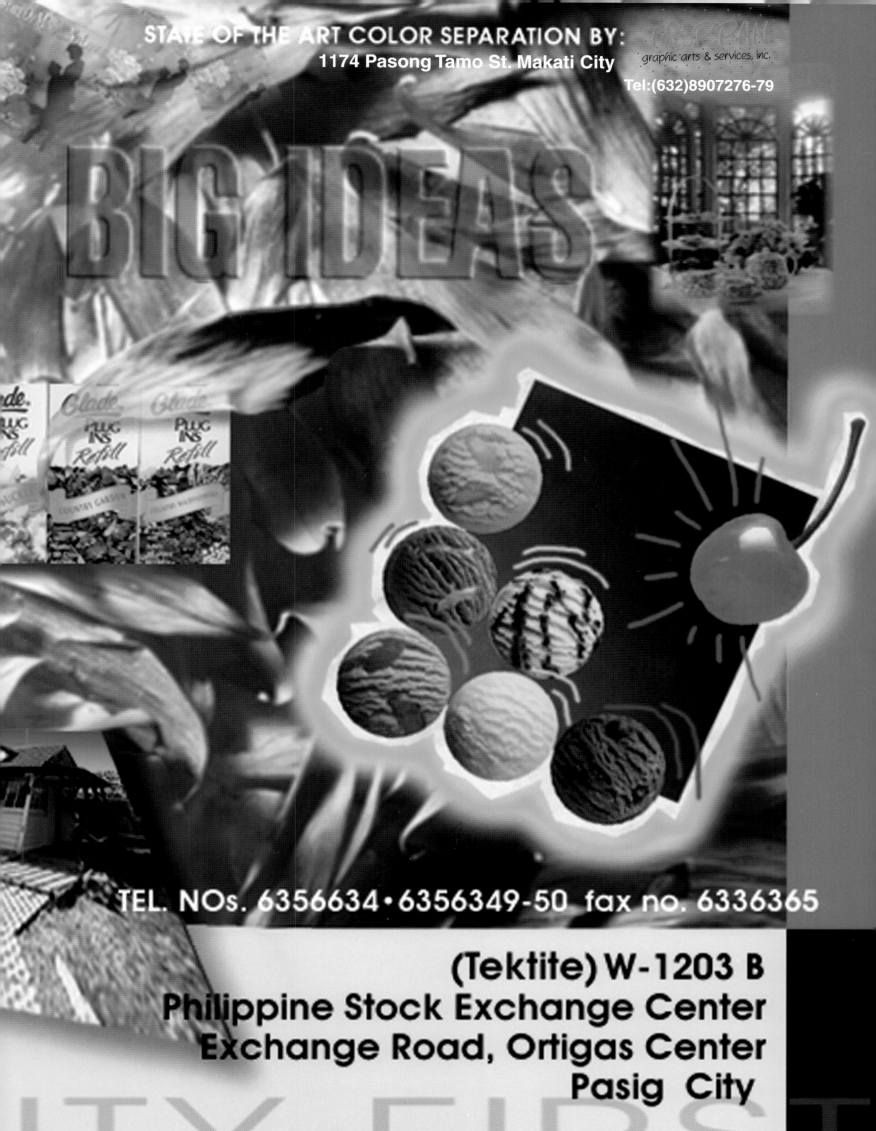

TAPESTRY OF BESTSELLERS

We have been putting solid business sense and creative innovation into corporate logos, brochures,packaging,annual reports, labels, signages,and POP materials since 1973. It's the least we can do as the oldest and one of the pioneers in Philippine graphic design.

GRAPHIC ATELIER (MANILA) INC.
6TH FLOOR
SALAMIN BUILDING
197 SALCEDO STREET
1200 MAKATI, METRO MANILA
PHILIPPINES
TEL: 818•5634/37/38
FAX: 818•5624

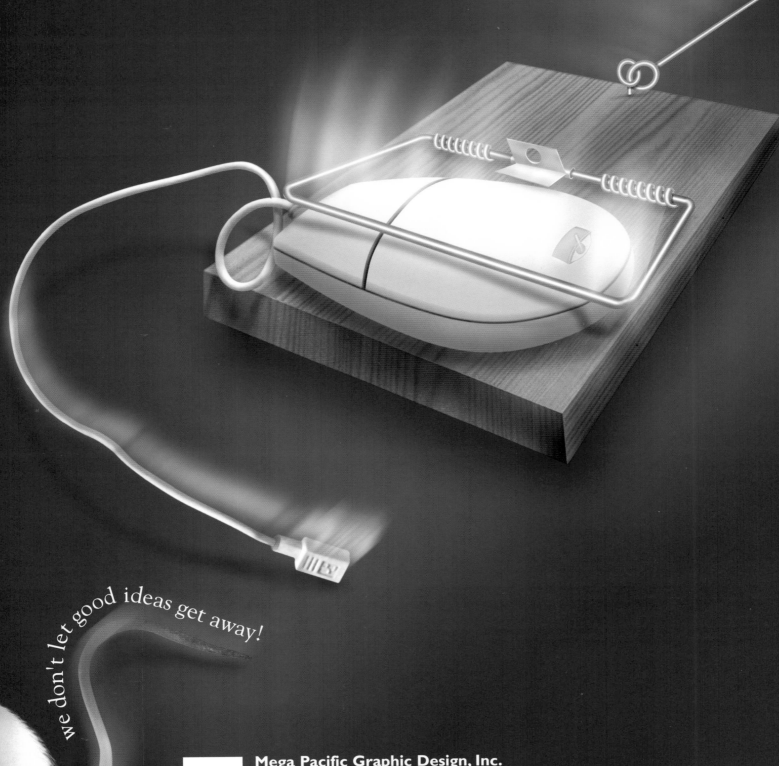

'meg-pac

we don't let good ideas get away!

Mega Pacific Graphic Design, Inc.
18th Floor, Strata 100 Bldg., Emerald Avenue, Ortigas Center, Pasig City, Philippines 1605
Tel. no.: (632) 633-3884; 631-4730; 633-4879; 633-6792; 633-4787; 633-4786; 631-2859; 633-4785
Fax no.: (632) 631- 2862

H E L L A S

▼ ▼ ▼ ▼

RÉPUBLIQUE HELLÉNIQUE

▼ ▼ ▼ ▼

Ä G Ä I S

▼

ELINA ZERVOU
creative studio

34, Griva str., Halandri
152 33 Athens Greece
Telephone: (01) 6812 193
Facsimile: (01) 6859 663

COMPANY PROFILE

Since 1990 a graphic design studio was formed for the purpose of offering creative solutions in the product promotion field, that is, from the idea right up to the final solution.

Our minds are committed to the area your interests lay so that we may provide you with company identity, informative documents, packaging, product presentation...

Our philosophy is that positive enthusiasm, friendly relationships with our clients and continuous effort, produce correct ideas that ensure the best results.

1. Product Presentation
2. Company Identity
3. Brochure
4. Packaging

Alta
Mare

Advertising

Digital Image Processing

Computer Graphics

Creative Art Work

Packaging

Lay Out

Logos

Studio
Image
&
Graphics

THOMPSON
communications

POINT OF SALE

PUBLICATIONS

PACKAGING

DIRECT MAIL

SEE
AND BE
SEEN

BRAND

OUTDOOR

BROCHURES

CORPORATE

DeLeMa / TBWA

DeLeMa Consultants Ltd
36 Grivas Dighenis Ave, P O Box 1674, 1512 Nicosia, Cyprus
Tel: (357-2) 459562, Fax: (357-2) 458136
e-mail: delema@spidernet.com.cy

Despo Lefkariti
Managing Director

Julia Papamichael
Art Director

Marina Christodoulides
Administration Director

Irene Karaoli
Media Director

Creative Energy

Full - service marketing communications agency, offering creative solutions to a variety of customers' needs, from Corporate Identity projects, to above and below-the-line campaigns.

Creative concept development, marketing strategy formulation and professional execution have ranked the agency third in terms of billings and first in creativity in Cyprus, after only 11 years.

Columbia Shipmanagement - brochures

Various Clients - identity

Regis - Velouté yoghurt - packaging
LIAA 1994 Finalist

Main Clients

Carlsberg Beer, BMW cars, Rover & Land Rover cars, Neskafé (Nestlé), Thera-Med (Henkel), Columbia Shipmanagement, Popular Bank, the Cyprus Government, Emirates Airline, Pizza Hut, Yves Saint Laurent perfumes, Elizabeth Arden cosmetics, Max Mara, KPMG Peat Marwick, Tiffany and Cartier jewelry.

Carlsberg Beer - 1990-1997 campaigns

EXCLUSIVE AFFILIATE
OF THE TBWA INTERNATIONAL
ADVERTISING GROUP

Popular Bank's - Action Club and Action Card - 1996 BMA Golden Coin Award

KPMG - brochures

Pizza Hut - printed material

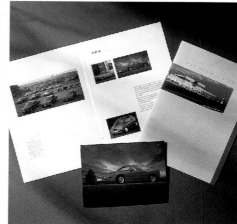

BMW - brochures

UNITED KINGDOM
▼ ▼ ▼ ▼
GRANDE-BRETAGNE
▼ ▼ ▼ ▼
GROSSBRITANNIEN

▼

image
+
design

art²g⁰

voice: (+44)171 386 7316   fax: (+44)171 460 0899   e-mail: art2go@dircon.co.uk

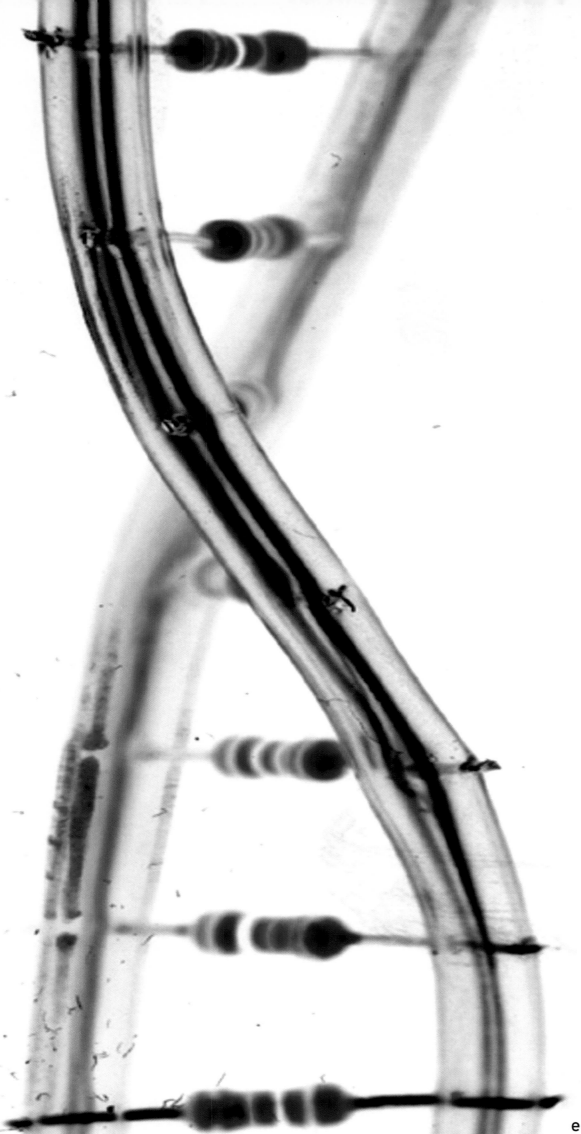

image created for ICA/Toshiba art & innovation commission

image
+
design

art²g⁰

voice: (+44)171 386 7316
fax: (+44)171 460 0899
e-mail: art2go@dircon.co.uk

- Graphic Design & Print
- Product Design & Development
- Packaging, P.O.S & Display
- Corporate Communications
- Training Packs & Games
- Presentation Material
- Sales & Publicity Literature

Brochure available on request

We enjoy the privilege of working for an impressive variety of companies. For well over a decade our quality of service has attracted dozens of high-profile names - and also plenty of less well known, but equally valued clients.

Some principal clients:
Alfred Dunhill
Abbey National
Forte
Harrods
Lloyds Bank
Parker
Selfridges
Tefal
Raymond Weil

Whether or not your business is a 'household' name, you can be assured of the highest quality of personal service from The Cole Design Consultancy.

We provide our clients with **CREATIVE and COST-EFFECTIVE** solutions to a wide range of design and marketing requirements.

T: +44 (0)1273 73 00 72

F: +44 (0)1273 73 00 02

email:coledesign@linkhouse.dial.iql.co.uk

THE COLE DESIGN CONSULTANCY
Creative & Strategic Marketing Services
Link House, 2 Norfolk Square, Brighton, East Sussex, BN1 2PB, England

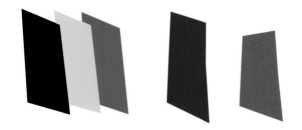

BELGIUM/FRANCE
▼ ▼ ▼ ▼
BELGIQUE/FRANCE
▼ ▼ ▼ ▼
BELGIEN/FRANKREICH

▼

PYTHAGORE

245, rue Jean- Jaurès
59491 Villeneuve d'Ascq - FRANCE
Tél. 03 20 20 36 75 - Fax. 03 20 20 36 78

PYTHAGORE
ART FINAL APPLIQUÉ

Luc LABYT
Manager
Bruno DUBOIS
Designer infographiste
Élise DESSAUVAGES
Responsable de production

Bienvenue à vos idées,

à vos envies de voir

la réalité changée,

revisitée, embellie…

Bienvenue aux images

qui vous poursuivent,

vous hantent et vous chantent :

pour tout changer

ou trois fois rien,

ensemble,

tentons de refaire le monde

à votre image…

Bienvenue chez Pythagore.

3 Suisses France

Epsilon pour LECLERC

Bahamas numérique pour HONDA

La Redoute

Studio Penez pour LLOYD CONTINENTAL

3 Suisses France

PICKWICK GIFT BOX "SPECIAL TEA" ASSORTMENT

MARIEN DESIGN
CONSULTANTS

PACKAGING DESIGN & CORPORATE IDENTITY

JAN VAN RIJSWIJCKLAAN 33 • 2018 ANTWERPEN BELGIUM • TEL. 03-248 19 92 • FAX 03-248 19 84

F R A N C E

F R A N C E

F R A N K R E I C H

Introduction

Design revival

As we approach the end of this century, strong currents of change are set in motion. The design profession has come of age. The businesses which call upon it have also come a long way. And the consumer has learned to distinguish true innovation from well-dressed fakery, to perceive the real benefits a new package or form can procure...Little by little we are embarking upon an era of difference. Where design occupies the forefront.

Innovation with substance

To shake off end-of-century lethargy, businesses are obsessed by four syllables : IN-NO-VA-TION: true innovation with real product plusses, tangible added value. This will-to-change recentres design at the heart of the creative process. Added to the fact that the consumer will just not be fooled. He has definitively tired of decoys, of old "new" products delivered by designers: products' wardrobe masters. The consumer has a shrinking budget, more time on his hands et does not want to be deceived : he will accept to pay more only where substantial innovation is proven. This is an irreversible trend which unmercifully excludes impostors. The design market is taking this turn after several painful years having attained a certain degree of maturity in the process. It has become an area of expertise. Businesses have a better grasp of the profession, they are more faithful, more appreciative of the value of lasting collaboration.

At the epicentre of modern business policy

Design has never been a panacea and one would hope that the extremism of the 60's and 70's, where the designer was looked upon as a kind of Mister Fix-all, will not resurface. On the other hand, he is clearly situated at the epicentre of corporate policy. Today's consumer knows what "new" means. If the term has no basis, she just might buy the product out of curiosity. But she won't be back for more. In such a context a product's commercial success correlates to a very simple but inescapable formula : tangible added product value + immediately perceptible added value through image, form, packaging or architecture.

Stimulating personnel awareness

Considering their strategic importance, design decisions, concerning new products or image evolution, will not really bear their fruit without true personnel awareness. Ideally, personnel awareness should be stimulated and implicated before decisions are made. Those who convey, use and sell corporate values must be the first concerned. The claim that image has the capacity to promote company unity proves true. But one must act along these lines in order that the personnel may recognize itself in the image construct and adopt it as its own.

Choosing the right partner

More than ever, choosing an agency is a source of anxiety. Are they creative enough and strategically qualified, will they fully fathom the problem, should one necessarily choose an agency with experience in the sector?

On that last point, it seems quite clear that market knowledge is an advantage. But it is neither sufficient nor a necessity. Past references can give a good idea of an agency's capabilities and drive : this is why we ask contributors to this guide to define their services as clearly as possible. But beyond references, sensitive, sharp analysis will always make the difference, whatever the sector.

As far as creativity goes, one counts on the agency's ability to differenciate you from all the rest, to create new codes. Your collaboration will last a while and as in couple relationships, you must let yourself be guided by your affinities, by your desire to work together or by the enthusiasm aroused by a project. The agency/company union must be conceived in a kind of alchemy, to create in turn a bit of magic.

Competition : no more than three agencies

When one chooses a builder for a new home, what are the decisive factors involved in that choice? The price...but let's suppose their estimates are all about the same. Then we ask about methods, how the building site will be organized, timing...Never would we think of asking the builders in competition to build a bit of a wall, just to see... When you think about it this way, it's sometimes rather absurd to ask agencies in competition to present a "piece" of their creative response to your project. Transforming a brief into a concrete solution calls for in-depth analysis of the problem to be solved. If the agency is straightforward and talented, its proposition will be THE one.

Even when "compensation" is offered, a serious competition should never include more than three agencies, at least in its final stages. Competition has become a "natural" phenomenon, but it must comply to fair and honourable rules.

Respect and trust

To function well, as in successful cohabitation, your professional relationship must be founded on trust and respect. An agency is not just a creative supplier. No more is it an enlightened dictator, eternally directing corporate conduct. Communication must be well established between you to find the perfect balance.

A partner from the start

A design agency resolves your problems all the better if it has access to the heart of the company. Agencies often complain about badly thought-out briefs, or problems awkwardly put. Their force lies precisely in their ability to coax the company into revealing its soul. A fresh look from the outside offers the possibility to express aloud what many are thinking to themselves on the inside of your business : those lucid employees who, locked into hierarchic structure can't get their message through.

▶

How much does design cost? Too much or too little?

The agency is basically remunerated for its capacity to classify and organize data and problems to be treated. And then to translate them concretely. At a price which corresponds to specialized professional skills. But today everything is negotiated. Even talent. Budgets are cut back with pressure exerted by corporate leaders. They seem intent on imposing the end-of-century credo "bigger profit, less spending". Even if research into estimating image and sales impact is the perogative of advertising and does not yet truly concern design, its profitability is broadly established by facts and experience. It remains that businesses have to absorb the idea that relevant design and its counterpart, profit, have their price. It's up to agencies to impose it, and up to businesses to remunerate design work at its true value...

CATHERINE LHÉRICEL
DIRECTOR OF GUIDE DESIGN FRANCE

THE THREE DIMENSIONS OF DESIGN

graphic design

▶ **Visual Identity**

A sort of corporate fingerprint, visual identity conveys a company's vocation, values and corporate plan. The days where one started over from scratch, with the idea of redefining together the components of corporate identity, seem to be over. Ours is a period of reorganization, of strategic maintenance.

▶ **Corporate literature, publications**

Annual reports, brochures, newsletters...all forms of corporate communication must be coherent with its image. Less restrictive than packaging in format, they offer an ideal space for textual communication.

▶ **Packaging design**

Primary communicator of brand expression, the packaging transmits product reality. The quality, attractiveness and clarity conveyed by package design must incite consumers to buy. Especially when one considers the short life of a package : disposed of once the product is consumed. Businesses' renewed investment in innovation has increased the demand on agencies for new product development.

product design

Product design is probably the most important differenciating factor. It reflects businesses' intention to take users' needs into consideration and ideally, to anticipate new ones. Budgets remain small although design seems to have found a permanent niche in development allowances.

environmental design

For chain stores, commercial space design has become an essential. The point of sale, now recognized for its primary communications value, must combine a comfortable place to shop with the profitabilty of each square foot. There are several agencies operative in this highly specialized and very active area.

To obtain your copy of
DESIGN FRANCE' 97 or for
further details, please contact:

Catherine Lhéricel
Guide Director
DESIGN FRANCE
tel. : 33 (0) 1 46 26 32 37
fax : 33 (0) 1 46 23 88 31

*Design plays a vital rôle in
stimulating corporate image
and commercial development
which, in turn, have indubitably
positive effects on profitability
and durability.*

The choice of an agency can hardly be left to chance

DESIGN FRANCE' 97 features 50 of France's foremost agencies today, with design professionals covering every need, to assist businesses in their search.

Clear and easy to consult

The agencies appear in alphabetical order and are classified by specialization under four headings:

- Brand Name Creation
- Graphic Design
- Product Design
- Environmental Design

For practical reference the back cover shows a complete agency listing along with corresponding telephone and page number.

Industry's leaders attest design's positive role in development

More than a guide, DESIGN FRANCE' 97 is a tool created to stimulate corporate interest in innovation and design. It is the only reference work of its kind to present 15 corporate leaders eager to share their design experiences and attest benefits reaped.

An overview of a year of great design

The DESIGN FRANCE' 97 also features a "Creations of the Year" section presenting all the past year's most innovative design projects, offering a handy digest of noteworthy evolution in sectors that are sure to interest you.

Complimentary but selective distribution (OJD distribution)

The DESIGN FRANCE' 97 is distributed free of charge to over 7,000 corporate deciders, selected from an annually revised and updated mailing list.

DESIGN FRANCE' 97 is of special interest to the following:

- General Management
- Marketing Management
- Communications Management
- Research & Development
- Research Consultants
- Division Management
- Product Management

design
FRANCE

QUALITY
SELLS

THE GUIDE TO FRENCH DESIGN AGENCIES

brand name creation

DEMONIAK

RODOLPHE GRISEY
Director
Qualifications : ESLSCA, 1982.
Career Background : From 1985, contributes to the development of linguistics software. At the same time participates in the founding of Epilog and Kaos. In 1988, launches Demoniak, agency specializing in name research.

CHRISTIAN BERTOLINO
Creative Director
Qualifications : CELSA.
Career Background : With a background in languages and linguistics, specializes in publications and communications.

YANN BRILLAUD
Art Director
Qualifications : School of Applied Arts.
Career Background : A traditional educational background leads to the development of a broad range of technical skills in computer-assisted design.

ANNE OLIVRY
Director of Development
Qualifications : ESC Reims (Higher School of Commerce, Reims).
Career Background : A solid marketing base evolves towards comunications. With experience at the European level, joins Demoniak in 1994.

DEMONIAK
96 rue du Faubourg Poissonnière
75010 Paris
Tel. : 33 (0) 1 49 70 06 06
Fax : 33 (0) 1 42 85 47 83

APPROACH - Brand names are distinctive signs, very personal corporate property, conveying image and values to compete in domestic and international markets. For Demoniak, a good name is not just a stroke of good luck. It is the result of successful interaction, triggered by competent linguists, creative talent, the exploratory potential of specialized software, familiarity with and analysis of anteriorities and the high standards of marketing and communications specialists.

Our performances in name research (brands, corporate names), in linguistic assistance or in the creation of brand statements bear witness to an in-depth knowledge of brand environment. Language usage, working knowledge of foreign languages and their commercial applications are our speciality. Together with our various partners, we develop and optimize our semantic engineering concept via tools and computer-assisted advanced linguistic research material. The pooling of our savoir-faire and the complementarity of our fields of intervention make it possible for us to offer a complete range of services, at all levels of verbal expression, extending to all sectors of economic activity.

AREAS OF EXPERTISE - Creation of brand names, creation and follow-up of brand name portfolios, linguistic and creative assistance, name testing, graphic identitiy, maintenance of a world-wide market competition watch.

Turnover	in %
Creation of brand names	90
Graphic Design	
Visual Identity	10

SECTORS OF ACTIVITY - All sectors.

NEW BUSINESS IN 1996 - Acome, Beiersdorf, Bongrain, Eurodisney Sca, France Loisirs, Golay-Buchel, Hipp France, L'Oréal, Monsanto, Reynolds, RJ Reynolds Tobacco, Rochas, Samaritaine, Procter & Gamble, SFR, SmithKline & Beecham, VVF.

PERSONNEL - 6

TURNOVER - 1995 : FF2.8m / 1994 : FF2.3m

COMPANY STRUCTURE - A limited liability company, capital of FF50,000. Founded in 1988.

NETWORK - Lyon - Toronto - Montreal (Geyser)

MEMBERSHIP - Founding member of Brand Partners Club

Brand and product name creation for :

Aérospatiale
Air France
Bel
Belin
Brandt
Cacharel
Caisse Nationale du Crédit Agricole
Cargill
Chanel
Colgate
Danone
DCN International
Dior
EDF
Fichet
France Loisirs
France Telecom
Gan
Humex Fournier
J'ai Lu
JF Lazartigue
Lancôme
La Poste
M6 Métropole Television
Panzani
Peugeot
Piaget
Pommery
Procter & Gamble
RATP
RJ Reynolds Tobacco
Sommer
TDF
TDR
VVF

RODOLPHE GRISEY
Director

CHRISTIAN BERTOLINO
Creative Director

ANNE OLIVRY
Director of Clientele

Mr DUPONT didn't rack his brains
to find his brand new shop, in Paris, which is located just beneath his flat.
He feels good.
Neither did Mr DUPONT rack his brains
to find his shop a brand new name, this is a telecommunication company.
He is so happy.
Phony sounds both simple and dynamic and it rings a bell !
He found it all by himself,
and applied for a European registration, nothing less !
Since Mr DUPONT is convinced that telecommunications are about to soar,
he aims to be worldwide concern.
He has already set up a few partnerships with "Anglo-Saxons" and within two weeks,
he will announce to them the birth of his "Phony business",
and how he will manage his worldwide set up.

Good luck Mr DUPONT !

To set up abroad and get it right
don't forget to check the meanings of your brandnames !

CREATION OF BRANDNAMES - TRADEMARKS - MARKETING WATCH
96 RUE DU FAUBOURG-POISSONNIÈRE 75010 PARIS - TÉL. : 00 33 1 49 70 06 06 - FAX : 00 33 1 42 85 47 83

graphic design

CORPORATE IDENTITY

PACKAGING / VOLUME

PUBLISHING

ALLIANCE DESIGN

YVES GUÉNOT
*Managing Director and
Creative Director*

ÉDITH BRUDER
Consulting Director

XAVIER MARTICOU
*Environmental Design
Manager*

APPROACH - Communication through design :
- combining strategy analysis with creative impact to confer a unique quality of relations with the public,
- designing, developing, reactivating brand identity, corporate identity, products or events.

AREAS OF EXPERTISE
- Visual identity : logos, identity manuals, branding
- Packaging design
- Environmental design : stand, signage, POS
- Corporate publications : annual reports, brochures
- Industrial design
- Multimedia : CD Rom, Web sites

Turnover	in %
Graphic Design	
Visual Identity	29
Packaging Design	12
Publishing	21
Industrial / Product Design	9
Environmental Design	
Commercial Architecture	12
Signage	15
Other	2

SECTORS OF ACTIVITY - Institutions, industry, food, bank and finance, cosmetics, computers, humanitarian.

NEW BUSINESS IN 1995/96
- Europort Vatry (global design)
- Rosières (visual identity, graphic design, industrial design)
- Groupe Cofinoga (graphic design and annual report)
- L'Oréal (packaging design, POS)
- Générale Sucrière (annual report)
- Chambre de Commerce et d'Industrie de Paris (publications)

PERSONNEL - 7

GROUP GROSS PROFIT - 1996 estimate : FF 6 m / 1995 : FF 3,5 m / 1994 : FF 2 m

COMPANY STRUCTURE - Alliance Design is a department of Alliance, a limited company, capital of FF 1, 500, 000. Founded in 1977.

NETWORK - Alliance is a founding member of the TEN (Trans European Network) network, present in Germany, Great Britain, France, Spain and Italy.

GROUP - Groupe Alliance

Europort Vatry
(Global design)

Rosières
(Global design)

Ministère de la Justice
(Visual identity)

Présidence Française de
l'Union Européenne
(Visual identity)

Akzo Nobel
(Global design)

L'Oréal
(Packaging design, POS)

Syndicat interprofession-
nel de la Viande (Logo
viande bovine française)

Arscimed
(Multimedia)

ALLIANCE DESIGN
17 rue des Dames Augustines
92200 Neuilly-sur-Seine
Tel. : 33 (0) 1 41 05 73 00
Fax : 33 (0) 1 41 05 08 40

YVES GUÉNOT
Managing Director

ÉDITH BRUDER
Consulting Director

identité visuelle

CLIENT :
MINISTÈRE
DE LA JUSTICE

ACTION :
CRÉATION
IDENTITÉ
VISUELLE

CHARTE
GRAPHIQUE

ÉDITION

36.15 JUSTICE

design global

Europort Vatry

CLIENT :
EUROPORT VATRY

ACTION :
CRÉATION
IDENTITÉ
VISUELLE

CHARTE
GRAPHIQUE

ÉDITION

SIGNALÉTIQUE

ARCHITECTURE
COMMERCIALE

CD-ROM

OUTILS
D'AIDE À LA VENTE

ANTARCTIQUE

KEY PEOPLE

PHILIPPE BALLATOUR
Managing Director
Free-lance designer.
Founder of Antarctique

PHILIPPE DUPUIS
Studio Manager
Career Background :
18 years design experience.

SYLVIE LEVALLOIS
Project Manager
Qualifications : École des
Beaux-Arts, École
Supérieure de Marketing et
de Communication (School
of Fine Arts, Higher School
of Marketing and
Communications).

COMPANY PROFILE

APPROACH - Self-defined as bridging the gap between producers and consumers, Antarctique's vocation is to transmit via the product a true corporate image, paving the way to brand awareness and exchange between companies and their clients.

AREAS OF EXPERTISE - Antarctique creates signs and images to enhance products in the marketplace and to emphasize corporate specificity. Product "signatures" to establish their unique identity, pictogram vocabularies, symbols and logotypes, graphic interfacing, typographical design and research, publishing and package design.

Turnover	in %
Graphic Design	
Visual Identity	40
Package Design	20
Publications	40

SECTORS OF ACTIVITY - Since 1988 Antarctique has successfully collaborated with France's major industrial firms. Whether in the automobile industry or in consumer durables, in machinery tools or in services, the agency has the capacity to act promptly upon a project, pooling all its resources and graphic design skills.

NEW BUSINESS IN 1995/96

- Renault Research and Development / Hybrid vehicles (Event identity / signature)
- Bull Multimedia (Internet sites, graphic design and specifications)
- France Télécom (Package design and specifications)
- Call (Publications, brochure design)
- Cap Sesa (Software products, graphic design and specifications)

PRINCIPAL CLIENTS

Porcher / Porcher
(New range identity /
graphic signature, analysis and concept)

Renault Design
Ludo & Modus
(Event identity /
graphic signature, design
and specifications)

Chaffoteaux & Maury /
Nectra
(New range identity /
graphic signature,
analysis and concept)

Renault Design / Spider,
Evado & Mégane
(Event, product identity /
graphic signature, design
and specifications)

SNCF
(Publications, Contact
sheets and catalogs,
in-house literature)

Renault Press / Renault
Boutique
(Press kit, design and
production)

CGFTE - Renault /
Praxitèle
(Event identity /
graphic signature,
corporate manual, design
and specifications)

CAT
(Publications, design of
in-house literature)

Éditions Larousse
(Publications, technical
art charter)

ANTARCTIQUE
88 Boulevard de la Villette
75019 Paris
Tél. : 33 (0) 1 44 52 52 80
Fax : 33 (0) 1 44 52 52 81

PERSONNEL - 7

TURNOVER - 1995 : FF 4,3 m / 1994 : FF 4,8 m

COMPANY STRUCTURE - A limited liability company, capital of FF200,000. Founded in 1988.

FRANCE TELECOM
Graphic signature design for the new
Amarys line of telephone terminals

RENAULT S.A
New typefont design for the branding
of the Renault motor vehicle range

CHAFFOTEAUX & MAURY
Graphic signature design for a new line of boilers

CGFTE
Visual identity concept
for the PRAXITÈLE programme

RENAULT RESEARCH & DEVELOPMENT
Visual identity concept
for the HYBRIDE programme

PORCHER
New product label design, with adaptation
to specific marking techniques

RENAULT S.A
Design and new derivation of the TWINGO logo
for the automatic transmission version: EASY

FRANCE TELECOM

Having designed the Amarys label,

designed and set up the user's graphic interface,

Antarctique also created a visual, highlighting elements

borrowed from France Telecom's product environment,

to illustrate packs and carrier bags designed for the range.

$$[b^3 + h^2]$$

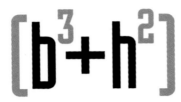

FRENCH HEAD

OLIVIER JOULIN
Director of Business Development
Qualifications : BTS, Bureau d'Études (Research) and complementary education.
Career Background :
7 years experience in design management.
Specialization : Packaging design and Design development.

COMPANY PROFILE

APPROACH - Great design alone resolves nothing. Successful design makes intelligent use of market research, putting a project on the right track from the start. We apply market values to our creative solutions and supervise production to our clients' greater benefit.

AREAS OF EXPERTISE - Consumer Products, Industrial Equipment, Package Design, Brand Identity and Brand Image, New Media Communications.

SECTORS OF ACTIVITY - Yours.

NEW BUSINESS IN 1996 - Several new accounts, but yours seems to be missing !

ACHIEVEMENTS - Our client's satisfaction is our greatest reward.

GERMAN HEAD

MICHAEL HARDT
Communication Design Consultant
Qualifications : Degree in Design.
Career Background :
20 years experience in marketing oriented design.
Specialization :
Multi-cultural Communications.

BARRAULT DESIGN
102 rue du Château
92100 Boulogne
Tel. : 33 (0) 1 46 03 86 20
Fax : 33 (0) 1 46 05 84 31

PERSONNEL - 6 in France and 5 in Germany
TURNOVER - 1996 : FF 4 Million in France and 600,000 DM in Germany
COMPANY STRUCTURE - Limited liability companies in France (SARL) and Germany (Gmbh)

HARDT DESIGN
Design Consultants
Kantstrasse 23a
D 66111 Saarbrücken
Tel. : (49) 681 936 57 12
Fax : (49) 681 936 57 11

h²

TIBHAR®   1973

WFS   1974

DeKowe®   1982

juris   1986

ORWO   1990

Urgomed   1996

our business
is the vision of
successful images

our business
is the vision of
tomorrows products

[It's not secret magic, it's simply the result of serious
methodology and the right management of the design process.]

b³

B C R

DIDIER BOULANT
Director of Clientele
École Supérieure de
Commerce, (Higher
School of Commerce),
ex-Director of Marketing,
agrifood sector.

MICHEL CALIBANI
Creative Director
25 years experience in
graphic design, six of
which were spent with
Raymond Loewy.

GUY RUAL
Director of Clientele
ex-Director of Marketing,
textile / sports sector.

APPROACH - Our management's first-hand experience from the client's point of view makes for practical and effective design.

AREAS OF EXPERTISE

- Institutional image : logotype, visual identity system, identity manual.
- Package design : form and graphics.
- Point of sale.
- Commercial publications.

Turnover	in %
Graphic Design	
Visual Identity	15
Package Design	75
POS and Publications	10

SECTORS OF ACTIVITY

- Agrifood
- Hygiene
- Beauty Care
- Maintenance
- Gardening
- DIY
- Fashion
- Pharmaceuticals…

NEW BUSINESS IN 1996

- Jacques Vabre (Package design and trademark, Café Primeur)
- Chambourcy (Package design and logo, Fruits du Soleil)
- Védial (Package design and trademark, Le Fleurier)
- Suchard (Package design, La chocolaterie)
- Eufodi (Visual identity for Poul' d'Or chain stores)
- Lactel (Espace Boissons, merchandising)

ACHIEVEMENTS - Janus of Industry 1995

Reckitt & Colman
(Néocide,
package design)

Nestlé
(P'tits Desserts,
package design)

Chambourcy
(Sveltesse Fruits du
Soleil, logo and
package design)

SmithKline Beecham
(Aquafresh,
graphic identity,
Popsy, Twist & Flex,
package design)

Bahlsen
(Curly Family,
package design)

Compagnie des
Fromages
(Le Coutances and
Neufchâtel,
package design)

Seita
(Picaduros,
package designs
and trademark)

Jacques Vabre
(100% Origine,
graphic identity and
package design for the
range)

Nestlé Rowntree
(Art Déco by Lanvin,
package design)

BCR
11-15 rue de la Rochefoucauld
92100 Boulogne
Tel. : 33 (0) 1 48 25 95 83
Fax : 33 (0) 1 48 25 95 81

PERSONNEL - 17

TURNOVER - 1995 : FF 13 m / 1994 : FF 12 m

COMPANY STRUCTURE - A limited liability company, capital of FF 300, 000.

Founded in 1987.

DIDIER BOULANT

GUY RUAL

PACO RABANNE : LOGO
AND IDENTITY SYSTEM RE-VAMP.
CREATION OF IDENTITY CHARTER
FOR ALL INTERNATIONAL LICENSEES.

«LE COUTANCES» AND
«NEUFCHÂTEL - EN - BRAY» : BRAND AND
PACK GRAPHICS REPOSITIONING.
TOWARDS GREATER IMPACT AND ACCESSIBILITY.
ASSERTING GENUINE VALUES.

THE AQUAFRESH TOOTHBRUSH
RANGE DESIGN
EXPRESSING THE TECHNICAL
ADVANTAGES
OF «FLEX» AND «TWIST & FLEX»:
SEGMENTING THE RANGE.

PACKAGE DESIGN FOR THE
INNOVATIVE «CAFÉ PRIMEUR».
ENRICHING JACQUES VABRE'S BRAND
COMMUNICATIONS TERRITORY.

RE-VAMP FOR LE FLEURIER RANGE.
PROJECTING A QUALITY IMAGE
WHILE MAINTAINING THE BRAND'S
DISTINCTIVE COLOUR CODES.

«A LONGER ROAD AHEAD»
WITH THE GRAPHIC DEVELOPMENT
OF A NEW CONCEPT APPLIED
TO THE ENTIRE WYNN'S ADDITIVES RANGE.

BLACK & GOLD

KEY PEOPLE

DANIEL DHONDT
Managing Director,
Creative Director
Career Background :
13 years experience as in-
house Creative Director in
package design. Founded
Black & Gold in 1990.

MURIEL GIRARD
Director of Clientele and
Marketing
Qualifications : Sciences
Politiques ; École de
Commerce, Lyon. (School
of Political Science ;
Business School, Lyon).
Career Background :
10 years marketing expe-
rience with major French
firms. Joined Black & Gold
in 1991.

CHRISTOPHE ALLISSE
Director of Business
Development
Qualifications : Masters
Degree in Economics.
Career Background :
2 years in advertising and
4 years in graphic design.

BLACK & GOLD
16-18 rue Quincampoix
75004 Paris
Tel. : 33 (0) 1 48 04 33 78
Fax : 33 (0) 1 42 71 04 28

COMPANY PROFILE

APPROACH - Each time we design a new package, we address the challenge : "Charm the consumer to sell the product". We mix marketing, design and technology to provide you with qualitative solutions that are both creative and effective. We offer to follow your product from concept through to merchandising : sales results are the best proof of the relevance and efficiency of our package designs.

AREAS OF EXPERTISE

- Strategy Consulting
- Package Design
- Visual Identity
- Publications
- Point of sale
- Store environment

SECTORS OF ACTIVITY - Our clients come from all areas (food, cosmetics, industry, leisure, services...).

NEW BUSINESS IN 1995/96

- Auchan
- B'A
- Ducros
- Jean Baptiste Delpierre
- Lactel
- Labeyrie
- Lanquetot
- Moët Hennessy
- Bosch
- Indola
- Labello

PERSONNEL - 14

TURNOVER - 1995 : FF 10,5 m / 1994 : FF 6,5 m

COMPANY STRUCTURE - A limited liability company, capital of FF300,000. Founded in 1990.

PRINCIPAL CLIENTS

Food Products
Auchan, B'A,
Besnier International,
Bizac, Boule D'or, Bridel,
Cap Océan, Claudel,
Ducros, E. Leclerc,
Eurofrais, Grosjean,
Félix, Fido,
Jean Baptiste Delpierre,
Lactel, Labeyrie, L.D.C.,
Lanquetot, Le Chatelain,
Lepetit, Lindt & Sprüngli,
Moët Hennessy,
Président, Rémy Martin,
Rians, Riblaire, Société,
Sodebo, Slim Fast,
Souchon,
Spillers Petfoods,
Sveltesse, Tendriade,
Tresch Alsacaves,
Valmont, Volcier.

Miscellaneous Products
Albal, Babivéa, Bosch,
Carrefour France,
Cristal Paris, Hansaplast,
Henkel, Impex, Indola,
Johnson, Labello,
Liliane France, Nivea,
Novémail,
Peintures TLM, Roc,
Rotring.

Other
Bouygues,
Dow Chemical,
La Française des Jeux,
Saggel Vendôme.

CONTACTS
DANIEL DHONDT
Managing Director,
Creative Director

MURIEL GIRARD
Director of Clientele

CHRISTOPHE ALLISSE
Director of Business
Development

6 ANS,
60 GRANDES MARQUES

PRÉSIDENT
Lifting gamme packaging

LACTEL
*Création identité
visuelle et packaging
lait Bio*

SOCIÉTÉ
*Création identité visuelle
et packaging Roquefort
Cave Baragnaudes*

B'A
*Création concept
packaging et design
volume*

IMPEX
*Création identité visuelle
packaging et forme
de la gamme
"New Design"*

BLACK & GOLD

C'CAPITAL

KEY PEOPLE

PHILIPPE DEVISMES
*Chairman and
Managing Director*
Career Background :
Published author of,
«Packaging Mode d'Emploi»
(How-to Guide to
Package Design), Editions
Dunod,1991.

MIGUEL CRUZ
*Associate,
Production Manager*

FRANÇOIS THIAUDIÈRE
*Associate,
Financial Director*

COMPANY PROFILE

APPROACH - To assure you of the highest level of expertise, C'Capital has chosen to specialize in package design. At every stage of your project, our team is involved in strategic analysis, following through from conception to production.

AREAS OF EXPERTISE - Our experience covers total product environment at the point of sale : package design, merchandising, point of sale and information at point of sale.

Turnover	in %
Graphic Design	
Brand Identity	20
Package Design	65
Publications	10
POS and IPOS	5
International	20

SECTORS OF ACTIVITY - Package design for the mass market : agrifood, hygiene / beauty care, DIY-gardening, motor vehicle industry...

NEW BUSINESS IN 1996
- Bébé Confort
- La Française des Jeux
- Lindt
- Marie Brizard
- Reckitt & Colman
- Stendahl
- Xylochimie...

ACHIEVEMENTS
- Honorable Mention, Stratégies Grand Prize 1994 for Touch' by Schweppes
- First Prize, Package Design Challenge, Luxury Packaging Night 1994
- Best Design Agency, 1992
- Gold Quojem Award1992, design category, for Brio
- Silver Metre Award1991, merchandising category, for OCP Répartition

PRINCIPAL CLIENTS

Food
- Lindt (Les Carrés)
- Marie-Brizard
  (Pulco Citron CHR,
  Polish vodka)
- Interco (Donati rice)
- Europâte (Croustipâte)
- Danuta-Barilla
  (Malma) Poland,
- Beghin Say (Sucre Ligne)
- Calixte (Cochonou)
- Fralib (Lipton Ice Tea)
- National Food Products
  Company (Lacnor milk
  and fruit juice ranges),
  United Arab Emirates,
- Motta (MAX ice cream
  range), France and
  International.
- Schweppes
  (Touch', Schweppes)

Other sectors
- Reckitt & Colman
  (Blanco, O' Cédar)
- Santé Beauté
  (Émail Diamant)
- Xylochimie (Bondex,
  Xylophène, Véraline,
  Décapex)
- Ampafrance
  (Bébé Confort), France
  and International
- Stendhal
- Melitta (Handy Bag)
- Sagem (Eyquem spark
  plugs)
- Plan SPG (Caillard,
  Le Paysan)
- Citroën (motor car parts
  range), France and
  International
- Holt Lloyd (Holt's motor
  car maintenance
  products)
- Ralston Energy System
  (Energizer, Mazda, Ucar)

CONTACTS

PHILIPPE DEVISMES
*Chairman and Managing
Director*

CHRISTOPHE FINOT
Business Development

C'CAPITAL
5 passage Thiéré
75011 Paris
Tel. : 33 (0) 1 47 00 80 00
Fax : 33 (0) 1 47 00 83 30

PERSONNEL - 25

TURNOVER - 1996 estimate : FF 16 m / 1995 : FF 15 m

COMPANY STRUCTURE - A limited company, capital of FF1,199,600. Founded in 1988.

MEMBERSHIP - PDA

Santé Beauté
Creation of a new
reference corresponding
to the entire EMAIL
DIAMANT product line.

Lindt
Revamping of the
"Les Carrés" line.

C'CAPITAL
DESIGN PACKAGING
IDENTITY/PUBLISHING

Cogesal
New packaging creation for
Max de MOTTA ice cream
(France and International).

Reckitt & Colman
New packaging creation
for a new Blanco
reference.

Xylochimie
Packaging and brand
identity revamping for
the DECAPEX line.

Holt-Lloyd
New packaging creation
(graphics-volume) for the
HOLTS automobile
maintenance product line.

CALYPSO

KEY PEOPLE

DANIEL JACQUIN
Chairman,
Creative Director
Founder

CLAUDE LOUIS-FERNAND
Director of Strategy
Qualifications : ESSEC
(Higher School of
Economic Sciences)
Career Background :
Marketing, Danone Groupe
(6 years), Director of
Marketing, Bridel (4 years),
Director of Marketing,
Casino (4 years).

JACQUES LLORENTE
Creative Director,
Product Design
Qualifications : CNAM, ICG
Career Background : Serge
Mansau Design Studio
(4 years). Llorente Design,
Founder

COMPANY PROFILE

APPROACH · Calypso bases its approach on brand enhancement. To fully grasp the brand, its history, its environment, each project begins with careful listening sessions, where we learn all we can about the problem to be solved. This analysis ensures the relevancy of our creative research and its ability to express the brand strategically and powerfully, with originality.

AREAS OF EXPERTISE · Calypso extends its expertise to brand strategy consulting and to all areas of visual expression : product design, identity, package design, publishing. It is backed by in-depth understanding of mass marketing as well as of selective or specialized merchandizing.

SECTORS OF ACTIVITY · Agrifood, luxury goods, hygiene, perfume, non-food.

ACHIEVEMENTS

- Stratégies Grand Prix for Package Design, agrifood category, 1995
- Stratégies Grand Prix for Design 1992
- Stratégies Graphic Design Prize 1992
- Oscar for Package Design
- LSA New Products Oscar
- Janus for Industry

PRINCIPAL CLIENTS

Mass Market

BN

Bridel

Entremont

Fromagerie des Chaumes

Fromarsac

Genlis

Harris

Pasquier

Starissima

Tipiak

Luxury Goods

Camus

Hermès

Parfums de Gency

Valrhona

Van Cleef & Arpels

Tobacco

SEITA

Santé

Laboratoire Monot

Laboratoire Septodont

CALYPSO
151 rue de Billancourt
92100 Boulogne
Tel. : 33 (0) 1 46 04 03 03
Fax : 33 (0) 1 46 04 82 64

PERSONNEL · 20

COMPANY STRUCTURE · A limited company, capital of FF 6,001,500. Founded in 1978.

CONTACTS
DANIEL JACQUIN
CLAUDE LOUIS-FERNAND

CALYPSO

La recherche de l'efficacité dans l'esthétisme

PASQUIER
Relifting de l'identité visuelle de marque et du packaging de la gamme viennoiserie de Pasquier.

CHOC'LAND - BN
Repositionnement de l'identité de marque et des packagings de la gamme Choc'land.

FRUITOON - TEISSEIRE
Création de l'identité de marque et du packaging des sucettes à glacer.

GAMME A.O.C. - ENTREMONT
Création du design emballage et des packagings de la gamme fromages A.O.C.

CALYPSO

La recherche de l'efficacité dans l'esthétisme

XO - CAMUS
*Création du design forme
du cognac XO.*

**FIRST
VAN CLEEF & ARPELS**
*Création du design forme
et du packaging du parfum.*

HERMES
*Création du design forme
et du packaging du parfum.*

VALRHONA
*Création du design de forme
et des packagings des boîtes
de bonbons de chocolats
et des carrés Manjari / Jivara.
Création du packaging
de Celaya.*

CALYPSO

La recherche de l'efficacité dans l'esthétisme

NIÑAS - SEITA
*Création des packagings
de la gamme cigare.*

**PLIZ ET FEE DU LOGIS
JOHNSON**
*Relifting des identités de
marque et des packagings des
gammes Pliz et Fée du logis.*

**SAINT-ALBRAY
FROMAGERIE DES CHAUMES**
*Relifting de l'identité
de marque et du packaging
de Saint-Albray.*

SURPRIZ' - YOPLAIT
*Création des packagings
des fromages frais aromatisés
et des crèmes desserts.*

CARRÉ NOIR

KEY PEOPLE

GÉRARD CARON
*Chairman and
Co-Founder of Carré Noir*

MICHEL ALIZARD
*Creative Director and
Co-Founder of Carré Noir*

MICHEL DISLE
*Creative Director and
Co-Founder of Carré Noir*

JEAN-LOUIS AZIZOLLAH
Managing Director

JACQUES CHARTOL
Managing Director

JEAN-PIERRE LEFEBVRE
Director of Clientele

SYLVAIN LABONNE
*Director of New
Technologies*

ALBERT BOTON
Creative Director

MICHEL COLLET
Creative Director

**JEAN-CHRISTOPHE
CRIBELIER**
Creative Director

BÉATRICE MARIOTTI
Creative Director

COMPANY PROFILE

APPROACH - Observatory for major consumer trends, Carré Noir assists business development strategy in the art of mastering of visual signs. Carré Noir creates total corporate, product and environmental design identity programmes.

AREAS OF EXPERTISE

- Visual identity : logotype, identity manual, brand image.
- Products : package design, new products, form design, industrial design.
- Commercial space design : POS image, signage, POS display.
- Corporate Literature : brochure, annual report, catalog.
- Multimedia : on-line, off-line.
- Special events.

Turnover	in %
Graphic Design	
Visual Identity	26
Package Design	47
Publishing	5
Product Design	
Luxury goods and Industrial	3
Environmental Design	
Commercial Space Design and Signage	16
Other	
Multimedia	3

SECTORS OF ACTIVITY

- Services : Finance-banking-insurance, hotels and catering, leisure-sports, transportation, multimedia communications.
- Industrial products : energy, computers, transportation, domestic consumer durables.
- Luxury goods : Textiles/fashion, cosmetics/perfumes, spirits.
- Mass market : Food, pharmaceuticals/hygiene, tobacco.

Turnover	in %
Services	26
Industrial products	21
Luxury goods	7
Mass marketing	46

ACHIEVEMENTS

- 3M France, Package design award
- Bon Marché, Best Euro (logo category)

PERSONNEL - 116

GROSS PROFIT - 1995/96: FF66m (group figure)

COMPANY STRUCTURE - A limited company, capital of FF2,234,000. Founded in 1973.

FOREIGN OFFICES AND NETWORK - Carré Noir Brussels - Carré Noir London - Carré Noir New York - Carré Noir Paris - Carré Noir Tokyo - Carré Noir Torino

MEMBERSHIP - Gérard Caron, president of the Carré Noir group, is this year's president of the PDA (Pan European brand Design Association).

PRINCIPAL CLIENTS

FRANCE
Product design
Saint Gobain Glass, Martell.

Publishing
SNCF train network

Visual identity
Alouette Fm, Dalloz Sirey, Cerruti, Delsey, Neuflize Schlumberger Mallet, Lafarge.

Environmental Design
Carnet de vol, Myrys.

Package Design
Eminence, Cogedep, Kraft General Foods (J. Vabre), Saint Mamet, Elle et Vire.

Multimedia
Peugeot

**INTERNATIONAL
ACCOUNTS**
Visual identity
American Express, Banque de Luxembourg, European Space Agency, Business Objects, Toshiba Europe
Package Design
Bernard Matthews Frozen Foods, Henkel, Shisheido.

Environmental Design
Agrokor (Croatia)

Publishing
Tag Heuer

Product Design
Taylor Made

CONTACTS

JEAN-LOUIS AZIZOLLAH
Managing Director

JEAN-PIERRE LEFEBVRE
Director of Clientele

CARRÉ NOIR
Square Monceau
82 boulevard des Batignolles
75850 Paris Cedex 17
Tel. : 33 (0) 1 42 94 02 27
Fax : 33 (0) 1 42 94 06 78

L'ARCHIPEL
DUTY FREE SHOP

Logotype for Paris Airports

TOKYO
OPERA
CITY

Corporate Identity
for Cultural and Business district

AEROSPATIALE

CARRÉ
NOIR

MIR plus

MIR plus

Corporate Identity and Architecture for hypermarkets

LANCÔME
PARIS

Product design
and merchandising
for Delsey

Packagings and product design for Coty cosmetics

Signage for Shell formula

Architecture for optician Mikissimes
at the Carrousel du Louvre

Multimedia design
for Automobiles Peugeot

Corporate Identity
for Méridien Hotels

PLANETE BLEUE

Corporate Identity
for Air France's programm

NIHON L'ORÉAL

Logotype and Corporate Literature for the Japanese subsidiary of L'Oréal

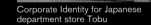

Corporate Identity for Japanese
department store Tobu

C B ' A

KEY PEOPLE

LOUIS COLLINET
*Chairman and
Managing Director*
Career Background :
Founder of CB'A.

ARNAUD TOURTOULOU
General Manager
Qualifications : ESCP
(Higher School of Business
and Advertising). Masters in
Business Law.
Career Background :
Marketing with Lesieur
Cotelle, Colgate Palmolive
and Côte d'Or.

COMPANY PROFILE

APPROACH - For 15 years CB'A has consistently combined strategic rigour and creative force to stimulate product sales and reinforce brand image.

SECTORS OF ACTIVITY

- Agrifood

- Mass market

- Cosmetics, Perfumes, Pharmaceuticals

- Finance, Banking, Insurance

- Computers

- Institutions

Turnover	in %
Graphic Design	**(70)**
Visual Identity	30
Package Design	60
Publishing	10
Product Design	**(15)**
Luxury goods	100
Environmental Design	**(15)**
Commercial Space Design	60
Signage	40

ACHIEVEMENTS

Three citations for Product of the year 1995

- La Croix Fraîcheur Lavande

- Paic Excel

- Findus Cuisine Créative

PRINCIPAL CLIENTS

Corporate identity :
Continent,
Conforama,
Mondial Moquette,
INPI, CANAM,
Douanes et Droits
Indirects, CCF SAM,
Bayard Presse,
Ecomax, Institut Pasteur,
Montecristo Restaurant
Café, Ministry of Labour,
Ministry of Foreign Affairs,
Disneyland Paris:
Nestlé Baby Comfort
Stops,
Permanent Assembly of
Chamber of Agriculture,
Fil à Fil, Concorde
Hotels, Banque de
France,
Wafabank Group...

Product identity :
Agfa,
Kraft Jacobs Suchard,
Colgate Palmolive,
Grand Metropolitan,
Gemey,
Champagnes and Spirits
Associated,
Fralib, Findus,
Nestlé, Lesieur,
Henkel, Rubson,
BN, Diépal,
Ducros, Miko-Cogesal,
Bourjois, Valrhona,
CPC, Pernod,
SVF, Bongrain,
Cora,
L'Oréal Technique
Professionnelle,
Lancôme, Biotherm...

PERSONNEL - 87

TURNOVER - 1995 : FF66.2m / 1994 : FF49.7m

GROSS PROFIT - 1995 : FF45.3m / 1994 : FF35.2m

COMPANY STRUCTURE - A limited company, capital of FF2,000,000. Founded in 1982.

FOREIGN OFFICES AND NETWORK - Paris - Brussels

MEMBERSHIP - PDA

CB'A
94 avenue de Villiers
75017 Paris
Tel. : 33 (0) 1 40 54 09 00
Fax : 33 (0) 1 47 64 95 75

CONTACTS
LOUIS COLLINET
ARNAUD TOURTOULOU

Création du logotype et mise en place du système d'identité visuelle de Continent

Création du logotype et mise en place du système d'identité visuelle des Relais Bébé Nestlé

Création de la campagne de fidélisation des Hôtels Concorde

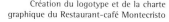

Création du logotype et de la charte graphique du Restaurant-café Montecristo

the graphic designers' index 11

COCKPIT DESIGN

KEY PEOPLE

SIMON BOUANICH
Chairman and Managing Director, Founder
Qualifications :
École Supérieure d'Art Moderne (Higher Scool of Modern Art).
Career Background :
11 years as Creative Director.

SOPHIE BELLOT
Director of Clientele, Associate
Qualifications : École Supérieure de Publicité (Higher School of Advertising).

COMPANY PROFILE

APPROACH - Our clients' success. Cockpit Design is convinced of the importance of corporate culture and values. We put our strategic and creative ability to work to enhance and reinforce these values through package design, visual identity and different promotional media such as publications and point of sale communications.

AREAS OF EXPERTISE

- Package Design
- Visual Identity
- Publications
- Point of sale communications

Turnover	in %
Graphic Design	
Visual Identity	10
Package Design	60
Publications	15
Other	
Merchandising, POS	15

SECTORS OF ACTIVITY

- Agrifood
- Hygiene / Beauty care
- Industry
- Franchise networks
- Cultural
- Fashion

Turnover	in %
Agrifood	50
Industry	20
Culture, Fashion	15
Hygiene, Beauty care	15

NEW BUSINESS IN 1996

- Lanquetot (New product design)
- TF1 (Film, video, CD collection)
- CCI (Informative brochure)
- Diapositive (Visual identity, point of sale communications)
- McDonald's (BDDP. Point of sale communications, inaugural kit)

PRINCIPAL CLIENTS

La Française des Jeux
(Graphic revamp of Loto media)

Carrefour
(Creation of a decorative biscuit tin collection with "Fabrics of the World" theme)

Monoprix
(Visual identity for children's products, "Les Monop's")

Fnac
(Corporate brochure)

Valéo
(Package design, domestic and international brand management

S.C. Galec
Brand design and management: agrifood, cosmetics and hygiene)

France Loisirs
(Quarterly point of sale communications programme)

Cibié
(Range design for the Spanish market)

Biscuiterie Bouvard
(Creation of various biscuit ranges)

Biscuiterie Tanguy
(Creation of traditional Breton biscuit ranges)

RJR Nabisco
(Point of sale communications, launch of new fashion label : Camel Vêtement)

COCKPIT DESIGN
64 rue Tiquetonne
75002 Paris
Tel. : 33 (0) 1 40 13 04 94
Fax : 33 (0) 1 40 13 07 94

PERSONNEL - 10

TURNOVER - 1995 : FF7.8m / 1994 : FF7.2m

COMPANY STRUCTURE - A limited company, capital of FF500,000. Founded in 1986.

CONTACTS

SIMON BOUANICH
Chairman, Project Manager

SOPHIE BELLOT
Director of Clientele, Associate

COCKPIT
DESIGN

· LECLERC - PÊCHE OCÉAN ·

· LECLERC - PLANTATIONS ·

· GERBE ·

· LECLERC
LES RECETTES GASTRONOMIQUES ·

· LECLERC - IROISE ·

· NESTLE SOURCES ·

· VALEO ·

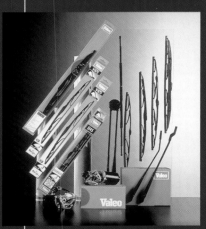
· VALEO ·

· BRASSEURS DE FRANCE ·

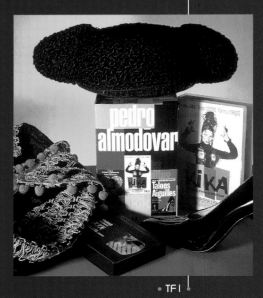
· TF1 ·

· McDONALD'S ·

DESGRIPPES GOBÉ & ASSOCIATES

KEY PEOPLE

JOËL DESGRIPPES
Chairman
Founder

LAURENCE WAHL
Partner
Corporate Identity

ALAIN DORÉ
Partner,
Creative Director

FRANÇOIS CARATGÉ
Partner
Consumer Brands

COMPANY PROFILE

APPROACH - A global approach to brands, multiple skills, and an international know-how define the agency's strenghts. Our passion and ambition is to put them to work for our clients with the highest degree of exigency, sensitivity, and professionalism. To reveal the universe of expression which both identifies and differentiates the brand from all the others, the agency makes use of an original process : SENSE (Sensory Exploration, Need States Evaluation), which centres the brand at the core of all research and leads to the definition of the brand's emotional territory and distinctive style through its multiple means of expression.

AREAS OF EXPERTISE - Desgrippes Gobé & Associates, ranking among the very top international design agencies, specialises in the global image management of brands for companies, products, and services. The programs are developed by integrating brand strategy with the definition of the territory of expression through all forms of communication design. Their goal is to expand and optimise the presense of the brands in their respective markets.

SECTORS OF ACTIVITY - In more than 20 years the agency has acquired a solid background in a broad range of areas, such as : fashion, perfume, beauty care, mass-market products, pharmacology, large financial institutions, industry and services, cultural and sporting events, our clients reaping the benefits of our eclectic experience and a constantly renewed outlook.

NEW BUSINESS IN 1995/1996 - CNCC (identity programme), Colart International (hobby line from Lefranc & Bourgeois), Ducros (range repositioning), Elida Fabergé (Impulse range), Henkel (Fa range), McCain (pizza range), Montevrain Papeterie, Nestlé (Friskies range), Renova - Portugal (global repositioning), Taittinger Champagne, UCPA (identity programme),...

ACHIEVEMENTS - Numerous awards including : Stratégies Grand Prix Design - Cosmétique News Design Award - Eurobest - Best of Show International Packaging Award (USA) - Packaging Oscar and Worldstar for Packaging.

PERSONNEL - 70 in France and 150 within the Group.
TURNOVER - 1995 : 24,8 million $
COMPANY STRUCTURE - Independent, capital of FF 1,000,000. Founded in 1971.
FOREIGN OFFICES AND NETWORK - The Desgrippes Gobé & Associates Group has offices in France (Paris and Lyon), in the United States (New York), in Japan (Tokyo), in Korea (Seoul) and in Hungary (Budapest). We are represented in Tunisia (Tunis) by Media Plus.
MEMBERSHIP - ADC (France), PDA (Europe), PDC and AIGA (US) and JPDA (Japan).

PRINCIPAL CLIENTS

Akai,
Beiersdorf Nivéa,
Bel Fromageries,
Belin Lu Biscuits,
Boucheron, Bourjois,
Cartier, Chronopost,
Club des Créateurs,
CNCC, CNP, Coca-Cola,
Commercial Union,
CPR, Crédit Agricole,
Danone Group,
Etam 1.2.3., Fila Sport,
Fragonard,
Galderma Laboratories,
Gillette, Givenchy,
Henkel,
Hoffmann La Roche,
IBM, Olympic Games of Albertville,
Journal Officiel, Kenzo,
Kraft Jacobs Suchard,
L'Oréal, La Poste,
Laboratoires Polivé,
Lacoste, Lindt,
McCain Foods, Ministry of Youth and Sports,
Monoprix,
Nathan Jeux,
Nestlé France, Novotel,
Optic 2000,
Procter & Gamble,
Pacific,
Reckitt & Colman,
Renova, Revillon,
Rhône Poulenc Rorer,
Ricard, Rodier,
Seafrance, Selles, SNCF,
Technal, UCPA,
Vania Expansion, Vittel,
Henri Wintermans.

CONTACTS

JOËL DESGRIPPES
ANNETTE KLEK

Corporate Identity :
LAURENCE WAHL

Consumer Brands :
FRANÇOIS CARATGÉ

Lyon Office :
GILBERT FLORÈS
Tel. : 33 (0) 4 78 89 62 72

DESGRIPPES GOBÉ & ASSOCIATES
18 bis, avenue de la Motte-Picquet
75007 Paris
Tel. : 33 (0) 1 44 18 44 18
Fax : 33 (0) 1 45 51 96 60
WWW : http://www.dga.com

CHRONOPOST

*Programme d'identité corporate, évolution du logotype en fonction
de deux axes de positionnement : l'international et l'humanisation*

CHRONOPOST
LES MAÎTRES DU TEMPS

signes extérieurs
de personnalité

CRÉDIT AGRICOLE
*Programme
d'identité corporate*

COCA-COLA
*Image Management Program
hors-médias*

IBM Aptiva
*Repositionnement mondial et
création d'une communication
de proximité*

COCA-COLA
*Repositionnement mondial
de SPRITE*

HENKEL
*Repositionnement
international
de la gamme FA*

McCAIN
*Création de la marque
et de la gamme
Gina Paterson*

SEAFRANCE
*Programme d'identité corporate
pour la compagnie ferry SEALINK
devenue SEAFRANCE*

DESGRIPPES GOBÉ & ASSOCIATES
IMAGE MANAGEMENT AND STRATEGIC DESIGN

Tél : 01 44 18 44 18 - Fax : 01 45 51 96 60

DESIGN BOARD

KEY PEOPLE

YVES SUTY
Acting Managing Director
Qualifications : Fine Arts.
Career Background : From
art direction to copywriting
to free-lance consulting.
From creative direction to
communications strategy.

CARL DELLAERT
Key Account Director
Qualifications : Advertising.
Career Background : From
advertising to marketing,
from marketing to design
marketing.

CHRISTINE DERCOURT
Commercial Director
Qualifications : MBA and
Business School.
Career Background : From
account executive to
account director in an advertising agency, from account
executive to commercial
director with Design Board.

ANN VAN NIEUWENHUYZE
Key Account Manager
Qualifications : Marketing.
Career Background : From
languages to sales, from
languages to development
and to client management.

ERIK VANTAL
Creative Director
Qualifications : Graphic Arts.
Career Background : From
graphics to art direction to
creative direction.

NICOLE MARTIN
Creative Director
Qualifications : Graphic Arts.
Career Background : From
graphics to art direction, from
art direction to client management to creative direction.

DESIGN BOARD
Avenue Georges Lecointe, 50
1180 Brussels
Tel. : (32 2) 375 39 62
Fax. : (32 2) 375 50 48

COMPANY PROFILE

APPROACH - Visual identity design is not an end in itself. It is the graphic expression of corporate marketing strategy. Design Board assists its clients in building their brand.

Linking two realities, the business of its clients and the marketplace, Design Board develops the corporate marketing strategy, the brand strategy and its visual expression.

Its methods are based on the creation of a task force, working from the strategic thinking to the creative process and using interactive techniques.

AREAS OF EXPERTISE

- Corporate : corporate name creation, visual identity, identity manual, editing, annual reports, architecture.
- Brand : brand name creation, brand identity, package design, brand management and extension, new product development, brand re-engineering, product design.
- Environmental Design : Architecture, com-mercial space design, systematization, stand design.

Turnover	in %
Graphic Design	
Visual Identity	30
Package Design	35
Editing	10
Product Design	
Luxury and Industrial	10
Environmental Design	
Commercial space	15

SECTORS OF ACTIVITY

- Corporate : All sectors.
- Brand : All sectors.

NEW BUSINESS IN 1996

- Campbell (Package design for D&L range)
- Total (Architecture for Shop in Shop)
- Café Colombie (Standardization)
- Sylvania (Package design for lighting range)
- Hoegaarden (Visual identity and package design for export)
- TIB (Visual identity and applications for Brussels Tourism)
- Belgacom (Telephone booth)
- SmithKline Beecham (Panadeine package design)

PERSONNEL - 33

TURNOVER - 1995 : BFr 210m / 1994 : BFr 168m

COMPANY STRUCTURE - A limited company, capital of BFr 960,000. Founded in 1968.

FOREIGN OFFICE AND NETWORK - Paris. IDP Network : Belo Horizonte - Bogota - Buenos Aires - Chicago - Cincinnati - Johannesburg - Lima - Madrid - Melbourne - Mexico City - New York - Rio de Janeiro - Santiago - Sao Paulo - Singapore - Sydney

MAJOR CLIENTS

Petrofina
(Corporate identity,
subsidiairies and network)

Mars
(Package design)

Johnson Wax
(Glade range)
(Canard - Duck -Pato)

Brossard
(Package design, biscuit
and frozen food ranges)

Bayer
(Natreen range)

Douwe Egberts
(Concept and space
design, corporate
package design for the
Jacqmotte Coffee
Houses)

Brandt
(Corporate identity,
subsidiairies, signage)

Procter & Gamble
(Package design)

Sara Lee
(Package design)

Sandoz Nutrition
(Package Design)

CONTACTS
Brussels :
CHRISTINE DERCOURT
ANN VAN NIEUWENHUYZE
CARL DELLAERT
Tel. : (32 2) 375 39 62
Fax. : (32 2) 375 50 48

Paris :
YVES SUTY
BÉATRICE FOURNIER
19 rue de la Dhuis
75020 Paris
Tel. : 33 (0) 1 40 30 47 47
Fax : 33 (0) 1 40 31 03 15

FOCI

PAS·DE·CALAIS

JPM

PARTNERS
ASSURANCES·VERZEKERINGEN

NOBRE

SAIMAZA

FINA

OBOURG

PUILAETCO

PATEK
PHILIPPE
GENEVE

DOMOTIK
EINE ANDERE DIMENSION DES WOHNENS

EURO SUCRE

CLYDA
PARIS

RCL

ENCYCLOPEDIES
BORDAS

SIDHOLE

Ville de Lille

TOURING
CLUB

EDITIONS
ATLAS

Marriott

BEKA

CORSE DU SUD

COFFEE HOUSE

Eternit

Groupe
Brandt

DESIGN BOARD

KEY PEOPLE

YVES SUTY
Acting Managing Director
Qualifications : Fine Arts.
Career Background : From art direction to copywriting to free-lance consulting. From creative direction to communications strategy.

CARL DELLAERT
Key Account Director
Qualifications : Advertising.
Career Background : From advertising to marketing, from marketing to design marketing.

CHRISTINE DERCOURT
Commercial Director
Qualifications : MBA and Business School.
Career Background : From account executive to account director in an advertising agency, from account executive to commercial director with Design Board.

ANN VAN NIEUWENHUYZE
Key Account Manager
Qualifications : Marketing.
Career Background : From languages to sales, from languages to development and to client management.

ERIK VANTAL
Creative Director
Qualifications : Graphic Arts.
Career Background : From graphics to art direction to creative direction.

NICOLE MARTIN
Creative Director
Qualifications : Graphic Arts.
Career Background : From graphics to art direction, from art direction to client management to creative direction.

DESIGN BOARD
Avenue Georges Lecointe, 50
1180 Brussels
Tel. : (32 2) 375 39 62
Fax. : (32 2) 375 50 48

COMPANY PROFILE

APPROACH - Visual identity design is not an end in itself. It is the graphic expression of corporate marketing strategy. Design Board assists its clients in building their brand.
Linking two realities, the business of its clients and the marketplace, Design Board develops the corporate marketing strategy, the brand strategy and its visual expression.
Its methods are based on the creation of a task force, working from the strategic thinking to the creative process and using interactive techniques.

AREAS OF EXPERTISE

- Corporate : corporate name creation, visual identity, identity manual, editing, annual reports, architecture.
- Brand : brand name creation, brand identity, package design, brand management and extension, new product development, brand re-engineering, product design.
- Environmental Design : Architecture, commercial space design, systematization, stand design.

Turnover	in %
Graphic Design	
Visual Identity	30
Package Design	35
Editing	10
Product Design	
Luxury and Industrial	10
Environmental Design	
Commercial space	15

SECTORS OF ACTIVITY

- Corporate : All sectors.
- Brand : All sectors.

NEW BUSINESS IN 1996

- Campbell (Package design for D&L range)
- Total (Architecture for Shop in Shop)
- Café Colombie (Standardization)
- Sylvania (Package design for lighting range)
- Hoegaarden (Visual identity and package design for export)
- TIB (Visual identity and applications for Brussels Tourism)
- Belgacom (Telephone booth)
- SmithKline Beecham (Panadeine package design)

PERSONNEL - 33

TURNOVER - 1995 : BFr 210m / 1994 : BFr 168m

COMPANY STRUCTURE - A limited company, capital of BFr 960,000. Founded in 1968.

FOREIGN OFFICE AND NETWORK - Paris. IDP Network : Belo Horizonte - Bogota - Buenos Aires - Chicago - Cincinnati - Johannesburg - Lima - Madrid - Melbourne - Mexico City - New York - Rio de Janeiro - Santiago - Sao Paulo - Singapore - Sydney

MAJOR CLIENTS

Petrofina
(Corporate identity, subsidiairies and network)

Mars
(Package design)

Johnson Wax
(Glade range)
(Canard - Duck -Pato)

Brossard
(Package design, biscuit and frozen food ranges)

Bayer
(Natreen range)

Douwe Egberts
(Concept and space design, corporate package design for the Jacqmotte Coffee Houses)

Brandt
(Corporate identity, subsidiairies, signage)

Procter & Gamble
(Package design)

Sara Lee
(Package design)

Sandoz Nutrition
(Package Design)

CONTACTS

Brussels :
CHRISTINE DERCOURT
ANN VAN NIEUWENHUYZE
CARL DELLAERT
Tel. : (32 2) 375 39 62
Fax. : (32 2) 375 50 48

Paris :
YVES SUTY
BÉATRICE FOURNIER
19 rue de la Dhuis
75020 Paris
Tel. : 33 (0) 1 40 30 47 47
Fax : 33 (0) 1 40 31 03 15

DESIGN STRATEGY

KEY PEOPLE

PHILIPPE RASQUINET
Chairman, Co-Founder

JIM WATERS
Managing Director,
Creative Director,
Co-Founder
Co-founder of one of the
top ten design bureaux
world-wide, Design
Strategy's culture and
experience are truly
international in scope.

DESIGN STRATEGY
41 rue Camille Pelletan
92300 Levallois-Perret
Tel. : 33 (0) 1 41 40 00 00
Fax : 33 (0) 1 41 40 00 01

STRATEGIC DESIGN PARTNERS
Square Sainctellette 1-2-3
1000 Bruxelles
Tel. : 32 2 219 24 51

MINALE TATTERSFIELD
The Courtyard
37 Sheen Road
Richmond, Surrey
TW91AJ
Tel. : 81 948 79 99

WINDI WINDERLICH
Bahrenfelder Chausee 49
Kônigliches Proviantamt
D 22761 Hamburg
Tel. : 040 8 99 04-0

COMPANY PROFILE

APPROACH · Our vocation is to assist businesses, institutions and brands in revealing their specific personality traits, in defining their image strategy and putting it to work via the creation and development of a powerful, relevant and lasting identity. We are convinced that design is a strategic management tool, instrumental in the corporate development process and effective in bringing brands to life.

AREAS OF EXPERTISE · Striving to respond individually or globally to all design needs, we have integrated the entire range of design services into our basic structure to better serve client strategy :
- Marketing and corporate studies
- Visual identity
- Signage
- Commercial space design and merchandising
- Product design
- Publications
- Package design

SECTORS OF ACTIVITY · By our very nature we are open to all businesses, institutions, civil services, local government, associations...in all sectors. Among areas best known to us are :
- the mass market
- the public sector
- banking and insurance
- transport
- industry

NEW BUSINESS IN 1996 · Aigle, Bourse de Casablanca, Office Chérifien des Phosphates, Lagardère, La Hénin, Eurisys, Neuflize-Schlumberger-Mallet, Exane, Chambre des Métiers, Banque Indosuez, Hachette Livre, Yamaha, Gewy, GIB Group, GTIE, Semtao, La maison autour du monde.

PERSONNEL · 30 (France), 120 (Europe).

COMPANY STRUCTURE · A limited company, capital of FF250,000. Founded in 1982.

MEMBERSHIP · ADC

PRINCIPAL CLIENTS

Visual Identity

Caisse d'Épargne

Banque Populaire

Banque Paribas

BNP

UAP

GMF

Lagardère

Eurostar

Transpole

Semvat

Sephora...

Environmental Design

Aigle

Armand Thierry
(for men and women)

La Hénin

Baiser Sauvage

Seita...

Consumer Goods

Gewy

Charal

Schweppes

Findus

Lancôme...

CONTACTS
PHILIPPE RASQUINET
JIM WATERS

ILLUSTRATION : OLIVIER DOUZOU

For **Eurostar**, the first European high speed train, an identity and graphic style expressing quality of service rather than high technology.

Strategic identity planning and management for **UAP**, one of the worlds' leading insurance groups.

Bourse de Casablanca

The Casablanca Stock Exchange is opening up to the financial world with a logotype based on the olive tree, symbol of life and wealth.

Through its architecture and environmental graphics, the new headquarters of **Hachette**, one of France's leading publishers, reflect the groups commitment to culture and communication.

DIALOG

KEY PEOPLE

DAVID LOCK
Chairman
Qualifications : BA Design
London College of Printing.

GRAND DODD
Director
Qualifications :
Bsc Econ Hons.

WILLIAM RICHARDSON
Creative Director
Qualifications : BA Design
London College of Printing.

MARY O'NEILL
Director
Qualifications :
Kingston University

CHRISTIAN DELCAMBRE
Director
Qualifications :
Institute Saint Luc.

COMPANY PROFILE

APPROACH - We believe the most important asset a corporation has is its name, its visual presentation, its inherent meaning and the culture is typifies. Consumers look to the corporate name for product purchase assurance. Employees look to it for performance guidance.

We create messages to help corporations define and differentiate themselves, develop internal communications to ensure employee understanding and action and design literature which is creative, campaignable, coherent and reinforces of the corporate brand values.

We make the corporate name talk. We research what external and internal audiences want to hear and how and not just what management wants to say. We create dialogue.

AREAS OF EXPERTISE

- Corporate positioning consultancy and creation
- Corporate culture creation and implementation
- Corporate identity creation and management
- Corporate change communication
- Internal communication
- External corporate communication

SECTORS OF ACTIVITY - Capital goods, Catering, Consumer durables, Engineering, Financial services, Information technology, Leisure, Pharmaceuticals, Telecommunications, Utilities.

NEW BUSINESS IN 1996 - British Steel, Cellnet, Compass Group, Telecom Italia.

ACHIEVEMENTS

- Art Directors Club New York merit
- DBA Design Effectiveness Awards 2 finalists
- Global Awards New York finalist
- Type Directors Club New York citation for excellence

PRINCIPAL CLIENTS

British Steel
(Automotive Brochure for new light steel)

Cellnet
(Strategic intent communications theme)

Compass Group
(Corporate Culture and identity programmes for Educational Segment)

IBM Euro co-ordination
(Internal communication)

Tupperware
(50th anniversary programme)

DIALOG
12 Peterborough Mews
London SW6 3BL
Tel. : 44 (0) 171 731 4495
Fax : 44 (0) 171 731 4533

171 quai de Valmy
75010 Paris
Tel. : 33 (0) 1 42 05 60 60
Fax : 33 (0) 1 46 07 65 88

PERSONNEL - 15 (London and Paris)

COMPANY STRUCTURE - A limited liability company, capital of £100,000.

MEMBERSHIP - DBA, IABC and D&AD

CONTACT

EMMA CANHAM
Business Development Manager

dialog

IT'S YOUR CALL

CELLNET The UK's leading mobile telephone network required a positioning statement to communicate their 5 year strategic intent. It formed the central message for a campaign comprising management road shows, newsletters, posters and deskdrops.

IBM EMEA Believe.Me is a communication programme being rolled out across the EMEA region. Infinitely flexible, it has been applied to a variety of media including a bi-monthly employee magazine Read.Me, a launch brochure Believe.Me and Watch.Me videos.

SIEMENS Asked to articulate their vision, mission and values (VMV), we produced a vision book to explain what it means to their customers and employees and how it contributes to business objectives. The analogy of the unused capacity of a baby's brain was used to illustrate the massive potential intellectual competence of the company.

TUPPERWARE TEAM To celebrate its 50th anniversary, Tupperware mounted a PR campaign by inviting international journalists to one of their major European manufacturing facilities at Tours. The Tour de Tours was preceded by a teaser mailing campaign culminating in a message in their latest cocktail shaker.

BRITISH STEEL In the drive for fuel efficiency and safety in cars, British Steel has produced a new lighter yet stronger steel. This brochure is targeted at their international automobile manufacturing customers to demonstrate their understanding of their customer's needs.

LIPOMATRIX Breast implantation is about the patient's desire to fulfil their self image. The LipoMatrix product contains a natural oil, Triglyceride. From the association with nature and wellbeing came the blossoming rose image, a universally recognised symbol of love and care. It was a DBA design effectiveness and New York Global finalist.

DIDIER SACO

KEY PEOPLE

DIDIER SACO
Art Director

LAURENT DUMTÉ
Creative Director

COMPANY PROFILE

APPROACH - "Every label, every brand, every business must create its own environment and emit its own specific signals. Universality, timelessness and eternity must be banished from the communications scene. The ephemeral, the particular, the unique are the best identifying signs." Christian Lacroix.

AREAS OF EXPERTISE

- Visual Identity
- Product Design
- Signage

SECTORS OF ACTIVITY

- Banking / Insurance
- Fashion
- Culture

Turnover	in %
Graphic Design	
Visual Identity	30
Publications	35
Product Desgn	
Fashion	20
Environmental Design	
Signage	20

Turnover	in %
Banking / Insurance	60
Fashion	20
Culture	20

PRINCIPAL CLIENTS

Agence Pour la Création Industrielle (Visual identity, publications)

Alfa Sante
(Global identity)

Bcen-Eurobank
(Global identity)

Caisse Nationale de Crédit Agricole (Visual identity, publications)

Christian Lacroix (Visual identity repositioning, magazine)

Compagnie Générale des Eaux (Visual identity, publications)

Confédération du Crédit Mutuel (Visual identity, publications)

Crédit Agricole du Nord Est (Global identity)

Fransabank
(Global identity)

Group Cofinoga (Visual identity, publications)

Groupe Crédit National (Visual identity, publications)

Institut du Monde Arabe (Visual identity for exhibits)

Institut français de la mode (French Fashion Institute) (Visual identity, publications)

La Géode
(Signage)

Yves Saint Laurent (Visual identity, package design)

DIDIER SACO
10 rue des Jeuneurs
75002 Paris
Tel. : 33 (0) 1 40 26 96 26
Fax : 33 (0) 1 40 26 95 26

PERSONNEL - 4

TURNOVER - 1995 : FF3.5m

COMPANY STRUCTURE - Free-lance consultants

CONTACT

DIDIER SACO

everything signifies

DRAGON ROUGE

PATRICK VEYSSIERE
Co-Chairman

PIERRE CAZAUX
Co-Chairman

DOMINIQUE MARCOT
Partner
Health & Beauty Care
Department Director

SOPHIE ROMET
International Development
Director

CHRISTIAN DE BERGH
Corporate Identity
Department Director

VÉRONIQUE LIABEUF
Health & Beauty Care
Department Director

DRAGON ROUGE
32, rue Pagès BP 83
92153 Suresnes Cedex
Tél. : 33 (0) 1 46 97 50 00
Fax : 33 (0) 1 47 72 05 03
E-mail : drweba dragonrouge.com
WWW : http://www.dragonrouge.com

APPROACH - We believe in effective brand design : we have a practical approach focusing on achieving our clients' commercial benefits.
We are a strategic design consultancy : we balance marketing and creation to design strategic solutions.
We believe in creativity, in both design and marketing.
We have the leading edge on new issues and trends, and continuously adapt our methodologies to best serve our clients' needs.
We are entrepreneurs, and our principals are involved in all programmes.
Above all, we believe in trust, ethics and building a true partnership with our clients.

AREAS OF EXPERTISE - Dragon Rouge specialises in :
Branding and packaging design :
- Mass-market
- Health and Beauty Care
Corporate Identity Programmes :
- Corporate Identities and Applications
- Collateral
- Interactive Design
- Signage
- Retail Environment

PERSONNEL - 110 in Paris, 15 in London
TURNOVER - 1995 : 98 MF
COMPANY STRUCTURE - A limited Company, Capital FF 5.250.000, Founded in 1984.
INTERNATIONAL NETWORK - Dragon Partners, including companies in the USA and Spain.
MEMBERSHIP - ADC

Corporate Identity :
Barclays,
Caroll (André),
Cetelem,
Coface,
Iridium (Aussedat-Rey),
La Poste,
Midas, Nestlé,
PMU, Renault,
Roland-Garros,
Valeo, Axa,
1998 World Cup.

**Branding and
Packaging :
Mass-market**
BASF, Bayer,
Belin-Lu (Danone),
Fromageries BEL,
GBG (Danone),
Henkel,
Kraft Jacob Suchard,
Kronenbourg (Danone),
Lever, Mölnlycke,
Nestlé Sources
International (Nestlé),
Panzani (Danone),
Repsol.

Health & Beauty Care
Chantelle, Colgate,
Henkel Cosmetics,
Laboratoires Garnier,
Laboratoires Vichy,
La Scad,
L'Oréal Parfumerie,
L'Oréal Coiffure,
Yves Rocher.

SOPHIE ROMET
Branding and Packaging /
Mass-market

VÉRONIQUE LIABEUF
Branding and Packaging /
Health and Beauty Care

JULIA BOCCARD
CHRISTIAN DE BERGH
Corporate Identity

Corporate identity

Health and beauty care

Mass market

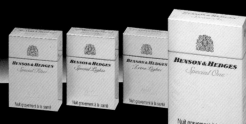

Official Mascot for the 1998 World Football Cup
Illustrator: Fabrice Pialot

EKONOS ET ASSOCIÉS

KEY PEOPLE

PASCALE BERNET
Associate Manager,
Director of Strategy

GÉRALD BOT
Creative Director

XAVIER LACOMBE
Creative Director

JEAN-MARIE MELIN
Associate Manager,
Director of Clientele and
Business Development

COMPANY PROFILE

APPROACH

- Strategic analysis and graphic diagnosis.
- Definition of image objectives.
- Powerful, attractive, relevant design.

Ekonos et Associés' specificity is founded on its three cornerstones : Design - Marketing - Communications.

AREAS OF EXPERTISE

Communication Design Consultants, Ekonos et Associés assist businesses in mapping out their particular "visual territory" potential for their brands and products :

- Image audit and strategy
- New product concepts
- Brand identity
- Product personality : Graphic and volume design
- Publishing
- POS
- Merchandising

Turnover	in %
Graphic Design	
Visual identity	10
Package Design	60
Publishing	25
Product Design	
Luxury goods and industry	5

SECTORS OF ACTIVITY

- Cosmetics, mass market, food, cosmetics, pharmaceuticals, consumer durables.
- Corporate identity for industry and services.

Turnover	in %
Food / Maintenance	50
Hygiene / Beauty care	20
Services	30

NEW BUSINESS IN 1996

- Mass market : Petit Navire, Coudray, Géant Vert, Kraft Jacobs Suchard, Besnier, Ancel, Lefranc & Bourgeois.
- Services : Paris Expo, ESCE, La Française de Jeux.

PRINCIPAL CLIENTS

L'Oréal
(P'tit DOP, Tec ni Art

Colgate
(Gama, Paic, Ajax, Génie)

Amora
(Brand territory)

Nestlé Maggi
(Saveurs du Monde, Les Marinades)

Nestlé Nescafé
(Speciality coffee range)

Raynal & Rocquelaure
(Pre-cooked food products)

Kraft Jacobs Suchard
(Malabar Kikroc)

Lotus
(Coton wool range)

Taittinger
(Champagnes and Whiskies)

Ancel
(Cake mixes)

Solvay
(Naoca salt)

Le Méridien
(Global image policy)

Automobiles Peugeot
(Accessories and auto parts)

Ravensburger
(Games)

EKONOS ET ASSOCIÉS
3 rue des quatre cheminées
92100 Boulogne
Tel. : 33 (0) 1 46 20 24 24
Fax : 33 (0) 1 46 20 01 28

PERSONNEL · 12

TURNOVER · 1995 : FF9m / 1994 : FF8m

COMPANY STRUCTURE · A limited liability company, capital of FF250,000. Founded in 1989.

MEMBERSHIP · PDA Europe

CONTACTS
JEAN-MARIE MELIN
FRANÇOIS FOUQUES DUPARC

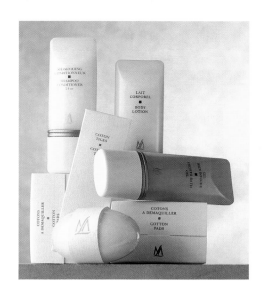

Le packaging* & l'édition

 Ekonos & Associés

EPOUDRY GUISLAIN DESIGN

KEY PEOPLE

GUY EPOUDRY
Creative Director,
Graphic Design
Career Background :
Designer, Roger et Gallet
Parfumeur, Printel Agency.
Co-founder of Epoudry
Guislain Design.

YVES GUISLAIN
Creative Director,
Industrial Design
Career Background :
Senior Designer,
J.L.Barrault.
Co-founder of Epoudry
Guislain Design.

COMPANY PROFILE

APPROACH - A team of experienced design practitioners and personality makers, who know how to balance the rigors of strategic analysis with well-channelled creative ardor.

AREAS OF EXPERTISE - A communications through design consultancy, Epoudry Guislain Design specializes in graphic and volume design, addressing all aspects of corporate, brand and product identity:
- Image audit and strategy consulting.
- Brand name research and creation.
- Logos and identity manuals.
- Package design, new products, re-design.
- Volume design, industrialization.
- Corporate publications, merchandising, POS - IPOS.

Turnover	in %
Graphic Design	
Visual Identity	5
Package Design	60
Publishing	15
Volume Design	
Bottle design and	
Consumer Durables	20

SECTORS OF ACTIVITY
- Food
- Gardening / Horticulture
- DIY
- Hygiene, Health and Beauty care
- Home maintenance
- Industry

NEW BUSINESS IN 1996
- Agrevo (Groupe Hœchst)
- Bongrain
- Henkel (Décap Four, Lavax)
- Chocolats Jacquot
- Or Brun
- Primagaz

PRINCIPAL CLIENTS

Food

Bongrain

Fromagerie Cloche d'Or

Gorcy Surgelés
(Groupe Danone)

Maître Pierre
(Laflam frozen goods)

Marie Surgelés
(Groupe Danone)

Chocolats Jacquot

Consumer goods

Benckiser

Blanc (Groupe SFA)

Colgate Palmolive

Henkel

Primagaz

Prolabo

Spengler

Triplex

Gardening / Horticulture

Agrevo (Groupe Hœchst)

Algoflash (Algochimie)

Jouffray Drillaud

Florentaise

Or Brun

CONTACTS
GUY EPOUDRY
Creative Director,
Graphic Design

YVES GUISLAIN
Creative Director,
Industrial Design

EPOUDRY GUISLAIN DESIGN
23 rue d'Alésia
75014 Paris
Tel. : 33 (0) 1 45 43 05 03
Fax : 33 (0) 1 45 43 06 01

PERSONNEL - 8

COMPANY STRUCTURE - A limited liability company, capital of FF50,000. Founded in 1978.

EPOUDRY
GUISLAIN
DESIGN

CRÉATION IDENTITÉ PACKAGING, **MARIE**
Expression généreuse d'une recette innovante,
invitation au voyage.

CRÉATION DESIGN FLACON, IDENTITÉ PACKAGING, **ALGOFLASH**
Valorisation de la marque, sublimation de
l'efficacité par l'expression concrète du résultat.
Gamme devenue leader du marché.

CRÉATION DESIGN FLACON, **Sᵀ MARC ULTRA**
Valorisation de l'efficacité produit,
ensemble compact, empilable, innovant.
Elu produit de l'année 1994 par les consommateurs.

CRÉATION MARQUE ET PACKAGING, **STERIPAN**
Codes couleurs traditionnels de
la parapharmacie pour conforter l'acte d'achat en GMS.

CRÉATION DESIGN PRODUIT, **PROLABO**
Destructeur d'aiguilles, l'ergonomie sécurisante.

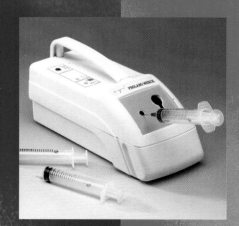

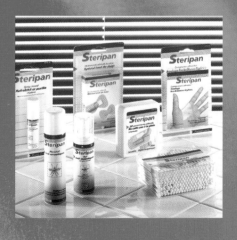

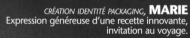

23, RUE D'ALÉSIA - 75014 PARIS - TÉL : 01 45 43 05 03 - FAX : 01 45 43 06 01

EPSIGN

KEY PEOPLE

ÉRIC PEAUCOUP
Chairman and
Managing Director,
Creative Director.
Qualifications : Over
20 years experience in
design.
Career Background :
Perfect mastery of graphic
production process :
Designer, Art Director,
Creative Director with major
design agencies.

BÉATRICE NICODÈME
Director of Clientele and
Business Development
Qualifications : École de
Communication, Commerce
et Gestion (School of
Communications, Business
and Management).

COMPANY PROFILE

APPROACH - Because seductive appeal is essential to sales, because each problem is different, because each element establishes and adds to corporate identity, because high-quality market studies, creative talent and working technical knowledge sum up our strong points, TOGETHER we will create the tools and the means best adapted to your specific needs, thus ensuring the economic success of your project.

AREAS OF EXPERTISE - Epsign is equipped to cover all aspects of visual identity : Package Design, Brand Image (logotypes), Product Design, Publications, Multimedia, Signage and Point of Sales / Display.

Turnover	in %
Graphic Design	
Visual Identity	15
Package Design	50
Publications	15
Design Produit	
Perfumes / Cosmetics	10
Environmental Design	
Signage	10

SECTORS OF ACTIVITY - Epsign's diversified expertise and multifaceted experience are adaptable to all areas of design activity.

PRINCIPAL CLIENTS

Andros

Bahlsen

Bel

Christofle

Colgate

Convatec
(Bristol-Myers Squibb)

Dekra

Eurosucre

Elida Fabergé

Ferrero

Friskies

Laboratoires Garnier

Guigoz

Kimberly Clark Sopalin

Laboratoires Leurquin
Mediolanum

Laboratoires Nutricia

Laboratoires Pfizer

Lafarge

Montévrain

Naf Naf

Nestlé France

Nike

Renault

RJ Reynolds Tobacco

SAFR (Groupe Bel)

SAFT (Groupe Alcatel)

SEITA...

EPSIGN
2 rue des Tennerolles
92210 Saint-Cloud
Tel. : 33 (0) 1 46 02 00 33
Fax : 33 (0) 1 46 02 57 23

PERSONNEL - 9

TURNOVER - 1995 : FF5m (30% in international revenues)

COMPANY STRUCTURE - A limited company, capital of FF2,500,000. Founded in 1990.

CONTACTS

ÉRIC PEAUCOUP

BÉATRICE NICODÈME

EPSIGN
STRATEGY/DESIGN/CONSULTANTS

différenc
uniqueness

Ensemble créons votre différence
Together, we create your uniqueness

Conception globale d'une opération événementielle pour **RJR**.
Overall concept for a special events program for **RJR**.

Un BéBé

Un Arbre

Création du logotype
"Un Bébé un Arbre" **GUIGOZ**.
Creation of the logotype
for **GUIGUOZ** " A Baby a Tree".

Réactualisation de la gamme **SUNSILK**.
Updating of **SUNSILK** line.

Concept nouveau
produit KINDER sur le
marché international
pour **FERRERO**.
KINDER new product
concept for the
international market
for **FERRERO**.

bel

elida

Repositionnement packaging de
la marque **St MORGON**.
Repositionning of **St MORGON** packaging.

Création Packaging de la nouvelle
gamme **ELIDA FABERGÉ** (33 références).
Packaging creation of **ELIDA FABERGE**
new range (33 references).

nestlé

Argumentaire pour un nouveau concept
de Purée en brique **NESTLÉ**.
Sails brochure for a new concept
of **NESTLÉ** bricked purées.

pond's

Plaquette événementielle pour le lancement
de 4 nouveaux produits **POND'S**.
Key-field information booklet for the
introduction of **POND'S** 4 new articles.

mod's hair

Redynamisation de la gamme **MOD'S HAIR**.
Re-energize **MOD'S HAIR** line.

Création d'un label
de qualité **CIRVIANDE**.
Creation of quality label
for **CIRVIANDE**.

Symboles brosses à dents
Enfants pour **COLGATE**.
Symbols for **COLGATE**
children's toothbrushes.

saft

PLV et mailing promotionnels **SAFT**.
SAFT promotional mailing
and display material.

l'EngagemenT
MUTUEL

Identité visuelle **RJR**.
RJR visual identity.

piuiɔ̣d

EURO RSCG DESIGN

KEY PEOPLE

GABRIEL BRUCKLER
Design Management

CHRISTINE DUFOUR
Graphic Design

ARMELLE GORAGUER
Graphic Design

XAVIER LAFORGE
*Consultant
Commercial Space
Design*

MARC LEBAILLY
Managing Director

AARON LEVIN
*Creative Director
Graphic Design*

MANUEL NOBLOT
Consultant
Brand Strategy

JACQUES NOËL
Graphic Design

JEAN-MARC PIATON
Managing Director

CHRISTOPHE PRADÈRE
*Marketing and
Sales Director*

JACKY SIGOT
Graphic Design

JÉRÔME WALLUT
*Director
Graphic Design*

COMPANY PROFILE

APPROACH - "To endure and prosper, brands require constant attention."

AREAS OF EXPERTISE - No form of design is unknown to us. We offer a wide variety of specializations : visual identity programmes, commercial space design, institutional space design, multimedia concepts and graphic manuals, signage, product design.

SECTORS OF ACTIVITY - "240 years of experience servicing brands in all areas".

NEW BUSINESS IN 1995/96

- Air Inter Europe (Visual identity programme)
- Amen Bank, Tunisia (Visual Identity Programme)
- BNP (Publications programme)
- Caja de Ahorro y Seguro, Argentina (Visual identity programme)
- Consolidar, Argentina (Visual identity programme)
- Crédit Local de France (International trademark audit)
- CGEA, Great Britain (Visual identity programme)
- FNAC (Publications programme)
- Havas (Visual identity programme)
- Infogrames (Visual identity programme)
- Infonie (Visual identity programme)
- Juncadella, Argentina (Visual identity programme)
- Lille 2004 (Visual identity programme)
- McDonald's (Visual identity programme)
- ODA (Visual identity programme)
- San in Godo Bank, Japan (Visual identity programme)
- Suravenir (Visual identity programme)

ACHIEVEMENTS - Contented clients who see their brands come to life and prosper.

PERSONNEL - 50

GROSS PROFIT - 1995 : FF 44 m

COMPANY STRUCTURE - A limited company, capital of FF 800,000.

FOREIGN OFFICES AND NETWORK - London (RSCG Conran Design) - Buenos Aires (Euro RSCG Design) - Lisbon (Euro RSCG Design) - Edinburgh (APEX Design) and the Euro RSCG network.

PROFESSIONAL MEMBERSHIPS - ADC and UFDI

GROUP AFFILIATION - Euro RSCG

PRINCIPAL CLIENTS

AGF

Air France

Bayard Presse

Beaufour Ipsen

Citroën

Crédit Commercial
de France

Crédit du Nord

Crédit National

Delmas

ELF

GAN

Gras Savoye

Jet Tours

La Cinquième

La Mondiale

Peugeot

PMU

RATP

Société Générale

Total

EURO RSCG DESIGN
84 rue de Villiers
92683 Levallois-Perret Cedex
Tel : 33 (0) 1 41 34 43 60
Fax : 33 (0) 1 41 34 44 47

CONTACT

JEAN-MARC PIATON

Air Inter Europe Programme
d'identité global

La Cinquième Chaîne du savoir
et de la connaissance

Peugeot Sport Système
d'identification

Havas Advertising 7ᵉ groupe
mondial de communication

Infogrames 1ᵉʳ éditeur français
de logiciels ludiques et culturels

Beaufour Ipsen
Laboratoire pharmaceutique

CFO Coupe du monde de football 1998

Bonux Evolution
de la gamme

La Caja 1ᵉʳᵉ compagnie
d'assurance Argentine

Oda La régie des Pages
Jaunes

Infonie Identité du 1ᵉʳ réseau on-line
français

EXTRÊME

KEY PEOPLE

FABRICE EMBERGER
Managing Director
Qualifications : ESAG (Higher
School of Graphic Arts).
Career Background :
Typogabor Communication.

NADÈGE SAVAGLIO
*Associate Managing
Director*
Qualifications : ILERI
Masters in Management,
Dauphine. DESS Sorbonne,
Degree in Russian.
Career Background :
Product Manager, L'Oréal.

CATHERINE DEBURE-GARRET
Creative Director
Qualifications : Institut d'Art
Visuel (Visual Arts Institute).
Career Background :
Lookmaker, Magellan.

MICHEL GIBOZ
*Director of Design
Department*
Qualifications : ESAA (Higher
School of Applied Arts).
Career Background :
Thomson, Matra.

CORINNE CERTA
Account Manager
Qualifications : Bachelor of
International Business,
USA. DESS Sup de Luxe.
Career Background : Regina
Rubens, Export Manager.

EMERIC BODINEAU
*Account Manager,
Pharmaceuticals*
Qualifications : IDRAC - DESS
in Pharmaceutical Marketing.
Career Background : Media 6.

LAURENT COLANGETTES
Account Manager
Qualifications : ESDI - CELSA.

EXTRÊME
127-129 rue du Mont Cenis
75018 Paris
Tel. : 33 (0) 1 49 25 80 50
Fax : 33 (0) 1 49 25 84 63

COMPANY PROFILE

APPROACH · Our Agency : Extrême is a place where inventiveness, creativity and communication have room to grow ; where we are sensitive to change and open to modern technology.
Our Approach : To enhance the assets inherent to our clients' products and services on local and international markets. To establish true product personality and evaluate brand future in relation to market trends.
Our Objective : To be dependable, efficient and receptive partners to our clients.

AREAS OF EXPERTISE

- Package Design (Form and Graphics)
- Product Environment
- Visual Identity
- Publications
- Point of Sale / Display

Turnover	in %
Graphic Design	
Visual Identity	20
Package Design	20
Publications	10
Product Design	
Luxury Goods	30
Environment	
Point of Sale / Display	20

SECTORS OF ACTIVITY

- Hygiene / Beauty Care Products
- Food
- Luxury Goods

NEW BUSINESS IN 1995/96

- BMW
- Pathé Cinéma
- Laboratoires Fumouze
- Sanofi Pharma
- Nestlé

ACHIEVEMENTS · 1996 Award by Cosmétique News for Narta Caresse (LaScad)

PERSONNEL · 39

TURNOVER · 1996 estimate : FF 30 m / 1995 : FF 24 m

GROSS PROFIT · 1996 estimate : FF 25 m / 1995 : FF 20 m

COMPANY STRUCTURE · A limited company, capital of FF300,000. Founded in 1983.

GROUP AFFILIATION · Extrême Communications Group, 1996 turnover estimate : FF 97 m

PRINCIPAL CLIENTS

Astor

C.P.C.

Créateurs de Beauté

Delacre

Fulmen

Gemey

Hermès

Kérastase

Laboratoires Vichy

Labosanté

Lancôme

La Roche Posay

LaScad

L'Oréal

Marc Delacre

Nestlé

Pathé Cinéma

Pierre Fabre

Rémy Martin

CONTACTS

NADÈGE SAVAGLIO
CORINNE CERTA
EMERIC BODINEAU
LAURENT COLLANGETTES

Lascad

Product design

Gel and foam distributors

Graphic design

Branding Mennen

pro-tech systeme

Packaging identity

Pierre Fabre

Product design

Perfume bottle

Graphic design

Brand identity

Roland Garros

Packaging identity

Delacre

Graphic design

International

packaging identity

for the Smurf

biscuits

Labosanté

Graphic design

Brand identity

Planet Kid

Range packaging

identity

GRIFFE

DANIEL CRESPY
Creative Director,
Chairman

MARIE BONHOMME
Director of Clientele

DENISE FRIQUET
Technical Manager

APPROACH - Griffe establishes a client-designer partnership based on an attentive listening capacity, creativity, quick response, and maintains its high standards through pertinent analysis, sound design, strict commercial and technical follow-up, amply justifying client trust at every phase of the creative process.

AREAS OF EXPERTISE

- Brand Image : strategy, definition of areas of expression, logotype and graphic system, standardization of applications.
- Research and development of product concept, product design and package design.
- Environmental design, signage, furniture design, display, point of sale, information at point of sale.
- Promotional, commercial and institutional literature.

BRS
(Brand image, corporate publications)

Chronopost
(Sales literature, signage for main office)

Elf / Antar
(Display for motorcycle dealerships)

France Glaces Findus
(Exquise, Extrême, Mystère, Kim : Range structure, branding, package design, sales literature)

Intermarché
(Pâturages de France, Apta : brand image, package design)

Nestlé France
(P'tit Duo, Baccara, Soir de Gala, Pralinés Suisses : package design)

Pernod Ricard
(Havana Club : visual identity and package design)

Prodim
(8 à huit : visual identity, retail space design, standardization)

Vuarnet Extrême
(Image strategy, visual identity, package design, point of sale displays, stands, communications)

DANIEL CRESPY
33 (0) 1 40 95 27 28

MARIE BONHOMME
33 (0) 1 40 95 27 03

DENISE FRIQUET
33 (0) 1 40 95 27 05

GRIFFE
2 rue Maurice Hartmann
92137 Issy-les-Moulineaux
Tel. : 33 (0) 1 40 95 27 10
Fax : 33 (0) 1 40 95 74 07

PERSONNEL - 12

COMPANY STRUCTURE - A limited company, capital of FF 250, 000. Founded in 1970.

IDENTITÉS

ANTOINE ORTOLI
Managing Director

ALICE GAPAILLARD
Associate Director

ELISABETH SERRELL
Associate Director

APPROACH - Identités' rôle is to foster success for its clients and their brands through :
- examining problems from a global viewpoint. In matters of assessment and strategy planning, our analysis benefits from resources made available by our affiliation with the Astrie group;
- our experience with identity problematics, qualified by an in-depth knowledge of institutional and corporate needs;
- our marketing and creative consulting process which takes into account the consumer, the sales force, distributors and, of course, the product itself;
- our capacity for international brand and product management.
These resources, combined with our management's expertise, allow us to conduct a daily policy of anticipation and innovation with each of our clients.

AREAS OF EXPERTISE
- Brand: name search, visual identity, identity manual.
- Product: form design, package image, identity manual, sales tools.
- Environmental design: retail and commercial space design, signage and programming, stand.
- Publishing: corporate publications, sales and commercial publications.

Turnover	in %
Brand	20
Product	60
Environmental Design	5
Publications	15

SECTORS OF ACTIVITY - Mass market, Hygiene and Beauty care, Tobacco, Leisure, Industry, Services, Institutions.

NEW BUSINESS IN 1996
Nina Ricci, Nestlé (Grands Chocolats), Warner Home Vidéo, Disneyland Paris, Cofinoga, Euroquest, Datar, Groupe Central Villes Nouvelles, CCI Guadeloupe, Ministry of Agriculture.

Agrifood
CPC (Alsa), Nestlé (Grands Chocolats), Prisunic (Forza, Gault et Millau), Touquet Savour, Unisabi.

Home maintenance
Johnson (Wax).

Beauty care, Health
Mustela, Nina Ricci, Reckitt & Colman.

Tobacco
Seita, Reynolds.

Leisure
Disneyland Paris, Eastman Kodak, Kodak-Pathé, M.V.M. Tour operator, Warner Home Video.

Retail
Domaxel, Prisunic.

Industry
Allard, Isover, Reboul Cosmétique.

Services
Aéroports de Paris, Cofinoga, Euroquest, Fairlines, Mutuelles du Mans, Onyx, Servair, SNCF, TAT, TDR.

Institutional
Ademe, ANPE, Assedic, CBC, CCI Guadeloupe, CFES, Datar, Groupe Central des Villes Nouvelles, INA, Ministry of Agriculture, Ministry of Tourism.

IDENTITÉS
218 boulevard Jean Jaurès
92514 Boulogne Cedex
Tel. : 33 (0) 1 47 61 62 80
Fax : 33 (0) 1 47 61 62 81

PERSONNEL - 15

TURNOVER - 1996 : FF 14,5 m / 1995 : FF 14 m

COMPANY STRUCTURE - A limited company, capital of FF 250, 000. Founded in 1982

GROUP AFFILIATION - Astrie Compagnie

CONTACT
ANTOINE ORTOLI

THE
BRAND

MINISTÈRE DE L'AGRICULTURE

CORPORATE LOGO.
CORPORATE IDENTITY MANUAL.

To express clearly three basic and complementary missions.

M I N I S T È R E
DE L'AGRICULTURE
DE LA PÊCHE ET DE
L'ALIMENTATION

THE
PRODUCT

KODAK PATHÉ : SELF-SERVICE BLISTER-PACKED FILMS

PRODUCT DESIGN. GRAPHIC DESIGN.
PACKAGING MANUAL.

To bring an equal benefit to the consumer, the distributor
and the brand through innovation and information.

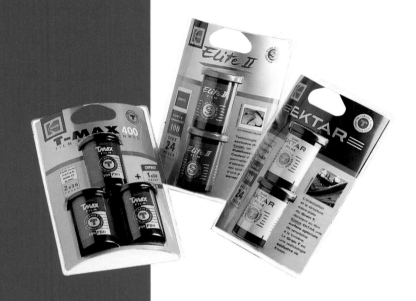

THE
PRINT

ADEME

PRINT MATERIAL PACKAGE FOR THE 1995 INTERNATIONAL SEMINAR.

To bring together specialists from the four continents to debate
on energy development policies for rural areas.

IDENTITÉS

IG DESIGN

IG DESIGN
3 bis, rue de l'Éperon
75006 Paris
Tel. : 33 (0) 1 44 07 24 00
Fax : 33 (0) 1 44 07 30 54

KEY PEOPLE

FRANÇOISE LEMAIRE
*Chairman and
Managing Director*

JEAN-MICHEL FARCE
Managing Director

FRANK LEROUX
*Business Development
Manager*

COMPANY PROFILE

APPROACH - For over 10 years, IG Design has developed three central ideas :
- the complementarity between creative graphics + structural design to offer a complete and coherent "approach".
- the transversality of markets to stimulate creativity and forecast trends.
- technical know-how to guarantee project workability.

AREAS OF EXPERTISE
- Product Design : concept, form and technology.
- Packaging Design : form and graphics.
- Visual Identity : product, brand, corporate and application norms.

Turnover	in %
Graphic Design	
Visual Identity	20
Packaging Design	40
Product Design	
Luxury Goods / Cosmetics	20
Industrial	20

FIELDS OF ACTIVITY - IG Design covers most spheres of activity and frequently contributes to multinational projects.

NEW BUSINESS IN 1996
- Belin-Lu
- Canson
- Colgate (Gama, Ajax)
- Compagnie des Fromages
- Douwe Egberts
- Ideval
- Kraft Jacobs Suchard
- Peugeot - POE
- 3M (Scotchgard)
- Searle
- Weleda

STAFF - 15

TURNOVER - 1996 estimate : FF 9,5 m / 1995 : FF 8,4 m

COMPANY STRUCTURE - A limited company, capital of FF 250, 000. Founded in 1983.

PARTNERSHIPS - K. Hartmann Design, Frankfurt - VISION, European Design Strategies.

MEMBERSHIP - Founding member of PDA (Packaging Design Association).

PRINCIPAL CLIENTS

Alcatel

Babolat

BASF
(France and Europe)

Biscuiterie Nantaise

Bristol - Myers Squibb

CEP Communication

Ciba Geigy Novartis

Colgate Palmolive

Facom

France Télécom

Groupe Bongrain

Henkel

Heudebert

Landis & Staefa

Mapa Hutchinson

Reckitt & Colman

Roche Laboratories

Sader Atofindley

Sanofi Beauté - YSL

Scholl

SmithKline Beecham

Soprat - Père Dodu

Synthelabo OTC

3M Europe

Vichy L'Oréal

Williams Holdings

WK France

CONTACTS

JEAN-MICHEL FARCE
Managing Director

FRANK LEROUX
*Business Development
Manager*

COLGATE-PALMOLIVE : Washing up liquid PAIC EXCEL : "shape-break" on the shelf. '96 Best Product Award-SECODIP.

1 **BASF** : Anti-freeze liquid GLYSANTIN : combination of image and use values to improve product benefit.

2 **WILLIAMS HOLDINGS** : Woodcare XYLADECOR range : design solution to convey both European identity and regional specifics.

3 **ROCHE LABORATORIES** : TILCOTIL tablet dispenser : innovative structural design for leading position.

4 **RECKITT & COLMAN** : Washing liquid : international harmonization of graphic codes.

LA COMPAGNIE DESIGN

KEY PEOPLE

PHILIPPE CERE
*Creative Director,
Founder*

FRANCIS POME
*Director of Business
Development*

COMPANY PROFILE

APPROACH - Concretely creative.
Both consumers and consumer markets evolve at breathtaking speed. A design agency must keep in touch with an ever-changing environment. La Compagnie Design tackles each project with a practical, operational approach where "visual reflexion", based upon analysis of environmental context, acts as a concrete stimulus for the creative team and guarantees rapid results.

AREAS OF EXPERTISE - Visual Communications : Visual Identity, Concept Research, Brand Design and/or Brand repositioning, Package Design, New Product Development or Update, Range Diversification and/or Expansion, Form Study and Research, Point of Sale, Publications.

SECTORS OF ACTIVITY
- Agrifood
- Health
- Industry
- Services

NEW BUSINESS IN 1996
- Danone International Brands : Development of package identity, Sarita range
- Poulain (Groupe Cadbury France) : Package development
- S.A.F.R. (Groupe Bel) : Brand identity concept, Samos 99 and package development for the range
- Vico : Package identity concept and development

PRINCIPAL CLIENTS

Belin-LU Biscuits France
(Groupe Danone) :
LU (Barquette, Hello!,
Brownies, Schooks,
Mikado Trio, Véritable
Petit Beurre Dans La
Poche) et TUC (Pops,
Crac'Fin)
(Package Identity)

Danone
International Brands
(Package identity, Sarita
range)

Gouaix Wines and
Spirits(Package identity)

Materne Fruibourg
(Groupe Hillsdown)
(Evolution Materne brand
image, package identity
development)

Monsanto Laboratories
(SEARLE) (Package
identity concepts)

Parsys Informatique
(Visual identity,
publishing)

Poulain (Groupe Cadbury
France) (Package
development)

Roussel Uclaf
Laboratoire Cassenne
(Package identity)

S.A.F.R. (Groupe Bel)
(Brand identity and
package development)

Tefal (Groupe SEB)
(Visual identity concept
for Tefal Baby Home,
identity manual, package
development)

Vico (Package identity)

LA COMPAGNIE DESIGN
Immeuble ATRIA
2 rue du Centre
93885 Noisy-le-Grand
Tel. : 33 (0) 1 43 05 00 11
Fax : 33 (0) 1 43 05 51 15

PERSONNEL - 8

COMPANY STRUCTURE - A limited company, capital of FF 150,000. Founded in 1992

CONTACTS

PHILIPPE CERE

FRANCIS POME

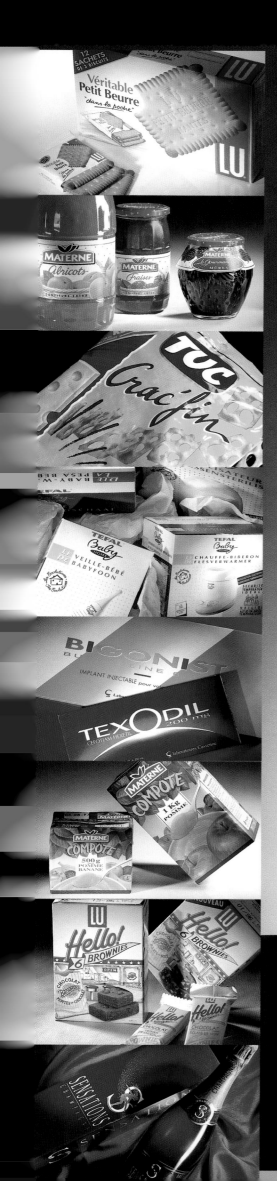

La Compagnie
DESIGN

La Créativité Concrète...

Un Art Consommé !

LOGIC DESIGN

SENDA HAMIDA
Creative Director,
Associate Managing
Director
Qualifications: ESDI
(Higher School of
Industrial Design).

JÉRÔME LANOY
Chairman and Managing
Director
Qualifications: ESDI
(Higher School of
Industrial Design).

MARIE-BÉATRICE
ULMER-THERMED
Director of Business
Development, Associate
Managing Director
Qualifications: Doctorate in
Comparative Literature.
MBA, HEC - ISA Business
School.

APPROACH - To create lasting design, drawing upon the logic inherent to a brand or product, to make a commitment.

AREAS OF EXPERTISE

Graphic Design

- Visual Identity : image evaluation, strategic analysis and advisory service, visual identity and applications.
- Package Design : package concept, graphics. Brand repositioning. Brand range management.
- Publications : a multi-dimensional approach to publishing with research into forms adaptable to corporate identity.

Turnover	in %
Graphic Design	
Visual Identity	20
Package Design	55
Publications	5
Product Design	
Luxury Goods	10
Industrial	10

Product Design

Perfume / Cosmetics / Industrial : An approach that begins with a product's function and its life on a shelf and elsewhere, implies an understanding of its ergonomics, research and analysis of material costs, optimization of industrial profitability, security in transport, adaptation to points of sale, and immediate awareness of product values.

SECTORS OF ACTIVITY - We have had the opportunity to work on exciting projects within the agrifood, pharmaceutical and textile industries, in beauty care and hygiene, road signage, building and public works sectors...

Turnover	in %
Food	45
Pharmaceuticals	20
Hygiene / Beauty Care	15
Maintenance	10
Services	10

It is not the area of activity that counts, but the actual project intention that ensures the best of our creativity.

NEW BUSINESS IN 1996

- Allibert (programme covering a new line of products)
- Ducros (package design for an innovation on the grocery shelf)
- Henkel (package design for Le Chat, home maintenance)
- Nestlé (package design for new non-dairy products)

Gelmer (Packaging)

Cacharel La Chemiserie
(Gift packs)

Cerruti (Brand image for
Signature)

Fournier-Debat (Logo,
packaging concept and
graphics for Erecnos)

Herta (Logo and package
design for Knacki,
traditional sausage range,
Ready to bake piecrusts,
Hams and Bacon bits,
Ingredients, Pâtés,
Breaded patties and Puff
pastries)

Kiwi France (Package
design for Quickies, Quick
Argile)

Lesieur (Package design
for Lesieur Olive Oil,
Counseling on form,
packaging and logo for the
Jardin d'Orante range)

Mon Verger (Logo and
package design for their
range of fresh fruit juices)

Prosign (Visual identity
programme)

SmithKline Beecham
(Logo, graphics and form
design for Valda, for the
Sauba ORL ranges,
Antigrippine, Lelong,
Pulmoll)

Yoplait (Package design,
Les Tentations, crème
fraîche range ; logo and
package design, Câlin
package design, Vitae)

LOGIC DESIGN
140 rue Galliéni
92100 Boulogne
Tel. : 33 (0) 1 46 04 88 04
Fax : 33 (0) 1 46 04 88 06

PERSONNEL - 8

TURNOVER - July 94 - June 95 : FF 4,7 m / July 95 - June 96 : FF 9 m

COMPANY STRUCTURE - A limited company, capital of FF 250,000. Founded in 1988.

MEMBERSHIP - Signee of Prodimarques Good Conduct Packaging Code

MARIE-BÉATRICE
ULMER-THERMED
Director of Business
Development

LESIEUR - Le Jardin d'Orante : Le goût naturel des herbes fraîches ◆ Création graphique, Recommandation volume ◆ Lancement

Laboratoires FOURNIER . DEBAT - Erecnos* : La dualité et le duo ◆ Identité, concept de conditionnement, packaging ◆ Lancement

HENKEL - Le Chat : La valorisation des parfums   ◆   Création graphique   ◆   Lifting

LONSDALE DESIGN

KEY PEOPLE

SONIA CHAINE
Co-Chairman,
Director of Strategy

GILLES RIEDBERGER
Co-Chairman,
Creative Director

COMPANY PROFILE

APPROACH - Rigorous strategic and graphic analysis join forces with creative talent to reveal underlying brand personality via powerful, relevant, enduring design. Design at an international level is made possible by TOTEM, an active network of complementary skills. Development of customized methodologies.

AREAS OF EXPERTISE
- Creation of brand names
- Concepts and products
- Image evaluation
- Visual audit
- Strategy analysis
- Packaging Design (Form and Graphics)
- Identity, Publications, Brand management

Turnover	in %
Graphic Design	
Identity	10
Packaging Design	80
Product Design	5
Other	
Creation of brand names, concepts and products	5

SECTORS OF ACTIVITY
- Food
- Health Care and Beauty
- Luxury Goods
- Industry and Services

Turnover	in %
Food	75
Heath Care and Beauty	10
Luxury Goods	5
Industry	5
Services	5

NEW BUSINESS IN 1995/96
- **Food :** Crespo, Fromageries Bel, Henkel, Orangina, SAFR, Segafredo, Sodebo, Spontex, Suchard.
- **Health Care and Beauty :** Bourjois, Kiwi.
- **Industry and Services :** IFGAP, Three Kings.

ACHIEVEMENTS
- Design Agency of the Year
- Grand Prix, design category (Stratégies)
- Oscar for Packaging
- Janus for Industry

PERSONNEL - 28

TURNOVER - 1995 : FF 18 m / 1994 : FF 16 m

GROSS PROFIT - 1995 : FF 13, 5 m / 1994 : FF 12 m

COMPANY STRUCTURE - A limited company, capital of FF 348,000. Founded in 1961.

NETWORK - TOTEM, International Design Network : Elmwood (GB), Vilaseca-Altarriba (Spain), Adriano Ruggero Design (Italy), Scandinavian Design Group (Norway), USA (pending), Japan (pending).

MEMBERSHIP - ADC and PDA

PRINCIPAL CLIENTS

Food :
Brasseries Heineken
Chambourcy (Nestlé)
Charal
Cogesal Motta
Diepal (Danone)
Henkel
Kraft Jacobs Suchard
Maggi (Nestlé)
Panzani (Danone)
Pernod Ricard
Saupiquet

Health Care and Beauty :
Ingrid Millet
Laboratoires Astra France
Laboratoires Deglaude

Luxury Goods :
Revillon
Terre Promise

Industry and Services :
Banque de Gestion Privée
Franfinance
Dassault Aviation
Fondation Serge Dassault
Corto Pacific

CONTACTS
SONIA CHAINE
Director of Strategy

GILLES RIEDBERGER
Creative Director

LONSDALE DESIGN
10 rue Jacques Bingen
75017 Paris
Tel : 33 (0) 1 40 53 02 02
Fax : 33 (0) 1 40 53 02 01

LONSDALE
D E S I G N

Pernod

Suze Tonic

An invitation to discover this thirst-quenching pre-mixed based on the classic french drink made from gentian.

Heineken

Amberley

A revised brand identity which endows stature to this speciality beer.

Cappuccino

Richness and preciosity à l'italienne.

KJS

Nestlé

Orangina

Orangina Rouge

Red-hot iron branding for the «bad-boy» of the range.

LC1

An international project which breaks the rules to create a unique new coding which expresses the products health improving advantages.

Saint Louis

Tutti Free

The pleasure of sugar without the calories.

Sara Lee

Savane

Flask, brand identity, packaging, an anthem to real explorers.

MBD DESIGN

KEY PEOPLE

YVES DOMERGUE
Chairman and
Managing Director
Qualifications : graduate of
ENSAD (Higher National
School of Decorative Arts).

JEAN-CLAUDE MARBACH
Managing Director
Qualifications : graduate of
ENSAD (Higher National
School of Decorative Arts).

COMPANY PROFILE

APPROACH - For over 20 years, MBD has worked jointly with all sectors of industry, with businesses of all sizes, from the small firm to the large company. The agency constantly confronts the components of management in its variety of approaches to design.

AREAS OF EXPERTISE - From the very start, our objective has been to create close relationships with companies in offering the essential design services they require : graphic design, product design, environmental design. As such, MBD Design has the capacity to effectively address problematics covering a product's function and ergonomics, its identity, its graphic codes.

Turnover	in %
Graphic Design	5,6
Product Design	11,7
Environmental Design	8,4

SECTORS OF ACTIVITY - Main areas :
- Agrifood
- Construction
- Railway Vehicles
- Industrial Equipment
- Small Appliances

ACHIEVEMENTS
- Janus 96 for "Sensoa" radiators for the bath (FINIMETAL).
- Design Batimat 95 Trophies for boilers (Chauffage Français).
- Stratégies Grand Prize for Design 94 for the gas cook-top "Linea Flamme" as well as a Janus of Industry and an Oscar from the Nouvel Économiste.

PERSONNEL - 27

TURNOVER - 1995 : FF 25,7 m

GROSS PROFIT - 1995 : FF 15 m

COMPANY STRUCTURE - A limited company, capital of FF 1,000,000. Founded in 1972.

MEMBERSHIP - OPQDI, PDA, FIF

PRINCIPAL CLIENTS

Lactel (Milks and flavoured milks, package design)

Suchard (Package design for Papillon and Blason)

Rougie (Foie gras package design)

Caron ("Pour Un Homme", package design)

Nassau (Tennis and ping pong balls, package design, decorative elements for balls...)

Muller (Package design for Cereals and Royal Snack...)

Zeneca Pharma (Visual identity and package design for 13 medical laboratory labels)

Chauffage Français (Boilers, brand image, stand)

Finimetal ("Sensoa" radiator for the bath)

Allègre Puériculture (Tigex infant care product range)

GDF / Sauter (Gas cook-top)

SNCF (Locomotive BB 36000)

SNCF / RATP (EOLE equipment for the new RER E line)

RATP (Métro BOA MF 88)

Alcatel DTV (vacuum pump range)

Strafor ("Prologue" desk)

CONTACTS

YVES DOMERGUE

JEAN-CLAUDE MARBACH

MBD DESIGN
11 rue Victor Hugo
93177 Bagnolet Cedex
Tel. : 33 (0) 1 48 57 30 00
Fax : 33 (0) 1 48 57 41 31

STRAFOR
Prologue

Office furniture design

MBD
design

ALLÈGRE
Puériculture

Design of Tigex babycare
products range

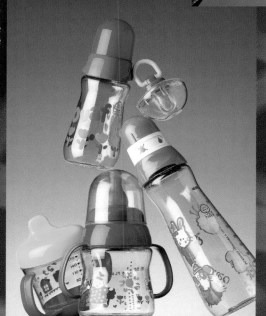

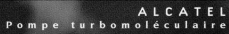

ALCATEL
Pompe turbomoléculaire

Industrial design, graphic identity and
packaging of Alcatel vacuum
technology products range

SNCF
Train Express Régional

Industrial design and graphic identity
of TER regional trains range

CARON
Pour un homme

Graphic updating of perfume,
After Shave and
new bath products line

SUCHARD
Papillon

Packaging and graphic design

LACTEL
Lait

Milk range graphic design

MEDIA PACK

KEY PEOPLE

JEAN-PAUL GUYARD
Chairman Media Pack

CAROLINE BOUSSICOT
Director of Clientele

CHRISTIAN CHABANETTE
Managing Director
Media Product

COMPANY PROFILE

APPROACH - In today's battle of the brands, the role played by visual identity and identification will be essential to victory. Media Pack can prove its creative relevancy and assert its experience in design strategy.

AREAS OF EXPERTISE

Package Design
- Graphics
- Form

Visual Identity
- Corporate
- Brand
- Product

Environmental design
- Points of sale
- Stands
- Corners

SECTORS OF ACTIVITY

Mass market, hygiene and beauty care, tobacco, leisure, industry, services, institutions.

ACHIEVEMENTS

- Andros, Prix Verre Avenir, 1994 (Glass Future Prize)
- Dynamic Ski Dynamic S94, Silver Medal, 1992 (best design out of 24,000 products) awarded by Pop Eye, Japan
- Andros, Prix Verre Avenir, 1992 (Glass Future Prize)
- Honoré Janin Tartelettes, Prix Prestige Helio, 1991
- Gourmandise, Oscar for Package Design 1991, Germany

PRINCIPAL CLIENTS

Agrifood
Andros
Blédina
Charal
Gayelord Hauser
Honoré Janin
Luang
Panzani
William Saurin

Non-Food
Boiron
Dynamic
Hospal
Groupe Prodef
Groupe Legris Industrie
Oxadis-Groupe Limagrain
Reti/groupe Akzo Nobel
Staubli

MEDIA PACK
97 rue Racine
69100 Villeurbanne
Tel. : 33 (0) 4 78 85 36 13
Fax : 33 (0) 4 78 85 35 79

ZI du Plateau
529 rue du Marché Rollay
94500 Champigny sur Marne
Tel. : 33 (0) 1 45 16 17 17
Fax : 33 (0) 1 45 16 35 99

PERSONNEL - 18

TURNOVER - 1995 : FF 16,5 m / 1994 : FF 15,4 m

COMPANY STRUCTURE - A limited company, capital of FF 250,000. Founded in 1974.

PARTNERS - Optima Conseil and Media Product

CONTACTS

JEAN-PAUL GUYARD
Lyon

CHRISTIAN CHABANETTE
Lyon

MARC GIRY
Paris

LABORATOIRES
BOIRON
DEPARTEMENT
PHYTOTHERAPIE

PACKAGING

COMAP

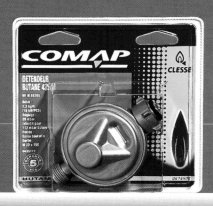

**CORPORATE
IDENTITY
APPLICATION
ON PACK**

DESIGN GRAPHIQUE

La nouvelle
tendance :
le CARVE
plaisir et
facilité

DYNAMIC

HOSPAL

**DESIGN
POINT OF SALES
STANDS
STORE CORNERS**

L'imperméabilisation
segmentée
par type d'usage

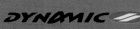

MEDIAPACK

MENU & ASSOCIÉS

KEY PEOPLE

JEAN-FRANÇOIS MENU
Chairman and
Managing Director

CATHERINE DE LA
BOURDONNAYE
Associate and Director
of Clientele

OLIVIER DEBIN
Associate and Director
of Strategy

OLIVIER PILLARD
Creative Director

COMPANY PROFILE

APPROACH - An approach combining creative proposals and strategic counseling, with the assistance of Check Pack Analysis® to bring out packaging strengths and weaknesses in its competitive environment.

AREAS OF EXPERTISE
- Recognized competence in dealing with consumer products.
- International project management.
- Brand and product concept development.

Turnover	in %
Graphic Design	
Visual Identity	13
Package Design	87

SECTORS OF ACTIVITY - All consumer product brands.

ACHIEVEMENTS - Elected Best Design Agency Of The Year, XVIIth Grand Prix "Agencies of the Year" Award (1996).

PERSONNEL - 15

TURNOVER - 1996 : FF10.8m / 1995 : FF7.1m

GROSS MARGIN - 1996 : FF9m / 1995 : FF5.8m

COMPANY STRUCTURE - A limited company, capital of FF300,000. Founded in 1993.

FOREIGN OFFICE - Milan, Italy.

MEMBERSHIP - ADC

PRINCIPAL CLIENTS

Orangina (Redesign of the Orangina range)

Astra-Calva (Package design for Aussi Bon Cru que Cuit)

Amora (New label design for vinegar range)

Danone (Redesign of the Kid range with new product launch)

Nestlé (Redesign of the Gourmet range for Europe)

Bahlsen (Redesign of the Stackers range)

Johnson Wax SC (Redesign of Raid range for Europe)

MENU & ASSOCIÉS
83 - 87 rue de Paris
92100 Boulogne-Billancourt
Tel. : 33 (0) 1 46 99 67 57
Fax : 33 (0) 1 48 25 93 33

CONTACTS

CATHERINE DE LA BOURDONNAYE

JEAN-FRANÇOIS MENU

ORANGINA
A LA PULPE D'ORANGE

ORANGINA FRANCE ET INTERNATIONAL
ORANGINA

Revitalize this historical brand.

Kid®
CRÉATION
DANONE

DANONE FRANCE
KID CRÉATION

Invent a new generation of
yogurts for children
conceived by children.

Friskies
GOURMET®
★ ★ ★

NESTLÉ
GOURMET

Increase appetite appeal and clarify
the understanding of
this European range.

ASTRA-CALVE
AUSSI BON CRU
QUE CUIT,
QUI L'EÛT CRU !

Establish a new generation
of spreadable fat.

MENU & ASSOCIÉS
Design et Stratégie

OVA'O

OLIVIER ORAIN
Associate Managing Director, Creative Director
Qualifications : ENSAAMA, Major, class of 1983.
Career Background :
1985 : Art Director, Carré Noir, Brand Design and Development.
1988 : Co-founder of Ova'o , Associate Managing Director and Creative Director.
10 years experience in Operational Brand Strategy.

SYLVIE BRISARD
Associate Managing Director,
Director of Clientele
Qualifications : ECV, Paris 1984.
Career Background : 1986 Carré Noir, development of visual identity programmes.
1988 : Co-founder of Ova'o, Associate Managing Director and Director of Clientele.
10 years experience in brand management programmes.

APPROACH · Creation and development of the first brand observatory. First market survey of brand identity taking stock of innovation programmes.

AREAS OF EXPERTISE

- Market Analysis / Brand Image Survey (Observatory)
- Brand Identity Concepts and Visual Identity Programmes
- Package Design
- Publications and Communications Design

Turnover	in %
Graphic Design	
Visual Identity	25
Package Design	30
Publications	20
Other	
Brand Image Marketing	15

SECTORS OF ACTIVITY · Ova'o develops brand and corporate strategy in all sectors, from the small local firm to large international groups eager to confirm and expand their image in the marketplace :

- Food
- Beverages
- Cosmetics / Perfume
- Interior Decoration
- Mass Market
- Financial / Insurance / Banking
- Hotels / Restaurants

- Industry
- Institutions
- Computers
- Leisure / Sports
- Health Care/ Hygiene
- Textile
- Services

NEW BUSINESS IN 1995/96 · With due regard for the confidential aspects at stake prior to project launching, Ova'o is unauthorized to disclose the names of new accounts at this time. They are large accounts of local and international scale.

ACHIEVEMENTS

The tangible results of identity programmes designed for our clients.

Groupe SB

Groupe des Sociétés de Bourbon

Groupe Expanscience

Centrale Système U

Groupe Lucien Barrière

Groupe Yves Rocher

Groupe Equad

Seiko Instruments

Colgate Palmolive

Nestlé France

GSM France Télécom

Laboratoires Doxia

Pharmygiène

Crinex

NAF-NAF

Biothérapie

Atochem

Armorial des As

International Man Search…

OLIVIER ORAIN
Creative Director,
Brand Image Marketing and Surveys

SYLVIE BRISARD
Director of Clientele and Development

OVA'O
261 rue Saint Honoré
75001 Paris
Tel. : 33 (0) 1 40 15 97 97
Fax : 33 (0) 1 40 15 97 22

PERSONNEL · 6

TURNOVER · 1996 : 5 MF / 1995 : 4 MF / 1994 : FF 3,5 m

COMPANY STRUCTURE · A limited liability company, capital of FF 250,000. Founded in 1988.

MEMBERSHIP · PDA Europe and Club des Prestataires de Marque (Brand Services Club).

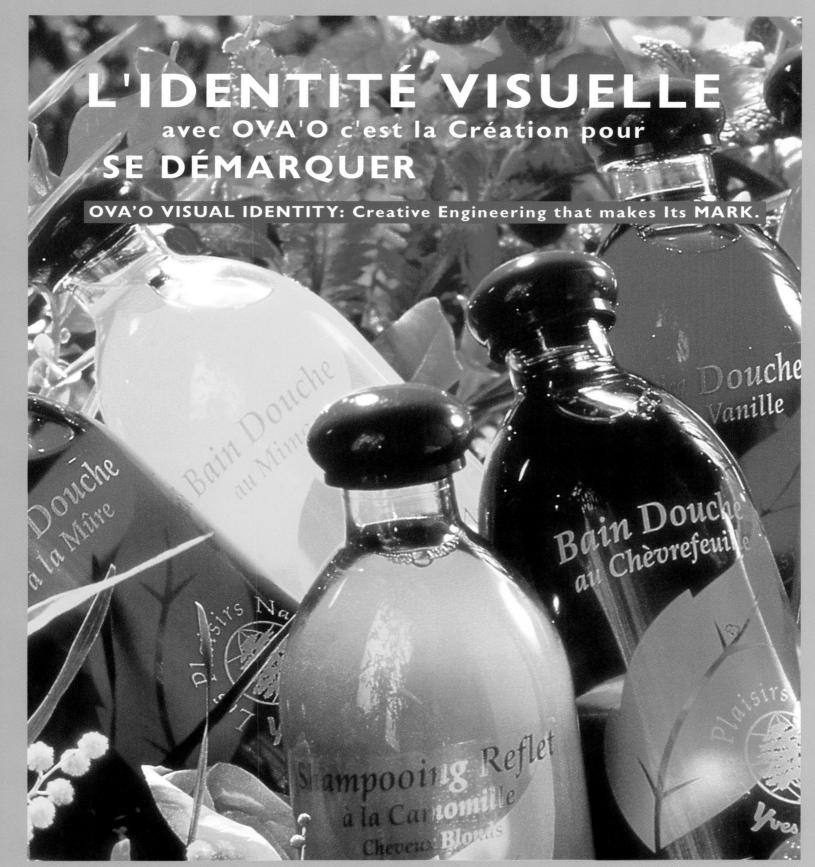

L'IDENTITÉ VISUELLE
avec OVA'O c'est la Création pour
SE DÉMARQUER

OVA'O VISUAL IDENTITY: Creative Engineering that makes Its MARK.

OVA'O

GROUPE SB
Stratégie de Communication de Groupe
Création Identité Visuelle - Hiérarchie de signature
Cahier des normes - Rapport Annuel d'Activité

ARMORIAL DES AS - TEAM DE COMPETITION
Création de nom de Marque - Création Identité Visuelle
Charte de Communication Edition de prestige
Programme Sponsoring

SOLENS
Création Identité Visuelle
Création gamme packaging segmentation

P'RÉFÉRENCE

KEY PEOPLE

FABRICE PELTIER
*President and
Managing Director*
Qualifications : École
Estienne, Paris.
Career Background :
Founder of
P'Référence, 1985.

MARCO KOMAR THLANG
*General Manager and
Financial Director*
Qualifications : Accounting
expertise, MBA, ESC
Rouen (Higher Busines
School, Rouen).

PIERRE MOUCHET
*Vice-President and
Project Manager*
Qualifications : ENSAAMA
(National Higher School of
Applied Arts and
Professional Arts).

PATRICE LE CORRE
*Clientele and
Marketing Director*
Qualifications : ISSEC.

DIDIER COSSON
*Product Design
Department Manager*
Qualifications : ESDI
(Higher School of Industrial
Design).

COMPANY PROFILE

APPROACH - "To make products that work". This standard leads us beyond basic intervention at the package design level (volume and graphics) to the establishment of a true product identity programme, covering and integrating all media destined to the sales force, to distributors, to consumers.

AREAS OF EXPERTISE - P'Référence is a global design agency which offers complete design services :
- Concept and trend boards
- Visual identity
- Package design (form and graphics)
- Publishing
- POS
- Merchandising

Turnover	in %
Graphic Design	
Visual Identity	5
Package Design	60
Publishing	10
Product Design	
Luxury goods	5
Industrial	10
Environmental Design	
Commercial Space Design	5
Signage	5

SECTORS OF ACTIVITY
- Hygiene / Beauty care
- Food
- Maintenance / DIY
- Sports / Leisure
- Industry and Services
- Tobacco
- All retail networks / chains

Turnover	in %
Hygiene / Beauty care	30
Food	25
Maintenance / DIY	20
Mass market	15
Sports / Leisure / Industry and other	10

NEW BUSINESS IN 1996 - Basic Homme Vichy (Restyling), Graphic Magic Gel, Garnier (Form and graphics), Sir Thomas Lipton, Fralib (Package design), Look Shoes (Product design), Toupret (Package design), Cristal Color, Garnier (Package design), CPC Knorr (Restaurant products design, form and graphics), Yves Rocher, 3 in 1 Shampoo (Form design), Thiriet (Package design).

ACHIEVEMENTS
- Award for Graphic Magic Gel, Laboratoires Garnier
- 1996 Cosmétique News Oscar for mass market packaging

PERSONNEL - 37

TURNOVER - 1995 : FF24.9m / 1994 : FF23.8m

COMPANY STRUCTURE - A limited company, capital of FF552,000. Founded in 1985.

NETWORK - EDD subsidiary for European, Asiatic and American markets.

MEMBERSHIP - PDA

PRINCIPAL CLIENTS

L'Oréal Perfection
Make-up (Form and
graphics)

Cils Demasq, Gemey
(Form and graphics)

Infinitif Perfume
(Package design)

Delacre
(Biscuit assortment
package design)

Astral, Akzo Nobel
(Package design and
merchandising)

Aigle boots
(Product design)

Charal heat and
serve cuisine
(Package design)

Havanitos, Seita
(Package design)

P'RÉFÉRENCE
45 rue des Apennins
75017 Paris
Tel. : 33 (0) 1 44 85 86 00
Fax : 33 (0) 1 44 85 86 44

CONTACT

PATRICE LE CORRE
Director of Clientele

Gamme BASIC HOMME pour VICHY • Restyling • Design graphique
BASIC HOMME for VICHY line • Restyling • Graphic Design ▶

Ligne de parfum INFINITIF pour COTY • Design graphique
INFINITIF perfume line for COTY • Graphic Design ▼

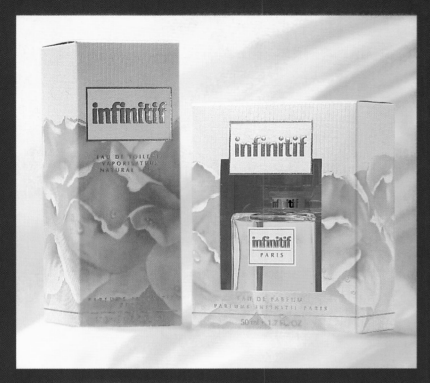

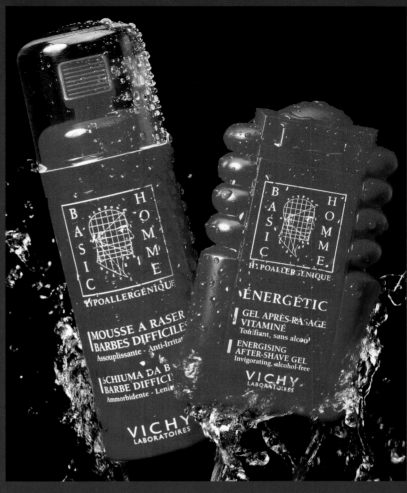

▲ Gamme bain et douches CONTINENT pour PROMODÈS •
Design volume et graphique
*CONTINENT Shower and bath line for PROMODÈS •
Volume and Graphic Design*

◀ GRAFIC MAGIC GEL pour les LABORATOIRES GARNIER •
Design volume et graphique
*GRAFIC MAGIC GEL for LABORATOIRES GARNIER •
Volume and Graphic Design*

PRÉFÉRENCE
AGENCE DE DESIGN

45, rue des Apennins 75017 Paris - Tél. : 01 44 85 86 00 - Fax : 01 44 85 86 44

PARIS VENISE DESIGN

KEY PEOPLE

STÉPHANE RICOU
Associate Managing Director
Qualifications : Sciences Politiques (School of Political Sciences)
Career Background : Havas, Carré Noir, Style Marque.

FRANCESCO MORETTI
Associate Director
Qualifications : Fine Arts, Venice.
Career Background : Advertising Agency, Italy.
Design Board, Belgium.
Style Marque.

PARIS VENISE DESIGN
4 bis, rue Descombes
75017 Paris
Tel. : 33 (0) 1 40 53 85 85
Fax : 33 (0) 1 40 53 85 84

COMPANY PROFILE

APPROACH - Increasing competition in marketplaces points to the necessary cohesion linking a project, production and people. Design is the tool which increases product quality and corporate image perception : it constitutes a relevant mean of connecting people and product. What is a modern business without effective corporate identity, for internal as well as public eye purposes ? What added value can a product project without a specific label, form or graphic expression ? What security lies in a commercial network lacking heart and soul ? Design is at the core of all communication and the brand has market value which integrates little by little corporate resources. As design professionals, our role is to make products and firms more able to compete and more attractive, through the enhancement of their true merits. Our methodology is built upon design strategy which balances visual emotion and rational marketing. The combined experience of Stéphane Ricou and Francesco Moretti, enriched by the presence of their talented team, ensures the creative quality, relevancy and accuracy of our work. With availability and efficacity at heart, we feel that our task is to offer our clients true partnership. Which is why our intervention field is very precise and focused on corporate identity and packaging, with a human sized structure made of specialists.

AREAS OF EXPERTISE - Creation, Evolution, and Management in Packaging Design, Brand Identity, Structural Design, Publishing and Standardizing.

Turnover	in %
Graphic Design	
Brand Identity	35
Packaging Design	60
Publications	5

SECTORS OF ACTIVITY - Food, Beauty Care, Luxury Goods, Health, Services.

NEW BUSINESS IN 1996 - Lu (Packaging Design), MKT (Corporate Identity), My-Épil (Brand Identity - Packaging Design), Riches Monts (Brand Identity - Packaging Design), Le Rustique (Brand Identity - Packaging Design), RATP/SNCF (Brand Identity), Snair (Brand Identity - Packaging Design).

WINNING DESIGNS

1992 : Lomudal
1994 : Arvie
1995 : U Tights, Carpené Malvolti
1996 : Decleor

PERSONNEL - 11

TURNOVER - 1996 estimate : FF 6,7 m / 1995 : FF 5,2 m / 1994 : FF 4,7 m

COMPANY STRUCTURE - A limited liability company

MEMBERSHIP - ADC

PRINCIPAL CLIENTS

Mineral Waters
Arvie, Evian, Italaquae (Italy), Salvetat.
Dairy
Bongrain Gérard, Candia, Danone, Ideval, Isigny Sainte Mère, Yoplait.
Grocery
Amora, Heudebert, Lu, Snair.
Alcoholic Beverages
B.G.I. Beer, Carpené Malvolti, Pernod, Rémy Martin.
Appliances
Arthur Martin.
Chemicals / Pharmaceuticals
Laboratoires Fisons.
Agriculture
Monsanto.
Automobile
Shell.
Hygiene / Beauty Care
Colgate, Decleor, Ella Baché, Henkel, Lancôme.
Luxury Goods
Alessandro Moretti, Carpené Malvolti, Fouquet's, Rémy Martin.
Publications
Les Saisons de la Danse.
Restaurants
Aux Moulineaux, Frantour.
Services
ADC Atlantique, Atelier 45°, Area, Cabinet Gröll, CTC, ESIEE, EFP, L'espace Thermal, Evian, Language Training Centre, MKT, Mutuelle de Seine et Marne, Prao Communication, Studio du Capitaine, Université de Paris Dauphine.
Tobacco
RJ Reynolds.
Textiles
Système U, Madoga.

CONTACT

STÉPHANE RICOU

PARIS VENISE

DESIGN

Création packaging.

Création forme.

Création marque, packaging et forme.

Création marque et packaging Italie.

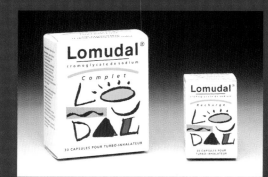

Création packaging France, Angleterre.

Evolution et gestion identité visuelle italie.

POINT MIRE

KEY PEOPLE

PHILIPPE GALLIEN
Chairman and
Managing Director
Qualifications : ESC
Toulouse (Higher Business
School) and Beaux Arts de
Toulouse (Fine Arts)

ÉRIC COURTOIS
Customer Director,
Technical Manager
Qualifications : École
Estienne

VALÉRIE RENAULT
Director of Strategy and
Business Development

VINCENT QUEFFELEC
Art Director

POINT MIRE
11 rue Moreau Vauthier
92100 Boulogne
Tel. : 33 (0) 1 46 99 18 40
Fax : 33 (0) 1 46 99 00 01

1530 des Rubis
Saint Hubert J4T 3S8 Quebec
Tel. : (514) 466 68 15

Unit A, 20/F, Empire Land
Commercial Center
81-85 Lockhart Road, Wanchai,
Hong Kong
Tel. : (852) 2866 6881
Fax : (852) 2529 5266

Seestrasse 36
D-13353 Berlin

Lopatecka 11a
147 00 Praha 4
Tel. : 42 2 61213949

COMPANY PROFILE

APPROACH - A methodology based on strategic and graphic analysis tailored to your needs. Relevant design combines with a sense of service and a pragmatic approach to design problematics.

AREAS OF EXPERTISE - International scope for export products, strategy consulting, creation, concepts, technical assistance and fieldwork in :
- package design and graphic identity
- visual identity
- advertising / promotional media
- brand merchandising

Turnover	in %
Graphic Design	
Brand name creation and visual identity	10
Package Design	30
Publishing	20
Environmental Design	
Ad / promotional media	15
Special appeal merchandising and signage	5

NEW BUSINESS IN 1996
- Fromageries Perreault (Chamois d'Or)
- Mundia (Disney doll range)
- GEB (DIY range)
- Armoric (Fresh crêpes range)
- Jean d'Erguet (Cocktail tray)
- Bricorama (Shop lay-out)
- Bulgomme (Shelf display)
- L'Oréal (Shelf display)

PERSONNEL - 12

TURNOVER - 1997 estimate : FF 11 m / 1996 : FF 10 m

COMPANY STRUCTURE - A limited company, capital of FF1,000,000. Founded in 1989.

PRINCIPAL CLIENTS

Food

Besnier (Fromagerie du Terroir)

Bongrain (Fromarsac, Fromagerie Paul Renard)

Bouguet Pau

Intermarché

Pescanova

Socopa

Consumer goods

Ets Turc (Truffaut)

Fian (Sigma Coatings)

Henkel (Pattex, Perfax)

L'Oréal (Phas)

Lardenois (Efidium)

Sodicam (Oxelia)

Unilever (Elida Fabergé)

V33 (Libéron / V33)

Institutional

Qualitel

Lion Assurance

OSIAQ

ECG

CONTACTS

PHILIPPE GALLIEN
Chairman and
Managing Director

VALÉRIE RENAULT
Director of Strategy and
Business Development

PHAS (l'Oréal)

POND'S (Élida-Fabergé)

ARMORIC

MUNDIA

GÉNIALTY (Intermarché)

POINT
MIRE
PARIS

CRÉATION VISUELLE

PUBLICIS DESIGN

PUBLICIS DESIGN
25 rue Plumet
75015 Paris
Tél. : 33 (0) 1 47 34 48 18
Fax : 33 (0) 1 47 83 51 99

KEY PEOPLE

PETER PETRONIO
Managing Director,
Creative Director

COMPANY PROFILE

APPROACH - "Seeing comes before words. The child looks and recognizes before it can speak." John Berger.

Design concerns all things that enter into our field of vision.

Design is an act of communication that influences our perception of and our attitudes towards institutions, products, services, people and ideas.

Design is more than the esthetic manipulations of forms and space ; of graphics, typography and colors ; of moving images on film ; or the envelope of our environment.

Design, like the alphabet, is the cement we use to hold our ideas together, in many cases design is the physical trace we will leave behind to mark our passage through time ; it is a reflection of our culture, our social, moral, esthetic and economic values.

AREAS OF EXPERTISE - Publicis Design is a strategic and creative resource offering clients the opportunity to profit from our collective experience in the areas of corporate and brand strategic planning and communications programs management.

Areas of activity include :
- New Product Development
- Brand Repositioning
- Volume Design
- Packaging
- Visual Identity Programs
- Corporate Publications
- Retail Environment and Architecture
- Point-of-Sale Presentations
- Brand Merchandising

PERSONNEL - 26

GROUP - Publicis Design is part of the Publicis International network, present on five continents.

PRINCIPAL CLIENTS

Consumer Goods :
Bongrain Gérard
Casio
Charal
Compagnie Laitière
Cuisimer
Henkel
Lindt
Materne / Confipote
Menier
Tabacalera, Spain
Villars, Switzerland

**Beauty/Cosmetics/
Fashion :**
Cacharel Perfumes
Dim
Giorgio Armani Perfumes
Lancôme
L'Oréal
Nivéa

Retail :
Groupe Flo
Shell
The Greenery
International, Netherlands
The Limited Stores, USA

Corporate Programs :
Drouot
Esselte
Lyonnaise des Eaux
French Ministry of
Foreign Affairs
National Office of
Moroccan Tourism
Perrier Vittel S.A.
SFR
Synthélabo

CONTACT
PETER PETRONIO

Conception of a commemorative metal box to celebrate the 150 years of existence of Menier chocolates.

Creation of a new visual territory for Montecristo cigarettes, for the pan-European market.

For Materne, the design of the packagings for their different lines of fruit desserts. Presented here are the adult, family and "ecological" products lines.

For Villars, Maître Chocolatier in Fribourg, Switzerland, the development of the visual identity and graphic design system for all their product lines; the supreme reference of authentic Swiss chocolate.

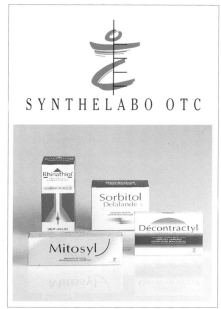

Creation of the visual identity for Synthelabo OTC, a division of L'Oréal, federating all of their pharmaceutic products.

le petit Flo
RESTAURANT

The visual identity for the most recent restaurant launched by the Flo Group, combining feminine fashion, cheerfulness, spontaneity.

the greenery
INTERNATIONAL

Visual identity program for a new international brand grouping Dutch vegetable producers, cooperatives and retailers.

CEGETEL

Creation of the visual identity CEGETEL, a subsidiary of the Compagnie Générale des Eaux, which unifies all their telecommunication activities (specifically SFR).

RAISON PURE INTERNATIONAL

KEY PEOPLE

GIANNI ROTTA
*Chairmanand and
Managing Director*
Qualifications: Art College
of London.

FRÉDÉRIC JENTGEN
*Associate Managing
Director*
Qualifications: Arts
Appliqués et Métiers d'Art
(School of Applied Arts and
Professional Arts).

LAURENT HAINAUT
*Associate Creative
Director*
Qualifications: Arts
Appliqués et Métiers d'Art
(School of Applied Arts and
Professional Arts).

COMPANY PROFILE

APPROACH - As Design Consultants, we research and define the visual concepts that best translate specific product and brand identities in a significant concentrate of form and function. The power of imagination thrives upon the agency's array of complementary skills, fundamental research and high qualitative standards, which combine to generate effective and innovative design.

AREAS OF EXPERTISE - Raison Pure serves all areas of brand identity, package design, bottle design, product design, point of sale display and publishing.

Turnover	in %
Beauty Care	50
Cosmetics	65
Perfumes	35
Agrifood	40
Other (publications)	10

SECTORS OF ACTIVITY

- Perfumes and Cosmetics (high-end and massmarket)
- Food and Consumer Goods
- Services

NEW BUSINESS IN 1995/1996 - Coty, Elf, Fleury Michon, France Loisirs, Guerlain, Heineken, La Française des Jeux, Miko.

ACHIEVEMENTS

- 1994 Janus Award (French Institute of Design), Worldstar for Packaging 1994 (World Packaging Organisation) for Fluokids, Synthelabo.
- Product of the Year 1996 : Petits Filous à Sucer, Yoplait.

PERSONNEL - 18

TURNOVER - 1995 : FF15m / 1994 : FF13m

COMPANY STRUCTURE - A limited company, capital of FF250,000. Founded in 1987.

FOREIGN OFFICES AND NETWORK - Raison Pure UK, LE16 7PT Leicestershire / Raison Pure USA , NY 10022 New York / Mythologies, 26 rue Édith Cavell, 92400 Courbevoie

RAISON PURE INTERNATIONAL
38 rue Lantiez
75017 Paris
Tel. : 33 (0) 1 42 63 45 45
Fax. : 33 (0) 1 42 28 18 60

PRINCIPAL CLIENTS

D&D (Lipsticks, Rouge Baiser)

Eau de Murano (Perfume range, bottle design, visual identity, package design, POS...)

Elf - Elf 500
(Visual identity)

Ella Baché - Radical Rides (Range revamp, packaging and visual identity)

Fleury Michon -
Les Fleurons (Range repositioning, package design)

France Loisirs (Photo products range, package design and publishing)

Guerlain - Champs Elysées (Package Design)

Guerlain - Habit Rouge (Repositioning, package design)

Heineken (Visual identity and new package design)

La Française des Jeux
(Tac O Tac)

Liebig Maille (Maille range)

Miko - Instants Choisis (Range repositioning, package design)

Reckitt & Colman - Marinessence (Range repositioning, visual identity and package design)

Seita - Gauloise Blondes 25 (Package design and POS)

Synthelabo - Fluokids (Toothbrush range, product design)

Yoplait - Petits Filous à Sucer (Package design)

CONTACTS

GIANNI ROTTA
FRÉDÉRIC JENTGEN
LAURENT HAINAUT

THE POWER

STYLE MARQUE

KEY PEOPLE

GÉRARD BOULANGER
Associate Technical
Manager
Qualifications : ESAM,
Reproduction and
packaging engineering
specialist.

JEAN PERRET
Associate Creative
Director
Qualifications : Professor of
Typography, École
Supérieur d'Art Graphique.
Brand image design
specialist.

YVES RONIN
Associate, Chairman
Qualifications : HEC School
of Business, brand
marketing specialist.

COMPANY PROFILE

APPROACH - Style Marque specializes in brand identity concepts, packaging and produces identity manuals within the framework of corporate policies of brand and identity renewal. Its management, with over 20 years of design experience in dealing with domestic and international brands, as well as with smaller businesses, contributes added strategic, creative and technical value to all projects. The agency is well-versed in computer-assisted design and has developed its own identity standardization software.

AREAS OF EXPERTISE

- Brand Identity
- International standardization
- Packaging (Form and graphics)
- Corporate Literature

SECTORS OF ACTIVITY - Style Marque has acquired major references in all branches of industry and services sectors.

NEW BUSINESS IN 1996 - Agnès B (Packaging), Conseil Général de l'Yonne (Brand identity, publishing), Fralib (Packaging), Joker (Packaging), Kindy (Brand identity, identity manual), Labonal (Brand identity, identity manual), Lapeyre GME (Brand identity), McDonald's (Brand identity, identity manual), Magasins Généraux de France (Brand identity), Paysan Breton (Brand identity, identity manual), Rémy Martin (Packaging), Renault Véhicule Industriel (Applications), Rougié (Packaging), Salins (Brand identity, identity manual), Teisseire (Packaging).

ACHIEVEMENTS

- Stratégies Grand Prix for French Design, 1991
- Glass Future Prize, 1992, Emballage Digest
- Oscar for Design, Evian glass bottle, 1993, le Nouvel Économiste
- Packaging Oscar for Trésor de Lancôme gift box, 1992

PRINCIPAL CLIENTS

Food
Glac Surgères (Packaging),
Paul Prédault
(Brand identity, packaging),
La Baleine (Brand identity,
packaging),
LU (Packaging),
Monoprix (Packaging)
Vivagel (Brand identity,
identity manual).

Beverages
BSN (Bottle design),
Canard-Duchêne
(Brand identity, packaging),
Évian (Bottle design),
Joker (Packaging),
Météor (Brand identity,
packaging),
Pernod (Brand identity,
packaging),
Rémy Martin
(Identity manual).

Cosmetics
Eau de Rochas (Packaging),
Kérastase (Brand identity,
packaging),
Mustela (Brand identity,
packaging),
PHAS (Brand identity,
identity manual),
Trésor de Lancôme
(Brand identity, packaging).

Institutional
Antar (Brand identity),
Camel (Identity manual),
Club Méditerranée
(Brand identity),
Renault (Brand identity),
Salins (Brand identity,
identity manual),
Sommer-Allibert (Brand
identity, identity manual),
Stim Batir (Brand identity,
identity manual),
Apsylog (Brand identity,
identity manual),
Longchamp (Brand identity,
corporate literature).

CONTACT

YVES RONIN
Chairman

STYLE MARQUE
10 rue des Moulins
75001 Paris
Tel. : 33 (0) 1 42 96 16 78
Fax : 33 (0) 1 42 60 17 10

PERSONNEL - 15

TURNOVER - 1996 estimate : FF12m / 1995 : FF11.5m

GROSS PROFIT - 1996 : FF9m / 1995 : FF5.8m

COMPANY STRUCTURE - A limited company, capital of FF800,000. Founded in 1980.

NETWORK - Brand Alliance (Germany, Benelux, Denmark, Great Britain, Italy)

LE SENS
DE LA MARQUE

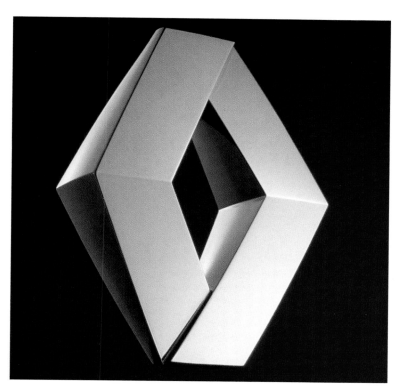

Pour la première marque automobile française ou pour un distillateur de Provence, Style Marque applique à la conception d'un logo une méthodologie exclusive. La recherche de sens, consacrée au fond et à la forme, en est le levier. Car plus le diagnostic est précis, plus la création s'impose, unique, originale, puissante, transformant le simple logo en marque remarquable.

TEAM CRÉATIF

KEY PEOPLE

NICK CRAIG
Chairman and
Creative Director,
Founder

SYLVIA VITALE-ROTTA
Managing Director,
Commercial Director,
Founder

OLIVIER GUERMONPREZ
Director of Business
Development

TEAM CRÉATIF
89 rue de Miromesnil
75008 Paris
Tel. : 33 (0) 1 42 89 90 00
Fax : 33 (0) 1 42 89 90 01

COMPANY PROFILE

APPROACH · Attuned to the exchange of ideas, thriving on feedback, team spirit permeates through to client / agency relationships - a matter of temperament. Drawing upon the very essence of a brand or product to assert uniqueness, define limits and extend visual boundaries - a matter of professionalism. Exacting, inventive creative forces combine with precision to endow strategic options with substance and meaning - a matter of perfectionism.
Many are the clients who have remained faithful to Team Créatif since 1986. Clearly, a matter of confidence.

AREAS OF EXPERTISE · Packaging and Product Design, Corporate Identity, Brand Creation.
In the past 10 years, Team Créatif has acquired a very solid experience in Consumer Goods Packaging Design and Brand Identity and has particularly developed a capacity for International Brand Management.

Turnover	in %
Graphic Design	**90**
Packaging Design	70
Visual Identity	20
Product Design	**10**

SECTORS OF ACTIVITY · Food, Hygiene / Beauty Care, Home Maintenance, Office, Leisure and DIY products.

ACHIEVEMENTS
- Several products voted "Products of the Year 1994"
- 1994 Grand Prix for Product Innovation
- 1994 Coup de Cœur (Special Favourite) Packaging Award for CarnaudMetalbox
- 1994 Hélio Prestige Award for CarnaudMétalbox

PERSONNEL · 43

TURNOVER · 1996 estimate : FF45m / 1995 : 43.5m

COMPANY STRUCTURE · A limited company, capital of FF2,000,000. Founded in 1986.

OVERSEAS OFFICES · Office in Bologna (Italy) and correspondants in England and the United States.

MEMBERSHIPS · ADC and EPDA

PRINCIPAL CLIENTS

Visual Identity
Danone Ultra Frais Europe, Biscuits Belin, Mars Ice Creams, Damart.

Packaging Design
Amora-Liebig-Maille (Groupe Danone),
Beghin-Say (Ferruzi),
Belin (Groupe Danone),
Colgate Palmolive :
Soupline/Paic/Axion,
CPC France : Knorr,
Diépal : Blédina
(Groupe Danone),
Danone Ultra-Frais Europe,
Fromageries Bel,
Galbani Italy,
Heudebert (Groupe Danone),
Kaysersberg,
Kimberly-Clark Sopalin :
Kleenex Europe,
Kiwi France (Sara Lee) :
Savane/Williams,
Kraft Jacobs Suchard :
Tonigum/Côte D'Or,
Lustucru (RCL) :
Pasta and Rice,
Mars Ice Creams,
Mars (World-wide) :
Whiskas/Kitekat/Aquarian/
Canigou/Chappi,
Reckitt & Colman Europe :
Maison Verte/Airwick/
Topp's/Jex/Glassex/Harpic,
Schweppes
(Cadbury Schweppes),
Teisseire : Tessalia/
Pressi/Golden Valley,
Volvic (Groupe Danone)
Yves Rocher.

Packaging and Structural Design
Alcatel Telephones
Hachette Jeunesse

CONTACTS

SYLVIA VITALE-ROTTA
Managing Director, Founder

OLIVIER GUERMONPREZ
Director of Business Development

SHERRY BAUDRY
Production Manager

TONNERRE DE BREST !

KEY PEOPLE

ZAKI ELIA
Creative Director

CHRISTOPHE SPETEBROOT
Art Director

ANNE MICHEL
Director of Clientele

PAUL MINOTT
Partner

JULES AKEL
Partner

COMPANY PROFILE

APPROACH · Our speciality is brand expression : conveyed by logo design, package design and by the objects bearing its name or point of sale / display.

Turnover	in %
Graphic Design	
Visual identity	10
Package Design	85
Publishing	5

SECTORS OF ACTIVITY · Cosmetics, mass market, prestige publications, sports events, humanitarian causes.

Turnover	in %
Cosmetics	90

NEW BUSINESS IN 1996

- Global design of a new hair care products brand from Laboratoires Garnier : Fructis (form, logo and graphics).
- Design of a new cigarette brand from R.J. Reynolds : V.O. (logo and graphics).
- Design of a hair care products range by Yves Rocher USA for the North American market : Biovital (logo and graphics).
- Graphic design concept for a new biscuit from LU : Pim's Barre.
- Volume design for the Vichy product range, Cosmétique Active Internationale.
- Volume design for the Vittel product range, LaScad.

ACHIEVEMENTS · 1995 Cosmetic Package Design Honourable Mention, French Design Grand Prix for P'tit DOP bath & shower.

PRINCIPAL CLIENTS

Global design : P'tit DOP shampoos, LaScad (logo, form, graphics)

Global design : P'tit DOP bath & shower, LaScad (logo, form, graphics)

Logo and form design : DOP shampoos, LaScad

Global redesign : Obao range, Laboratoires Garnier (logo, form, graphics)

Graphic revamp : Axion, Colgate Palmolive Detergents

Graphic concept for Hansaplast condoms, Beiersdorf Médical

Global design : Jacques Dessange product range, LaScad (volume and graphics)

Graphic concept for the Neutralia range, Laboratoires Garnier (logo, graphics)

Kellogg's Tour of Britain (poster and press pack)

The Earth Center, London (print identity)

Ascot Racecourse (logo)

Greenpeace (brochures and reports)

Marylebone Cricket Club (publishing)

TONNERRE DE BREST !
35 rue de la Fédération
93100 Montreuil
Tél. : 33 (0) 1 49 88 10 80
Fax : 33 (0) 1 49 88 11 43

PERSONNEL · 10

TURNOVER · 1995 : FF7.4m / 1994 : FF7m

COMPANY STRUCTURE · A limited liability company, capital of FF50,000. Founded in 1991.

FOREIGN OFFICES AND NETWORK · London partner : Akel Minott Elia, 26 Britton Street, London EC1M 5 NQ

CONTACT

ANNE MICHEL
Director of Clientele

La Scad
JACQUES DESSANGE
own brand identity
Three dimensional design

Laboratoires Garnier Paris
FRUCTIS
Brand identity
Three dimensional design

Laboratoires Garnier Paris
NEUTRALIA
Brand identity

Cosmetique Active Int.
VICHY
Three dimensional design

Sports for television
KELLOG'S TOUR
Poster design

Greenpeace
DANGEROUS WATER
Brochure

TRAPÈZE

KEY PEOPLE

MARYSE BRIGOT
Director
Career background: A
career in advertising
(agency and announcer)
followed by 10 years in
mass marketing.
Founder.

CHANTAL PIALOT
Director of Clientele
Career experience: CB'A
Packaging and by CB'A
Edition.

COMPANY PROFILE

APPROACH - The impact of creative simplicity combined with strategy and efficacity at the service of brands. The creativity of an experienced and enthousiastic team. And the simplicity of a small agency.

AREAS OF EXPERTISE

- Corporate visual identity
- Brand image
- Package design (graphics and volume)
- Institutional publications (brochures, annual reports...)
- Product literature (catalogs, brochures, sales kits...)

Turnover	in %
Graphic Design	
Visual identity	10
Package Design	55
Publishing	35

SECTORS OF ACTIVITY

- Mass market
- Industry and Services
- Hygiene
- DIY
- Home appliances

NEW BUSINESS IN 1996

- Lactel (New products)
- Raynal et Roquelaure (Package design)
- Roussel - Uclaf (Volume/Package design)
- Whirlpool (Package design)

PRINCIPAL CLIENTS

Distrivet - Groupe
Roussel Uclaf (Veterinary
range package design)

Harry's
(Festive end-of-year
package design)

Lactel (New product
package design)

Lever (Omo Micro range)

Nestlé France (Maggi -
dried dishes, soups and
cooking aids: package
design)

Nestlé
Visual identity for infant
range (Swiss market)

Raynal et Roquelaure
(Quenelle package
design)

Roussel-Uclaf (Volume
design)

Seita (New Meccarillos
products, package
design)

Stafford Miller (Corporate
logo and package design
for Coréga, Sensodyne)

Whirlpool (Catalogs,
brochures, package
design)

TRAPÈZE
12 rue des Pyramides
75001 Paris
Tel. : 33 (0) 1 42 60 73 73
Fax : 33 (0) 1 42 60 63 73

PERSONNEL - 8

TURNOVER - 1996 : FF7m / 1995 : FF6.3m

COMPANY STRUCTURE - A limited liability company, capital of FF250,000. Founded in 1986.

CONTACT

CHANTAL PIALOT
Development

TRAPÈZE

Packaging

▲ China Cup et India Cup
Un nouveau concept MAGGI.
Création marque et packaging.

▲ Mini Meccarillos
SEITA - Création du packaging.

Création de la ▶
nouvelle gamme
des quenelles
RAYNAL & ROQUELAURE :
Raffinement et Modernité.

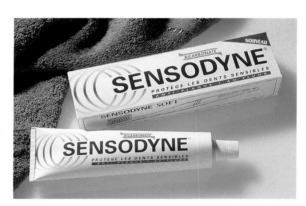

▲ Lifting du packaging
de la gamme
SENSODYNE.

◀ COMPAGNIE
FRANÇAISE
DU MÉTHANE
Rapport annuel 95.
Un univers institutionnel
et dynamique.

Edition

▲ TECHNOCOM :
Création d'une plaquette
institutionnelle.

product design

HYGIENE / COSMETICS / PERFUMES

INDUSTRIAL / CONSUMER PRODUCTS

C B ' A

LOUIS COLLINET
Chairman and
Managing Director
Career Background :
Founder of CB'A.

ARNAUD TOURTOULOU
General Manager
Qualifications : ESCP
(Higher School of Business
and Advertising). Masters in
Business Law.
Career Background :
Marketing with Lesieur
Cotelle, Colgate Palmolive
and Côte d'Or.

APPROACH - For 15 years CB'A has consistently combined strategic rigour and creative force to stimulate product sales and reinforce brand image.

SECTORS OF ACTIVITY

- Agrifood

- Mass market

- Cosmetics, Perfumes, Pharmaceuticals

- Finance, Banking, Insurance

- Computers

- Institutions

Turnover	in %
Graphic Design	**(70)**
Visual Identity	30
Package Design	60
Publishing	10
Product Design	**(15)**
Luxury goods	100
Environmental Design	**(15)**
Commercial Space Design	60
Signage	40

ACHIEVEMENTS

Three citations for Product of the year 1995 :

- La Croix Fraîcheur Lavande

- Paic Excel

- Findus Cuisine Créative

Corporate identity
Continent,
Conforama,
Mondial Moquette,
INPI, CANAM,
Douanes et Droits
Indirects, CCF SAM,
Bayard Presse,
Ecomax, Institut Pasteur,
Montecristo Restaurant
Café, Ministry of Labour,
Ministry of Foreign Affairs,
Disneyland Paris:
Nestlé Baby Comfort
Stops,
Permanent Assembly of
Chamber of Agriculture,
Fil à Fil, Concorde
Hotels, Banque de
France,
Wafabank Group...

Product identity
Agfa,
Kraft Jacobs Suchard,
Colgate Palmolive,
Grand Metropolitan,
Gemey,
Champagnes and Spirits
Associated,
Fralib, Findus,
Nestlé, Lesieur,
Henkel, Rubson,
BN, Diépal,
Ducros, Miko-Cogesal,
Bourjois, Valrhona,
CPC, Pernod,
SVF, Bongrain,
Cora,
L'Oréal Technique
Professionnelle,
Lancôme, Biotherm...

CB'A
94 avenue de Villiers
75017 Paris
Tel. : 33 (0) 1 40 54 09 00
Fax : 33 (0) 1 47 64 95 75

PERSONNEL - 87

TURNOVER - 1995 : FF66.2m / 1994 : FF49.7m

GROSS PROFIT - 1995 : FF45.3m / 1994 : FF35.2m

COMPANY STRUCTURE - A limited company, capital of FF2,000,000. Founded in 1982.

FOREIGN OFFICES AND NETWORK - Paris - Brussels

MEMBERSHIP - PDA

LOUIS COLLINET

ARNAUD TOURTOULOU

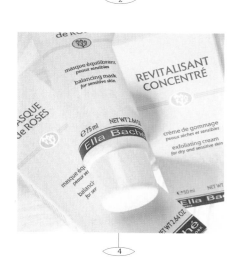

1

2

3

4

5

6

7

8

1. BOURJOIS

Création des noms, du design
volume des pinceaux et des boîtes,
et du design graphique.

2. BOURJOIS

Création du volume de la chemise,
des décors du tube et des étuis,
de la gamme Fond de Teint.

3. BOURJOIS

Création du design volume et du design
graphique de la Gamme Hygiène.

4. ELLA BACHÉ

Lifting des packagings des gammes
"Hydratation" et "Rosée du Matin".

5. L'ORÉAL

Création du packaging international
Epicéa Color pour un nouveau concept
de coloration à base de plantes.

6. GEMEY PARIS

Lifting des packagings des sprays
Jean-Louis David et proposition
du principe de colorisation des capots.

7. COLGATE

Création des packagings d'une gamme
de shampooings pour enfants.

8. ÉLIDA FABERGÉ

Création du packaging pour une
nouvelle gamme de brosses à dents
à la marque Sanogyl.

DIEDRE

KEY PEOPLE

FRANÇOIS BURON
Managing Director,
Founder
Qualificatations : Degree in
Design and Interior Design,
École Supérieure d'Art
Graphique (Higher School
of Graphic Art).
Career Background : Since
1984, teaches at the École
Nationale des Arts et
Métiers (National School of
Arts and Professional
Trades).

COMPANY PROFILE

APPROACH - Design : to develop a product's added value potential. **Creativity :** to better respond to consumer expectations and to accelerate the ageing process of competing brands. **Product marketing :** helps define innovative solutions to consumer expectations, is of assistance in range management and brings relevancy to brand differencion. **Product innovation :** for the implementation of the most effective technologies and taking forward the client's differenciating knowledge.

AREAS OF EXPERTISE - Diedre operates in close partnership with businesses, contributing both creative and reflective input :
- Product and package innovation.
- Definition of range graphic codes relevant to its positioning.
- Brand differenciation and expression of brand values at the point of sale.

Turnover	in %
Graphic Design	
Visual Identity	10
Package design	25
Product Design	
Industrial	65

SECTORS OF ACTIVITY - Motor Vehicles, Habitat Components, Appliances, Electronics and Telecommunications, Packaging, Office Furniture, Security and Home Automation, Signage and Urban Furniture, Sports and Leisure, Infant care and Toys, Comfort Products, Transportation.

Turnover	in %
Motor Vehicles	20
Sports	20
Infantcare	20
Habitat	15
Packaging	10

NEW BUSINESS IN 1996 - Reydel (New dashboards), Baby Relax (Push chair), Mavic / Groupe Salomon (Expressive Concept for expressionof wheel products), RMN Musée du Louvre (Educational game), Renault (Outdoor vehicle design) Pampryl (Corporate package design for the brand), MAPA (New improved glove design for better comfort), Carrefour France (Product design and toy range package design).

ACHIEVEMENTS
- Nominated for European Design Grand Prix, 1992
- 3 Oscars awarded by the Nouvel Économiste
- 9 Janus of Industry

PERSONNEL - 14

TURNOVER - 1995 : FF 8,5 m / 1994 : FF 8 m

COMPANY STRUCTURE - A limited liability company, capital of FF 100, 000. Founded in 1992.

FOREIGN OFFICES - Honk Kong - INRIE Foundation

MEMBERSHIP - OPQDI (pending)

PRINCIPAL CLIENTS

Aérospatiale (Workstation ergonomics)

Carnaud Metalbox (6 years joint collaboration on new products)

CEBAL - Groupe Pechiney (New toothpaste tubes)

IBM - Albertville Olympic Games (Interactive signage terminal concept)

Salomon (Formalization of design specifications)

SEB (Idea portfolio on toasters and barbecues)

Valéo (New air conditioner control panel)

VMC - Groupe Danone (Product enhancemnt for glassware)

Yacco - Groupe Total (New identity and identity manual, package design and Totem display)

CONTACTS

FRANÇOIS BURON
Managing Director and Consultant

BENOÎT COUSIN
Director of Business Development and Consultant

FRANÇOIS POTIE
Consultant

DIEDRE
89 rue Damrémont
75018 Paris
Tel. : 33 (0) 1 42 62 51 46
Fax : 33 (0) 1 42 54 94 06

PAMPRYL

Greater taste sensations and improved practicality set off to advantage new 1 litre juice containers made with a new composite material : Barex.
• Package and stopper design.

Contemporary, user-friendly and powerful : these are the attributes conveyed through design to differenciate this new generation of boiters for IDEAL STANDARD.
• Form and body design.
• Information and control interface design.

IDEAL STANDARD

Personnality, practicality and assertion of competitive spirit bring a modern touch to a well-known brand : YACCO.
• Logo design (YACCO).
• Package form design.
• Package graphics.

YACCO

Whimsy and glasswork's shimmer, to win over the homemaker and become a part of home decor.
• Product logo design (RIVIERA).
• Package design.
• Form and textural effects design.

VDG

The added value

of product

the graphic designers' index 11

MICHEL BLANC

MICHEL BLANC
Chairman and
Managing Director

GÉRARD WANTZ
Managing Director

MAHASTY REZAÏ
Commercial Attachée

APPROACH - We seek the best results for our clients.

AREAS OF EXPERTISE
- Image strategy
- Product concept
- Graphics
- Product design
- Publications
- Point of sale

Turnover	in %
Graphic Design	
Visual Identity	10
Package Design	30
Publications	5
Product Design	
Luxury goods	45
Environmental Design	
Commercial space design	5
Signage	5

SECTORS OF ACTIVITY
- Cosmetics
- Perfumes
- Luxury Goods
- Spirits
- Furniture
- Textiles
- Tobacco

NEW BUSINESS IN 1996
- RJR Nabisco (Camel Filters)
- Parfums Jacques Fath
- Parfums Christian Dior
- Moët et Chandon
- Dom Pérignon

Harley Davidson - SBI
(Product design and
graphics for Eaux de
Toilette range and
derived products)

FX by Studio Line - OAP
(Concept research, name
search and graphics)

Vogica
(Concept and publishing
for Bath and Kitchen
catalogs)

Brew n°1 - Irish Brewing
Beer (Brand strategy,
name search and
graphics)

Loulou Blue - Cacharel
(Graphics and point of
sale)

MICHEL BLANC
1 rue d'Anjou
92602 Asnières
Tel. : 33 (0) 1 47 90 66 87
Fax : 33 (0) 1 47 33 49 07

PERSONNEL - 14

TURNOVER - 1995 : FF26m / 1994 : FF18m

COMPANY STRUCTURE - A limited company, capital of FF756,000. Founded in 1977.

MICHEL BLANC
GÉRARD WANTZ
MAHASTY REZAÏ

1 Harley Davidson

2 Fresco Absolut

3 Acqua di Gio
de Giorgio Armani

4 Studio Line

5 Castorama

6 Loulou, pour Cacharel

7 Rémy Martin

8 Orlane Solaire

9 Cross

10 Irish Brewing

1 **Harley Davidson :** Brand positioning study, form and package design for the complote range.

2 **Fresco Absolut :** Concept created for the ad campaign, point of sale display and advertising / promotional strategy.

3 **Acqua di Giò de Giorgio Armani :** Package design, POS and sales drive media for the Eau Fraîche line.

4 **Studio Line :** Brand positioning study. Creation of the FX label and decor.

5 **Castorama :** Image evolution conveyed via new POS and catalog design for kitchen and bath.

6 **Loulou Blue :** Package design and POS for Cacharel created in synergy with the J.B. Mondino film commercial.

7 **Rémy Martin :** Worldwide sales drive tacking into account international market standards.

8 **Orlane Solaire :** Concept created for the ad campaign, point of sale display and advertising / promotional strategy.

9 **Cross :** European market penetration strategy for the American leader.

10 **Irish Brewing :** Brand and decor design created for Pure n° 1 beer.

environmental design

ARCHITECTURE INTERIOR AND EXTERIOR

SIGNAGE

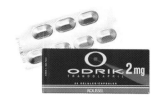

DRAGON ROUGE

KEY PEOPLE

PIERRE CAZAUX
Co-Chairman

PATRICK VEYSSIÈRE
Co-Chairman

GEORGES OLIVEREAU
*Managing and
Creative Director*

MARC CHALVIDAL
Associate Director

CHRISTIAN DE BERGH
Associate Director

COMPANY PROFILE

APPROACH - Environmental design demonstrates strong potential and is instrumental towards triggering brand awareness and establishing notoriety, thus increasing traffic flow and commercial activity.

Environmental design programmes require :

- The ability to assess points of sale with a good background in merchandising mechanisms.
- Strong creative solutions.
- Highly developed technical know-how.
- Permanent cost control.
- Retail experience.
- On the scene action leading to turnkey delivery of animated sites.

AREAS OF EXPERTISE - Environmental design covers a variety of areas :

- Signage for retail networks
- Signage and site planning
- Retail space design

Dragon Rouge is fully equipped to handle global intervention, from concept to distribution of that concept over a network.

PRINCIPAL CLIENTS

Renault

Total

La Poste

Yves Rocher

Groupe SCIC

Midas

Auchan

Nestlé

Pompes Funèbres
Générales

Kodak

Caroll
(Groupe André)

Lacoste
(Montaigne diffusion)

Marcelle Griffon
(Groupe Poch)

Serjent Major

Darjelling
(Chantelle)

Hypersanté
(Groupe Leduff)

DRAGON ROUGE
32 rue Pagès
92153 Suresnes Cedex
Tel. : 33 (0) 1 46 97 50 62
Fax : 33 (0) 1 46 97 50 81
E-mail : drweb@dragon rouge.com
www : http://www.dragon rouge.com

PERSONNEL - 110 in Paris, 15 in London.

TURNOVER - 1995 : FF 98 m

COMPANY STRUCTURE - A limited Company, Capital FF 5,250,000. Founded in 1984.

MEMBERSHIP - ADC

CONTACT
CHRISTIAN DE BERGH

Signage for commercial networks

Renault
A full corporate identity and architectural program extending
into all customer, executive and industrial contact points.

Midas
A re-staging of exterior signage of its European service network.

Kodak
Interior and exterior signage program for network
of independent distributors.

Retail environments

Sergent Major
Architectural and merchandising concept.

Caroll
Architectural concept and expansion program of 220 boutiques.

Yves Rocher
Architectural concept for 150m²-area boutiques.

Générale de Restauration
Architectural concept for college cafeterias.

Signage and site fitting-out

La Poste
Signage program for industrial and tertiary sites.

ENVIRONMENTAL DESIGN

GBGM

KEY PEOPLE

GÉRARD MORATILLE
Chairman
Qualifications : ENSAAMA,
ISG, ISM Environmental
Design and Marketing.
Career Background :
Environmental Design
Director, Lonsdale (1976-
1983) ; Environmental
Design Director, Design
Strategy (1984-1989),
founded GBGM with
Gérard Barrau in 1990.

MARIE-CLAUDE MORAZZINI
*Director, Communications
Department*
Qualifications : Institute of
Public Relations.
Masters in Psychology.
Career Background :
Joined GBGM in 1990.

COMPANY PROFILE

APPROACH - In just seven years GBGM has become a true specialist in retail concept and space design. The agency has developed its own methods and tools to produce relevant solutions, corresponding to both market needs and client objectives. GBGM supervises the construction of all his projects.

AREAS OF EXPERTISE - Our role is to perform market analysis, to comprehend corporate needs and structure, assess investment costs, define strategy planning in order to design high-performance, original, efficient space adapted to client positioning and specific markets.

Turnover	in %
Brand Name Creation	**10**
Graphic Design	
Visual Identity	30
Publishing	10
Environmental Design	
Commercial Architecture	40
Signage	10

SECTORS OF ACTIVITY

- Specialized Retail
- Restaurants
- Railway Terminals / Airports
- Industry
- Institutions

NEW BUSINESS IN 1995/96

- Saresco (Duty Free chain store concept, image, identity, design)
- Nota Bene (Store concept, image, identity)
- La Planète des Parfums (Store concept, image, identity)
- Issey Miyake (Merchandising, design of display elements)

PRINCIPAL CLIENTS

Institutions

RATP
(New ticket counter
concept)

SNCF
(Implantation study,
Commercial space,
Visual identity)

Specialized Retail

Parashop
(New store concept,
Visual identity, Signage)

Intersport
(New store concept)

Relais H
(Interior design,
Merchandising, Signage,
Industrialization)

Promo Metro
(Production of
commercial space and
specific concepts)

Process Blue
(Self-serve perfumery
concept, Visual identity,
Image)

Portrex
(Multi-service automat
space design : Dazibao)

Thomas Cook
(New ticket counter
concept)

Laurie
(Concept for specialized
lighting shop)

GBGM
28 rue Broca
75005 Paris
Tel. : 33 (0) 1 44 08 60 61
Fax : 33 (0) 1 44 08 60 89

PERSONNEL - 22

TURNOVER - 1996 estimate : FF 14 m / 1995 : FF 12 m

COMPANY STRUCTURE - A limited company, capital of FF250,000. Founded in 1990.

GROUP AFFILIATION - Group of three firms : Architral, Gérard Barrau SA and GBGM.

CONTACTS

GÉRARD MORATILLE
Chairman
MARIE-CLAUDE MORAZZANI
Director of Communications

Saresco : Duty Free store concept (gastronomy).

Saresco : Duty Free store concept (Wine, Spirits, Tobacco).

Thomas Cook : New foreign exchange desk.

Intersport : Merchandising, store concept.

Nota Bene : Store concept, identity and architecture.

SNCF : Set up proposals
      commercial space: Les Boutiques de Paris Est.

Process Blue : Self service perfume.
      Store concept, identity and architecture.

G B
G M

PDA : Pan european brand

The PDA (Pan european brand Design Association) has been founded in April 1991 as a non-profit professional organization consisting of specialists in packaging design and other visual communication expressions of the corporate image, in order to promote the profession to users, non-users and governments.

At least two times a year a general meeting is organized, each time in a different european country, in order to give the members the possibility to meet and to improve their professional skills and to better understand the profile of the country in which the meeting is organized.

The association draws its inspiration from PDC (Packaging Design Council), its counterpart umbrella organization of the design trade.

PDA, which endeavours to get design recognized as an essentiel tool of marketing strategy, today boasts 150 members.

THE PDA RULES

• provide opportunities for designers to meet and interact with their colleagues, to encourage professional respect among designers, to enable them to exchange information of intra-professional interest,

• set and maintain high standards of ethics and professional pratice,
• make the designer's function known and understood by business management and the general public,
• ensure credit and recognition for the designer's creative efforts,
• define areas of designer's responsibility to clients and consumers,
• maintain liaison with other professional organizations, trade and technical associations,
• offer guidance to design schools and colleges in the training of designers and to help and encourage those who are preparing to enter the field,
• create strong links with the EEC-authorities.

Contact : **Gérard Caron** - France.
Tel : 01 42 94 02 27. Fax : 01 42 94 06 78.

Exchanging experience

P. Dinand - Ateliers Dinand

P. Le Quément - Renault

H. Meyer - Gertsman, Meyer

C. Laroche - Le Bon Marché

L. Wallentin - Nestlé

SCANDINAVIA

S W E D E N

S U È D E

S C H W E D E N

▼

Markus Hillborg

AD på herrtidningen SLITZ. CD på musiktidningen STEREO.
Förutom att göra tidningar är jag bra på att prata.
Föreläsningar? Seminarium?
Ring 08-240 240.

EN PERSONLIG SYN PÅ GRAFISK DESIGN
- I EN BOK

Jeanette Palmqvist Copy
Kari Palmqvist Designer

Studio Bubblan gör grafiska designlösningar för företag, evenemang och utställningar. Vi arbetar manuellt och digitalt med form och ord.

Nu har vi samlat våra erfarenheter i en bok. Vi illustrerar tankar bakom vanliga fackuttryck i området kring grafisk design. Boken ska förhoppningsvis underlätta kommunikationen mellan uppdragsgivare och byrå.

Grafiska designböcker finns redan för den vetgirige. Vår bok är för den som vill veta mer, *utan att egentligen anstränga sig.*

Exemplen är hämtade från vår egen tjugoåriga produktion och ger personliga tolkningar av några viktiga begrepp. Med en humoristisk grundsyn; från julkort till corporate identity. Varje uppdrag kan och måste få ett eget uttryck för att kommunicera.

Beställ boken "OM - en personlig syn på grafisk design" direkt från oss.

Du når oss på telefon: 033 41 44 41,
fax: 033 13 29 68 eller
E-post: bubblan@studiobubblan.boras.se

STUDIO BUBBLAN

Sjunde Villagatan 28   504 54 Borås Sweden
Tel: +46 33 41 44 41   Fax: +46 33 13 29 68
E-mail: bubblan @ studiobubblan .boras .se

A PERSONAL APPROACH TO
GRAPHIC DESIGN - IN A BOOK

Studio Bubblan makes graphic design-solutions for companies, events and exhibitions. We work manually and digitally, with forms and words.

Our experiences are now gathered in a book. The idea is to show the thougths behind words and common terms used in the field of graphic design. It could be seen as a step to ease communication between the bureau and the client. Already existing books about graphic design can be looked at as complicated or small. *Our is neither way.*

By examples from our twenty-years production, we give our personal view to different ideas. With a humourous tuch; from christmas-cards to corporate identity. Every commission should and must, to communicate, have an expression of its own.

Order the book "OM - a personal approach to graphic design" directly from us.

You reach us on phone: +46 33 41 44 41,
fax: +46 33 13 29 68 or
E-mail: bubblan@studiobubblan.boras.se

verksamhetens minsta gemensamma nämnare, centrifugerad, utkristalliserad:
en **S**ymbol

Öga för färg
känsla för form
lyhördhet för nyanser
smak för kontraster
och näsa i blöt

redan eva frestade
och adam åt,
han ville bli klok
macintosh frestar med sitt **Ä**pple
och vi biter,
inte blir vi klokare för det

det ser bara så ut

en strategi

en handlingsplan

en **H**elhet

corporate identity

Phisk

Grøn

DESIGNER ‡ ARTIST ‡ PHOTOGRAPHER

P GRØN
Box 17
S-790 20 Gryxbo
SWEDEN
Tel:46+23-40006,40060
Fax:46+23-40002
e-mail:pgron@p-gron.se

http://www.dalnet.se/~pgron

KRISTIAN RUSSELL
▼ ▼ ▼ ▼ ▼ ▼ ▼ ▼ ▼ ▼ ▼ ▼ ▼ ▼ ▼ ▼ ▼

GHETTO DESIGN
Ateljén, Svartensg. 4
S-116 20 Stockholm
Tel: +46-8-644 4404
Mobil: +46-708-129 294
Fax:+46-8-641 6814

BA (Hons) Graduate active in Sweden since 1995 specialising in Fashion & Newspaper illustration, Music artwork and Advertising

THE DIGITAL GENERATION IN DOWNTOWN TOKYO GO CRAZY DURING THE INTERNATIONAL ARTIST'S VISIT TO JAPAN BY PLUGGING THEIR WALKMANS STRAIGHT INTO THE P.A ..FOR A HYAAAAHHH BETTER NIPPON SOUND HHIAAHH.

KRISTIAN RUSSELL

▼ ▼ ▼ ▼ ▼ ▼ ▼ ▼ ▼ ▼ ▼ ▼ ▼ ▼ ▼ ▼

GHETTO DESIGN
Ateljén, Svartensg. 4
S-116 20 Stockholm
Tel: +46-8-644 4404
Mobil: +46-708-129 294
Fax:+46-8-641 6814

BA (Hons) Graduate active in Sweden since 1995 specialising in Fashion & Newspaper illustration, Music artwork and Advertising

LESS IS MORE

DETONATOR DESIGN GROUP
▼ ▼ ▼ ▼ ▼ ▼ ▼ ▼ ▼ ▼ ▼ ▼ ▼ ▼

Slipgatan 3
S-117 39 Stockholm
Tel: +46 8 629 55 33
Fax: +46 8 98 57 12

Futuristic / minimalistic graphic design
for printed and interactive media.

F+

Själagårdsgatan 8A
111 31 Stockholm
Tel 08-21 31 31
Fax 08-21 00 11

Ricky Tillblad
Designer

Nina Ramsby
Designer

Anna-Zarah Tillblad
Sister

Primal Music®

Primal® SubDivision

AMEN VACUUM
TAKEN FROM THE FORTHCOMING ALBUM "LAKEFRONT"

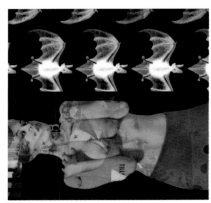 

AMEN LAKEFRONT

CLAES G.

Claes Gustavsson
Fatburs Kvarngata 16 e
S-118 64 Stockholm, Sweden
Tel. +46 [8] 720 36 46

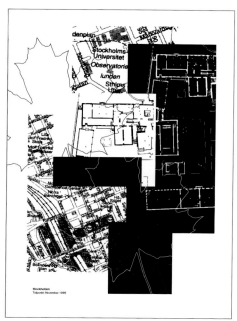

Annual report. Client: Stockholm – Cultural Capital of Europe 1998/Sandler Mergel.

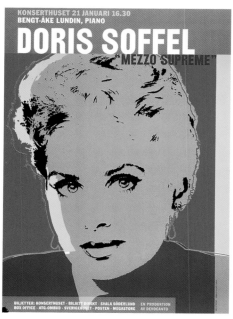
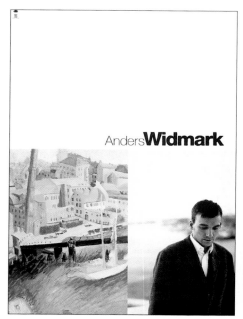
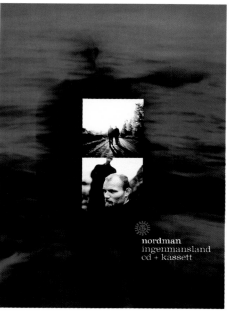

Promotional posters. Clients: Sandler Mergel/DevoCanto, Polar/Stockholm Label Group, Sonet/Stockholm Label Group.

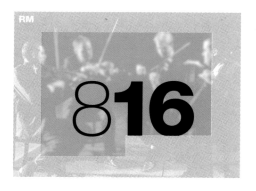

CD-ROM. Yggdrasil String Quartet. Client: Sandler Mergel/Norstedts.

OMNIBUS TYPOGRAFI

Box 135 · S-13523 Tyresö · Svedio / Sweden
Tel. +46 8 742 8336
Fax +46 8 712 3993
franko@omnibus.se · http://www.omnibus.se

Marknadsför samtliga typsnitt tecknade av den svenske typsnittstecknaren Franko Luin.

Läs vad han säger om sitt arbete med bokstäver:

99 När jag skapar egna typsnitt har jag stor frihet att bestämma den enskilda bokstavens karaktär. Men jag är hela tiden bunden till de bokstavsformer som följt oss alltsedan renässansen, och det samtidigt som jag strävar efter att åstadkomma något nytt.

Det är inte lätt. Under mer än 500 år har formgivare jobbat med samma grundformer och strävat efter samma sak. När jag ser resultatet av mitt arbete och jämför det med andra formgivares resultat, är jag benägen att hålla med F. W. Goudy, att 'våra förfäder har knyckt våra bästa idéer'.

Men ändå: det finns alltid detaljer som gör att ett nytt typsnitt, trots att det liknar ett annat, ger ett annorlunda intryck. Vad som till sist räknas är ju helhetsbilden, inte den enskilda bokstaven.

Att återskapa historiska typsnitt, särskilt de allra tidigaste, är en annan sorts utmaning: att med modern teknik återge mer eller mindre kända bokstavsformer, att göra dem tillgängliga för dagens växande skara av typsnittsanvändare. Och även om en bokstavsform redan finns i en eller annan tolkning, finns det alltid utrymme för fler tolkningar.

Det är ju tack vare olika tolkningar av Nicolas Jensons och efterföljares bokstavsformer som vi idag har vårt rika utbud av typsnitt.

Merkatigas la tiparojn, kiujn desegnis la sveda desegnisto Franko Luin.

Legu, kion li mem diras pri sia laboro:

99 *Kiam mi kreas tiparojn, mi povas libere difini la trajtojn de unuopa litero. Sed ne tute libere. Mi ne rajtas tro devii de la konataj formoj de literoj, en uzo de la renesanco aŭ pli frue. Mi ja volas, ke la tekstoj kompostitaj per miaj tiparoj estu legeblaj. Samtempe mi provas krei ion novan, unikan.*

Tio ne estas facila tasko. Dum pli ol 500 jaroj desegnistoj deiris de la samaj formoj kaj celis la samon. Ofte, kiam mi vidas la rezulton de mia laboro kaj komparas ĝin kun la rezultoj de aliaj, mi emas samopinii kiel F.W. Goudy, konata usona desegnisto de tiparoj, ke 'niaj antaŭuloj ŝtelis niajn plej bonajn ideojn'.

Tamen: ĉiam ekzistas detaloj, pro kiuj unu tiparo, eĉ se laŭ unua impreso simila al alia, donas malsaman finrezulton. Kio gravas, estas la aspekto de la tuto, ne la unuopa litero.

Interpreti klasikajn literformojn, precipe la plej fruajn, estas alispeca defio: per moderna tekniko rekrei la malnovajn literojn, tiel ke ili taŭgas por nuntempa komputora uzo. Kaj kvankam iuj historiaj tiparoj jam ekzistas en pluraj versioj, ekzistas ĉiam ebleco vidi ion novan en ili.

Diversaj interpretoj de la literformoj de Nicolas Jenson kaj posteuloj ja signife kontribuis al nia hodiaŭa abundo de tiparoj. Kaj pliaj konstante survojas...

Marketing the whole range of typefaces designed by the Swedish typeface designer Franko Luin.

Read what he says about his work:

99 When I design my own typefaces I am free to determine the details of a particular character. But not totally free, since I must keep track of the character shapes in use since the Rennaissance – and that while I am trying to create something new.

It isn't easy. Typeface designers have been working for 500 years with the same basic shapes and with the same aim. When I see the result of my work and compare it with what other designers have achieved, I am inclined to agree with F. W. Goudy that 'the elders have stolen our best ideas.'

Nevertheless, there are always details by which a new typeface – even when resembling another – leaves a different look. What matters in the end is the overall impression, not the single character.

Recreating historical typefaces, especially the earliest ones, is another kind of challenge: to use modern technology for reproducing more or less known character shapes and make them available for the ever growing number of typeface users. And even if a typeface already exists in one or another rendering, there is always place for some more.

Many designers have tried to improve on the basic design of Nicolas Jenson and his followers. It's thank to them that we can choose among all the typefaces available today.

Brand identity and packaging design solution for
products in the health sector. Client: Friggs (Semper).

Corporate identity programme
which links up 200 individual optician's.
Client: Din optiker.

This new brand identity programme has been made for
a Paris based fashion designer. Client: Marcel Marongiu.

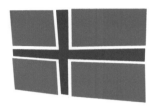

N O R W A Y

N O R V È G E

N O R W E G E N

BRUNO OLDANI

▼▼▼▼▼▼▼▼▼▼▼▼▼

Bruno Oldani Communication & Editorial Design
Photography, Industrial Design
Bygdøy allé 28B N-0265 Oslo, Norway
Phone: +47 22 55 01 26 Fax: +47 22 56 02 01

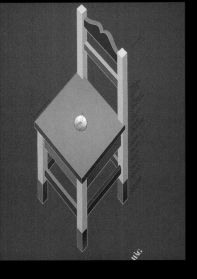

BRUNO OLDANI

▼ ▼ ▼ ▼ ▼ ▼ ▼ ▼ ▼ ▼ ▼ ▼

Bruno Oldani Communication & Editorial Design
Photography, Industrial Design
Bygdøy allé 28B N-0265 Oslo, Norway
Phone: +47 22 55 01 26, Fax: +47 22 56 02 01

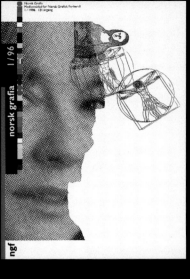

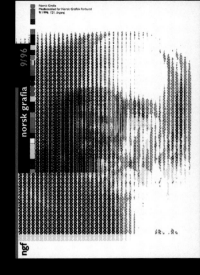

BRUNO OLDANI

▼ ▼ ▼ ▼ ▼ ▼ ▼ ▼ ▼ ▼ ▼ ▼ ▼

Bruno Oldani Communication & Editorial Design
Photography, Industrial Design
Bygdøy allé 28B N-0265 Oslo, Norway
Phone: +47 22 55 01 26 Fax: +47 22 56 02 01

ad Notam

Bruno Oldani Designstudio
Bygdøy Allé 28B
0265 OSLO 2

Nordisk Dirigentkon...

Bergen 20...

Sekretariatet

Postboks 5190, Majorstua

N - 0302 Oslo, Norway

Telefon: + 47 22 46 40 55, linje 430

Telefax: + 47 22 46 36 3...

Bank: 6074 06 411...

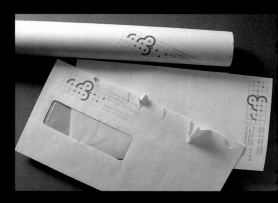

to my Birthday P...

Paris and Cologne...

Invitation to my Birthday Party!

Bruno Oldani
Am Wasser 105
CH-8049 Zürich

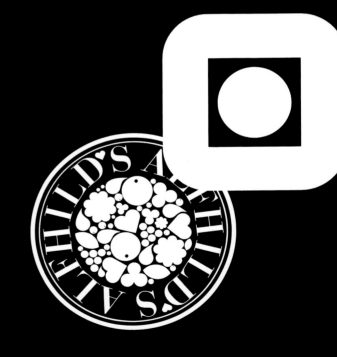

déville design

Medarbeidere

Ellen Rongstad
Partner/Designer
Utdannelse:
School of Visual Arts,
New York

Nippe Pahle
Partner/Designer
Utdannelse:
Westerdal Reklameskole,
Oslo

Stian Bråthen
Partner/Illustratør
Utdannelse:
Westerdal Reklameskole,
Oslo

Jostein Fossnes
Senior Designer
Utdannelse:
Oppegård Videregående

Hanne Dillan Pedersen
Junior Designer
Utdannelse:
Westerdal Reklameskole

Lin Kroken
Prosjektassistent

déville design
Parkveien 62 A
0254 Oslo
Tlf: 22 12 82 50
Fax: 22 55 18 20
e-mail: deville@sn.no

déville design

déville design as ble etablert i 1988, og er idag et av landets 10 ledende designstudioer. Vi er 6 medarbeidere som har bred erfaring med visuell kommunikasjon innen fagområdene grafisk design og illustrasjon. Innovasjon og nytenkning basert på solid erfaring ligger til grunn for våre designløsninger, og vi har markert oss som et av de få retningsgivende studioene i Norge. déville baserer designprosessen på samarbeid og gjensidig kommunikasjon: å sette opp forutsetninger og å definere oppdrag gjøres best i nært samarbeid med kunden. Vårt hovedmål er alltid at resultatet av designprosessen er i tråd med den enkelte kundes behov og forventninger. déville har markert seg sterkt innen kultursektoren og mange av våre designløsninger er belønnet med priser i inn- og utland. Kreativitet, kvalitetsbevissthet og erfaring er krav vi stiller til våre medarbeidere - og som resultat presenterer vi innovative, markedsorienterte designløsninger med et høyt estetisk nivå.

Antall ansatte: 6
Omsetning 1996: 3,5 mill.
Selskapsform: Aksjeselskap

Kundereferanser

Apotekjubileet 1995
Arbeidsmiljøsenteret
Arcus Produkter AS
Aschehoug forlag
Bare Bra Musikk AS
Bokåret 1993
Burson Marsteller
Cappelens forlag
Dagens Bok
De norske Bokklubbene
Hov + Dokka
Høgskolen i Oslo
JBR Reklamebyrå
Kunstindustrimuseet/Alessi
Kunstnernes Hus
Kunstnernes Informasjonskontor
Leo Burnett
Norsk Form
New Media Science
Reuters
Sony Music
Statsbygg
Tiden forlag
Tomten AS
Trondheimsjubileet 1997
Universitetsforlaget
Utenriksdepartementet
Utsmykkingsfondet for
offentlige bygg

P O R T U G A L

P O R T U G A L

P O R T U G A L

▼

COMMUNIQUÉ IS A FAST EXPANDING ANGLO/PORTUGUESE DESIGN GROUP

ESTABLISHED IN 1990 AND BASED IN THE ALGARVE, WITH A NUCLEUS OF SIX

DESIGNERS SUPPORTED BY AN EXPERIENCED PRODUCTION DEPARTMENT.

COLLECTIVELY, THE COMMUNIQUÉ TEAM HAS A WEALTH OF EXPERTISE IN ALL

ASPECTS OF GRAPHIC DESIGN AND MARKETING - FROM CORPORATE IDENTITY,

ADVERTISING AND MULTIMEDIA TO PACKAGING AND PRINT PRODUCTION.

OUR PHILOSOPHY IS THAT DESIGN IS ONLY TRULY EFFECTIVE WHEN

CORRECTLY TARGETED - GREAT EMPHASIS IS THEREFORE PLACED UPON

DETERMINING THE INDIVIDUAL AIMS OF EACH CLIENT AND IDENTIFYING

THEIR SPECIFIC MARKET. CREATIVE VISUAL SOLUTIONS ARE CONSISTENTLY

PRODUCED TO THE HIGHEST OF STANDARDS REFLECTING OUR SCRUPULOUS

ATTENTION TO DETAIL AND COMMITMENT TO EACH AND EVERY COMMISSION.

PRINCIPLE CLIENTS INCLUDE ALTO GOLF & COUNTRY CLUB (MOWLEM)

BOVIS ABROAD · CHAMPAGNE INFORMATIONBÜRO · ESPICHE GOLF · HOTEL

QUINTA DO LAGO · JARDIM VISTA · MCINERNEY · MARRIOTT HOTELS & VACATION

CLUB INTERNATIONAL · MILTOURS · MULTIOPTICAS · PESTANA HOTELS &

RESORTS · PINHEIROS ALTOS · SHERATON PINE CLIFFS · THE VIGIA GROUP

CONTACT EVAN JONES OR ISABEL PEREIRA AT COMMUNIQUÉ DESIGN &

MARKETING · RUA NOVA 3 · LOJA B · BOLIQUEIME · 8100 LOULÉ · PORTUGAL

TELEPHONE 089 366993 · FAX 089 366996 · E-MAIL communique@telepac.pt

THINKING
Creative
+
MARKETING
Targeted
+
DESIGN
Fine
+
PRODUCTION
Quality
=

COMMUNIQUE

The Formula for Success

Homo habilis
design de comunicação lda

Homo habilis
design de comunicação, lda

rua da meditação 48, 3º
4150 porto

telefone / fax 02. 6006416

http://www.imediata.pt/homohabilis

Livro *Prime Time*, 10º Ano - Inglês, **Porto Editora**

Papel de carta, cartão de visita e embalagens de tinta, **Norticor**

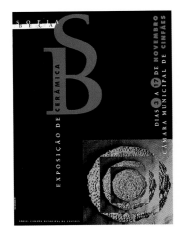

cartazes: Promoção do Bar **Escola de Windsurf** • Exposição de cerâmica de **Sofia Beça** • Promoção do CD *Danças no Tempo*, **Frei Fado d'el Rei**

Pormenor do Logotipo **X Trod** (streetwear)

Desdobrável promocional, **Joaquim Pombal**

Álbum *Danças no Tempo*, **Frei Fado d'el Rei**

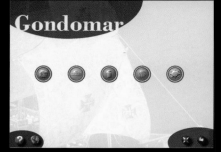

Design dos quiosques interactivos autárquicos de: C. M. de Gondomar (ecran de entrada e eventos culturais) • Associação de Municípios da Terra Quente (turismo)

Design dos quiosques interactivos autárquicos de: C. M. de Matosinhos (ecran concelho e mapa de cidade) • C. M. de Gaia (ecran concelho)

Consola para *Quiosques Camarários Pro*

início | localizar | inform. | ajuda | língua | som

Logotipos: **Adisil** (produtos químicos) • Restaurante **Benditas Proteínas** • Restaurante **Dom Carlos** • **Costafil** (têxteis) • **Escola de Windsurf** (bar/escola) • **Frei Fado d'el Rei**
Globo (Gelados) • **Institut Français de Porto** • **Irla** (construção civil) • **Joaquim Pombal** (azulejaria) • **Libervida** (clínica de repouso) • **Max Plano** (consultoria) • **Norticor** (tintas)
Prit Gest (gestão) • **TZA** (ferragens) • **Viebel** (produtos de beleza)

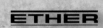

ANTERO FERREIRA DESIGN

ANTERO FERREIRA
DESIGN LIMITADA
RUA DE RORIZ 203
P-4100 PORTO
PORTUGAL (EC)
T +351.2.6104657
F +351.2.6104757

João Machado, Design Lda.

Rua Padre Xavier Coutinho, 125
4150 Porto
Telef. • 6103772/78, Fax • 6103773
nop34278@mail.telepac.pt

Rua do Viriato, 27 – 1°B
1050 Lisboa
Telef. • 3556942

Áreas de actuação Imagem corporativa, Design de 3 dimensões, Design Gráfico: cartazes, folhetos, catálogos, livros, Relatórios e Contas, embalagens, ilustrações, Rótulos, Revistas **Direcção** João Machado **Colaboradores** António Nunes, José António Seixas, Marta Machado, Susana Leão Machado, Ricardo Tadeu Barros **Contacto** Joana Leão

O Rosto da Máscara
Centro Cultural de Belém

Colecção
Asa Literatura

O Palácio da Bolsa
Associação comercial do Porto

O Palácio da Relação e a Cadeia do Porto
IPPAR

Os Irmãos Borges
Banco Fomento Exterior
Banco Borges & Irmão

Corvo – A Ilha da Sabedoria
Jornal da Cultura

Relatório e Contas 1994
Maconde Confecções, SA

Colecção Ciclo de Óperas
Lisboa 94

Fundação de Serralves

Pavilhão Rosa Mota

RTP

Bolsa de Valores do Porto

Rota do Vinho do Porto

Comunicar é preciso

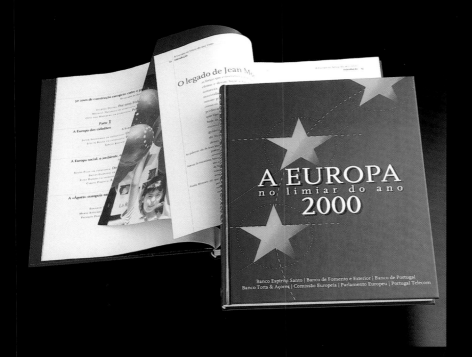

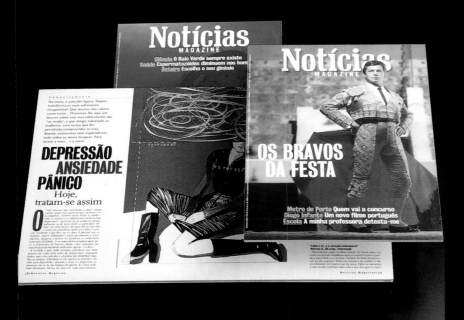

Caixa **ALT**

Caixa
Desenho Gráfico e Publicidad
Rua Américo Durão, 16 B, 1º
1900 L
tel 01-840 21 84 fax 01-84

Para comunicar connosco co
José Cardoso ou Fernando

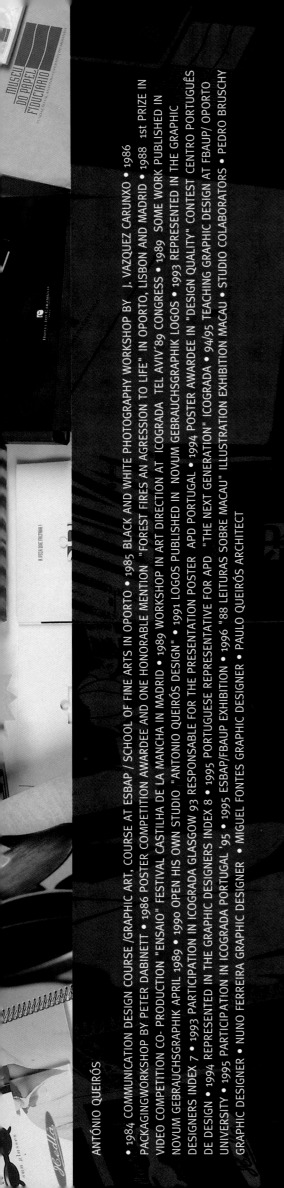

ANTÓNIO QUEIRÓS

• 1984 COMMUNICATION DESIGN COURSE /GRAPHIC ART, COURSE AT ESBAP / SCHOOL OF FINE ARTS IN OPORTO • 1985 BLACK AND WHITE PHOTOGRAPHY WORKSHOP BY J. VAZQUEZ CARUNXO • 1986 PACKAGINGWORKSHOP BY PETER DABINETT • 1986 POSTER COMPETITION AWARDEE AND ONE HONORABLE MENTION "FOREST FIRES AN AGRESSION TO LIFE" IN OPORTO, LISBON AND MADRID • 1988 1st PRIZE IN VIDEO COMPETITION CO- PRODUCTION "ENSAIO" FESTIVAL CASTILHA DE LA MANCHA IN MADRID • 1989 WORKSHOP IN ART DIRECTION AT ICOGRADA TEL AVIV'89 CONGRESS • 1989 SOME WORK PUBLISHED IN NOVUM GEBRAUCHSGRAPHIK APRIL 1989 • 1990 OPEN HIS OWN STUDIO "ANTONIO QUEIRÓS DESIGN" • 1991 LOGOS PUBLISHED IN NOVUM GEBRAUCHSGRAPHIK LOGOS • 1993 REPRESENTED IN THE GRAPHIC DESIGNERS INDEX 7 • 1993 PARTICIPATION IN ICOGRADA GLASGOW 93 RESPONSABLE FOR THE PRESENTATION POSTER APD PORTUGAL • 1994 POSTER AWARDEE IN "DESIGN QUALITY" CONTEST CENTRO PORTUGUÊS DE DESIGN • 1994 REPRESENTED IN THE GRAPHIC DESIGNERS INDEX 8 • 1995 PORTUGUESE REPRESENTATIVE FOR APD "THE NEXT GENERATION" ICOGRADA • 94/95 TEACHING GRAPHIC DESIGN AT FBAUP/ OPORTO UNIVERSITY • 1995 PARTICIPATION IN ICOGRADA PORTUGAL '95 • 1995 ESBAP/FBAUP EXHIBITION • 1996 "88 LEITURAS SOBRE MACAU" ILLUSTRATION EXHIBITION MACAU • STUDIO COLABORATORS • PEDRO BRUSCHY GRAPHIC DESIGNER • NUNO FERREIRA GRAPHIC DESIGNER • MIGUEL FONTES GRAPHIC DESIGNER • PAULO QUEIRÓS ARCHITECT

ANTÓNIOQUEIRÓS DESIGN

Av. Comendador Ferreira de Matos 68 2f · 4450 Matosinhos Portugal · Tel (351 2) 9383525 Fax (351 2) 9383531

MUSEU DO PAPEL FIDUCIÁRIO
Linha Gráfica · Corporate Identity

HOTEL DO CARAMULO
Manual de Identidade · Corporate Identity Manual

HOUSE CAFFE
Linha Gráfica · Corporate Identity

CABELTE
Relatório e Contas · Annual Report

SPGM
Catálogo · Catalogue

RHINO
Linha Gráfica · Corporate Identity

HEDLA
Catálogo · Catalogue

**Business
Innovation
Centre**

Algarve-Huelva

ICOMATRO

*Hospital
Particular
do Algarve*

ATELIER DO SUL

*Esplanada de Sta Maria
8100 Boliqueime, Algarve, Portugal.
Tel: (351) (0)89 366123
Fax: (351) (0)89 366439*

s:	*Specialising in:*	*Especialistas em:*	*Contactos:*
orate:	*Corporate Identity,*	*Imagem Institucional,*	*Design, Imagem:*
9 366123	*Graphic Design,*	*Design Gráfico,*	*Fred Phillips 089 366123*
	Sign Projects,	*Projectos de Sinalização,*	
Projects:	*Corporate Interior Design,*	*Interiores/Exteriores Comerciais,*	*Projectos de Sinalização:*
9 328118	*Point of Sale, Packaging.*	*Ponto de Venda, Embalagem.*	*Célio Portela 089 328118*

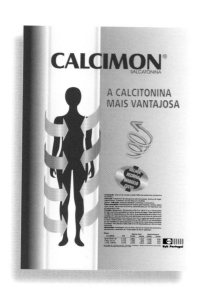

 papeis de escritório
impressão e cópia

CREATIVE INDEX-PORTUGAL'96/97

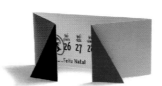

RECORDS

A F I N A L

DESIGN & PUBLICIDADE

RUA CÂNDIDO DE FIGUEIREDO, 78, 2º DTO.

TELEFS. 778 82 81 - 7740311 • FAX 7784036

1 5 0 0 L I S B O A • P O R T U G A L

imagem corporativa
packaging relatórios e contas
brochuras ilustração
sinalização
exposições e stands

SPAIN
ESPAGNE
SPANIEN

▼

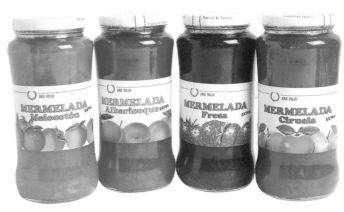

SPOT
AKIMOTO y
MOTORETA G.A.C

SPOT
TRANSPORTES AZKAR
Y AZKAR MODA

EL TRANSPORTE DE MODA

SPOT
COCO ICE
ZAHOR

STUDIO GRAFICO PUBLIBI

Imagen corporativa
Campañas publicitarias
Fotografía e ilustración
Retoque fotográfico

STUDIO GRAFICO PUBLIBI

Pº Zumaburu 14-bajo
20160 Lasarte (Guipúzcoa)
Teléfonos 360206/360207
Fax 36 02 05

DOBLE SENTIDO

Avda. Lehendakari Aguirre, 133
48015 Bilbao
Telf: (94) 476 11 61
Fax: (94) 476 03 94
e-mail: invesco1@sarenet.es

ASESORES DE COMUNICACION

Martín ESCRIBANO
Director

Joseba KANPO
Director Comercial

Mikel DIAZ DE ARGANDOÑA
Director Creativo

Ramón ZUMALABE
Director Arte

BILBAO ESKUALDEKO HILTEGIA
MATADERO COMARCAL DE BILBAO

EUSKADIKO FUTBOL FEDERAKUNDEA
FEDERACION VASCA DE FUTBOL

JEZ
SISTEMAS FERROVIARIOS

ALLIGRAF

DINALAN

INGENIERIA DE SOFTWARE

IRUDI
ESTAMPACION METALICA

GARLOA
ENCUADERNACION

promociones
SOLLUBE S.A.

residencial
LANDETXE

AutoZENTRUM
EDIFICIO RAG

MANAGEMENT ICSA

Txapala
ARTESANIA MEXICANA

Baliak
HIPERMERCADO

AudiCenter

VILLA
MENDIALDE

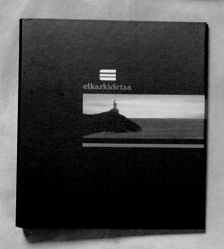

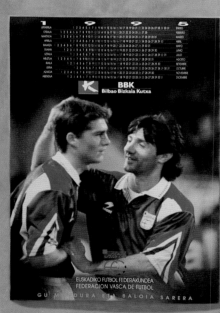

Damos forma
a sus ideas

- *Imágenes Corporativas*
- *Catálogos y Folletos*
- *Cartelería*
- *Campañas Publicitarias*
- *Revistas*
- *Imagen de Congresos*
- *Ilustración*
- *Páginas Web*

1LUNE
Diseño

C/ Marcelo Celayeta, 75 (Edificio IWER)
Tfno.: (948) 14 30 22 / 14 39 80
Fax: (948) 13 32 44
E. mail: ilune@abc.ibernet.com
31014 PAMPLONA (Navarra)

edizioGrafikoa
ZUBIAURRE

S.Klara 40-3.
Tf • Fax: 943-744444
20870 Elgoibar
GIPUZKOA

ZUBIAURRE *edizioGrafikoa* 1990an jaiotako entrepesa dugu, beren helburua preinpresioari dagozkion gaiak lantzea delarik.

Hortarako bereak diren kliente orori, bere experientzia eta baliabideak eskeintzen dio.

Sorkuntza prozesoaren etapa guziak kontrolatzen ditugu, beharrezko ditugun baliabide eta neurri guziak martxan jarriz (argazki erretokeak, liburuak, infografia, irudi korporatiboak...).

Gure klienteak sektore guzietan banatzen dira:

❖ Erakunde ofizialak (Elgoibar, Mutriku, Soraluze ...Udalak).

❖ Mondragon Corporacion Cooperativa. (Fagor, Ideko, Danobat..)

❖ Herramienta-makinaren sektorea (Geminis, Aisiakin, Etxetar...).

❖ Beste Entrepresak (Balzer-Elay, Alura, Elkor, eta abar ....).

❖ Besteak: Kilometroak 96 aren irudia, margo zein argazki erakusketen publizitatea (Oteiza-Ormazabal, Luziano...)

Empresa honetan parte hartzen dugunok:

Luis Z., **Sabela M.**, **Gerardo S.**, **Edurne A.** eta **Allande O.**

■ Calle Luchana, 4 - 3° Izda.
48008 Bilbao
Tel : (94) 416.60.57

■ Servicios de Diseño Gráfico, Diseño
Editorial, Ilustración, Identidad Gráfica
Corporativa y Packaging.

TABIRA
Animation

Microfarma

SORMEN SA CREATIVOS
DISEÑO & IMAGEN

Andalucía, 2. bajo.
Tel.: (945) 27 01 55
Fax.: (945) 27 01 55
P.O. Box. 234
01003 Vitoria Gasteiz

Sormen Creativos, S.A. está formado por un grupo de profesionales del diseño, que lo desarrollan en dos campos diferentes claramente marcados por sus divisiones de:
* División de Diseño Gráfico
* División de Diseño de Museos y Exposiciones.

Comenzó su andadura en el año 1988.
Cuenta con un amplio equipo de personal cualificado que permite la realización de servicios integrales, en estos campos.

EQUIPAMIENTO

Equipamiento informático Macintosh y PC.
Plató y laboratorio fotográfico.
Talleres especializados.

SERVICIOS

DIVISION DE DISEÑO GRAFICO

* Diseño Editorial.
* Diseño Gráfico Empresarial.
* Campañas de Imagen.
* Identidad Corporativa.
* Diseño Páginas Web.
* Facsímiles de Documentos Impresos.

DIVISIÓN DE MUSEOS Y EXPOSICIONES

* Diseño, realización y montaje de instalaciones fijas. Museos.
* Diseño, realización y montaje de espacios efímeros. Exposiciones Temporales.
* Musealización de Patrimonio Monumental.
* Medios Audiovisuales y Multimedia.

HEMOS TRABAJADO PARA

* Gobierno Vasco.
* Diputación Foral de Alava.
* Junta de Extremadura.
* Ayuntamientos de:
  Irún, Santa Pola, Samaniego, Vitoria-Gasteiz, Bergara, Llodio, Salvatierra...
* SMC España,S.A.
* Holtza, S.A.
* URSSA, S.Coop
* Caja Vital Kutxa
* Bodegas:
  Herederos del Marqués de Riscal, Artadi, Remelluri...
* Museos:
  Museo Vasco, Santa Eulalia, Santa Pola, Santa Elena, Quejana, Pipaón, Arqueológico de Alava, Armería de Alava, La Hoya, Iruña, Heráldica Alavesa, Remelluri, entre otros.

PERSONA DE CONTACTO

Cristina Llanos Urrutia.

DIVISION DE DISEÑO GRAFICO

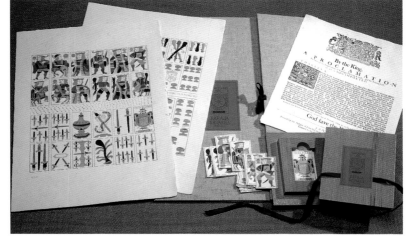

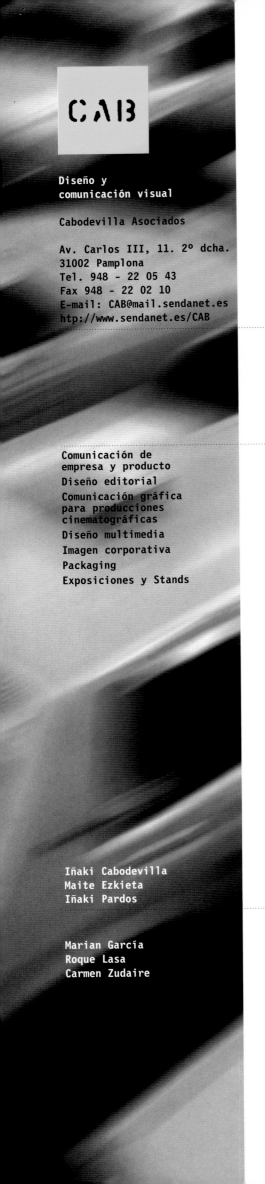

CAB

Diseño y
comunicación visual

Cabodevilla Asociados

Av. Carlos III, 11. 2º dcha.
31002 Pamplona
Tel. 948 - 22 05 43
Fax 948 - 22 02 10
E-mail: CAB@mail.sendanet.es
htp://www.sendanet.es/CAB

Comunicación de
empresa y producto
Diseño editorial
Comunicación gráfica
para producciones
cinematográficas
Diseño multimedia
Imagen corporativa
Packaging
Exposiciones y Stands

Iñaki Cabodevilla
Maite Ezkieta
Iñaki Pardos

Marian García
Roque Lasa
Carmen Zudaire

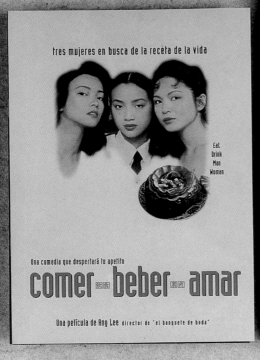

tres mujeres en busca de la receta de la vida

Eat
Drink
Man
Woman

Una comedia que despertará tu apetito

comer beber amar

Una película de Ang Lee director de "el banquete de boda"

JUAN LUIS PANERO

MICHI PANERO   LEOPOLDO M.ª PANERO

Después de tantos años

Una película de Ricardo Franco

MONTAJE: Daniel Cebrián · MEZCLAS DE SONIDO: Patrick Ghislain
MÚSICA: Eva Gancedo · JEFE DE PRODUCCIÓN: Marta Blasco
SONIDO: Gilles Ortion · DIRECTOR DE FOTOGRAFÍA: Gonzalo F. Berridi
PRODUCIDA por Imanol Uribe y Andrés Santana · Dirigida por Ricardo Franco
Una Producción AIETE FILMS y ARIANE FILMS con la participación del I.C.A.A. y Canal + España

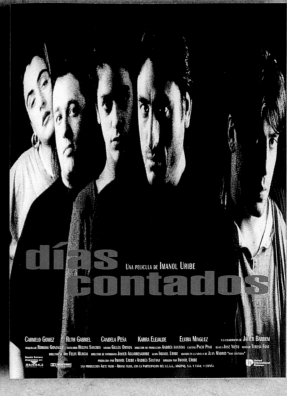

días contados

Una película de IMANOL URIBE

CARMELO GOMEZ   RUTH GABRIEL   CANDELA PEÑA   KARRA ELEJALDE   ELVIRA MINGUEZ   y la colaboración de JAVIER BARDEM

206

Sistema de apertura por clave electrónica de hasta 8 dígitos y cerradura de puntos con llave marca S.T.S. Con cerradura de emergencia y bloqueo electrónico en caso de intento de robo.

208

Sistema de apertura por clave mecánica de 4 discos y cerradura de gorjas con llave de doble paletón.

sobreponer basic

Legislación de las Comunidades Autónomas

Esencial

ARANZADI EDITORIAL

Repertorio Cronológico de Legislación

Imprescindible
en el día a día

ARANZADI EDITORIAL

Fundaciones y
Mecenazgo

Análisis Jurídico - Tributario de la
Ley 30/1994, de 24 de noviembre

ANTONIO MARTÍNEZ
LAFUENTE

ARANZADI
EDITORIAL

Procedimiento de
Elecciones a
Representantes de
Trabajadores y
Funcionarios

Mª José Rodríguez Ramos
Gregorio Pérez Borrego

ARANZADI
EDITORIAL

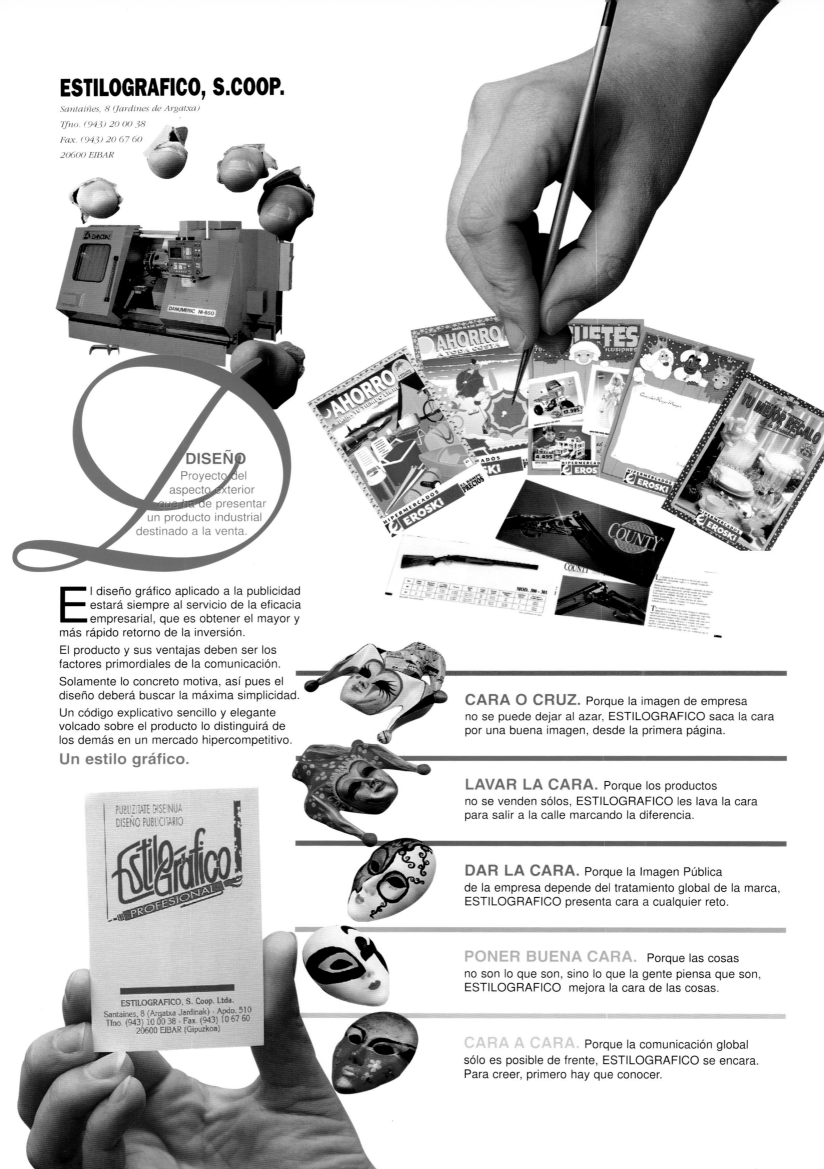

ESTILOGRAFICO, S.COOP.

Santaiñes, 8 (Jardines de Argatxa)
Tfno. (943) 20 00 38
Fax. (943) 20 67 60
20600 EIBAR

DISEÑO
Proyecto del aspecto exterior que ha de presentar un producto industrial destinado a la venta.

El diseño gráfico aplicado a la publicidad estará siempre al servicio de la eficacia empresarial, que es obtener el mayor y más rápido retorno de la inversión.

El producto y sus ventajas deben ser los factores primordiales de la comunicación.

Solamente lo concreto motiva, así pues el diseño deberá buscar la máxima simplicidad.

Un código explicativo sencillo y elegante volcado sobre el producto lo distinguirá de los demás en un mercado hipercompetitivo.

Un estilo gráfico.

CARA O CRUZ. Porque la imagen de empresa no se puede dejar al azar, ESTILOGRAFICO saca la cara por una buena imagen, desde la primera página.

LAVAR LA CARA. Porque los productos no se venden sólos, ESTILOGRAFICO les lava la cara para salir a la calle marcando la diferencia.

DAR LA CARA. Porque la Imagen Pública de la empresa depende del tratamiento global de la marca, ESTILOGRAFICO presenta cara a cualquier reto.

PONER BUENA CARA. Porque las cosas no son lo que son, sino lo que la gente piensa que son, ESTILOGRAFICO mejora la cara de las cosas.

CARA A CARA. Porque la comunicación global sólo es posible de frente, ESTILOGRAFICO se encara. Para creer, primero hay que conocer.

PUBLIZITATE DISEINUA
DISEÑO PUBLICITARIO

EstiloGráfico
PROFESIONAL

ESTILOGRAFICO, S. Coop. Ltda.
Santaines, 8 (Argatxa Jardinak) - Apdo. 510
Tfno. (943) 10 00 38 - Fax. (943) 10 67 60
20600 EIBAR (Gipuzkoa)

RECURSOS

Elementos y medios
que constituyen la
riqueza o la potencia
de una empresa.

La creatividad es el recurso
natural que sólo el ser humano
es capaz de aportar.

Un equipo de profesionales
especializados en comunicación gráfica,
una tecnología acorde con los tiempos
y una esmerada exigencia de calidad,
unificará, evitando la dispersión,
el tono y el estilo con el que deberán
expresarse las marcas
a través del tiempo.

La persecución de un producto
digno y deseado,
por la perfección de su acabado,
será el objetivo a cumplir.

Un estilo de calidad.

**POSIBLEMENTE,
LE INTERESE
CONOCERNOS**

L&Adiseño

luis alonso

ilustración

diseño gráfico

multimedia

infografía

Virgen de Begoña, 10 - Tel./Fax 94 479 04 29 - 48006 BILBAO

HORIXE DISEÑO

Benito Goñi
Javier Unzué

Diseño y comunicación gráfica

Manuel Iribarren, 12-14 bajo
31008 Pamplona • Iruña
Tel.: 948 - 17 27 09
Fax: 948 - 17 17 24

ESPECIALIDADES

Equipo profesional de diseño
con más de veinte años de
experiencia en el campo de la
Comunicación
Identidad corporativa
Diseño gráfico
Diseño editorial
Embases y embalajes

PRINCIPALES CLIENTES

Altuna Hnos.
Caja Pamplona
Editorial Altafaylla
Editorial Txalaparta
Editorial Verbo Divino
Federación Navarra
   de Municipios y Concejos
Gobierno de Navarra

Industrias Lotu
Maison de la Qualité
   Sindicato Vinícola de Burdeos
Mancomunidad de la Comarca
   de Pamplona
Movies Distribution
M. Torres Diseños Industriales
Parlamento de Navarra
Semillas Zulueta

Publicaciones periódicas, diseño de colección editorial...

Catálogos, folletos promocionales, envases...

Logotipos.

CLAM

C/Londres 17 • Bajo izquierda

28028 MADRID

Tel.: (91) 356 01 37

Fax: (91) 356 01 37

SERVICIOS

Agencia de Publicidad
de servicios plenos:

- Publicidad
- Estudios de Mercado
- Spots TV
- Cuñas de Radio
- Imagen Corporativa
- Diseño Gráfico
- Diseño Editorial
- Ilustración
- Packaging

Javier De Lacy Boville

Director Ejecutivo

Santiago Calvo Osorio

Director Creativo

ALGUNOS CLIENTES

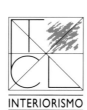

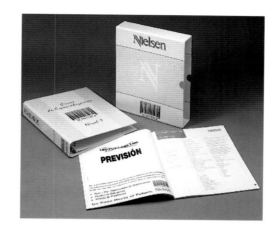

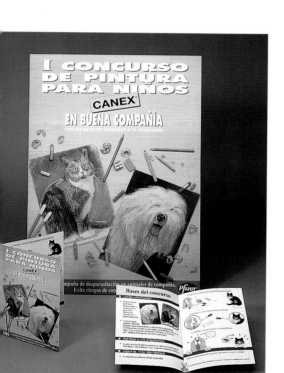

A L T O
CONTRASTE
ESTUDIO GRAFICO

ACTIVIDADES:

RETOQUE DIGITAL COLOR

RETOQUE DIGITAL B/N

DISEÑO GRAFICO

CLIENTES:

ASOCIADOS, EQUIPO 3, EUREKA,

EURO RSCG, LINTAS, McCANN

ERICKSON, RUIZ NICOLI, SLOGAN,

TAPSA, TBWA, SOLUCION, ETC.

CONTACTO:

PEDRO CARRETERO

PABLO RODRIGUEZ

EDUARDO LOPEZ

Cochabamba, 24 - Bajo B

28016 MADRID

Tel/Fax: 458 88 92

SPAIN General Palanca, 42. Atico. 28045 Madrid.   Tel. **91** 528 1207 / 528 3337.   **NYC** 3C

Street. Apli 1022. New York 10024. Tel. **212** 580 5672. E-MAIL 1930f11f@mail.sendanet.es

Trapping

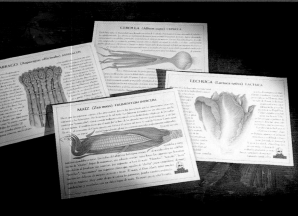

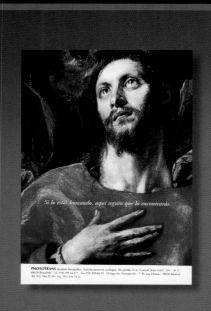

TRAPPING S.L.
Diseño & Comunicación
C/ Zurbano 26-1º Dcha.
28010 Madrid
Telf. y Fax: 310 10 30

DIRECTORES
Carlos Rúa
Gabriel Rivera Bernic

PRINCIPALES CLIENTES
Over MKTG
Grupo Negocios
Diario Negocios
Semanario Dinero
Radio Intereconomía
Naya C.I.S.A.
Todosandwich S.L.
Graphic Meeting
Fondo Formación

Citrícola Garupa s.a.

Over MKTG

92.7 FM Serie Oro

Mercado Nacional de Hacienda

Naya C.I.S.A

Puerta del Sur

Todosandwich S.L.

ANTONIO LAX

DISEÑADOR

Castelló, 38 - 4º D
28001 - Madrid
Tel. (91) 435 71 38
Fax (91) 435 35 97

SERVICIOS

Diseño de Marcas y Logotipos
Programas de Identidad Corporativa
Diseño Editorial
Libros
Memorias
Revistas y Publicaciones Periódicas
Discos
Folletos
Carteles y Vallas
Señalética
Diseño Publicitario
Fotografía e Ilustración
Producción Gráfica

COLABORADORES

Fotografía
Francisco Ontañón
Hervé Tirmarche
Miguel Zavala

Ilustración
José Luis Saura

Multimedia
José Manuel Collazo
Antonio Reina

CLIENTES PRINCIPALES

Renfe
Confederación Española de Cajas de
Ahorros (CECA)
Universidad Pontificia Comillas
Instituto Universitario de Administración
y Dirección de Empresas (ICADE)
I+D Teléfonica Investigación y
Desarrollo
Ayuntamiento de Madrid
Compagnie pour la Communication
(Francia)
Tecnitasa, S.A.
Grupo Santillana
El Pais/Aguilar
Editorial Diaz de Santos
Grupo Anaya

PERSONAS DE CONTACTO

Antonio Lax
José Manuel Collazo

[diseño **editorial**
libros, revistas y publicaciones periódicas]

[diseño **corporativo**]

memorias CECA 95
y su aplicación en **CD-ROM**

[folletos de imagen **CECA** y **TECNITASA** sa]

[**anuarios** para **ICADE**]

[**edición y aplicaciones multimedia**]

[**memoria RENFE 95**
informes económico y de gestión]

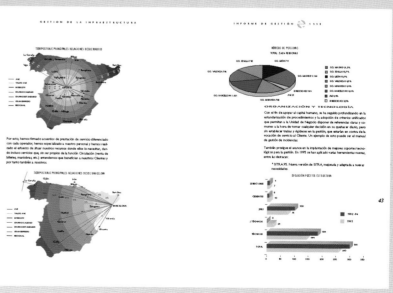

Arké

Glorieta de Bilbao, Nº5,
4º Izda. 28004 Madrid
Tel. 447 68 78 - 26 68
Fax. 447 67 68

arké

Amalia Camacho
Director de Cuentas

José Manuel Noriega
Director de Arte

Gonzalo Aliaga
Director de Producción

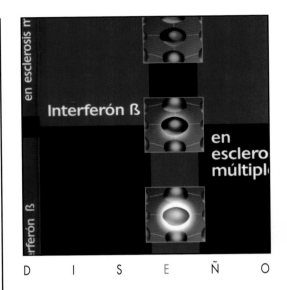

D I S E Ñ O

E D I T O R I A L

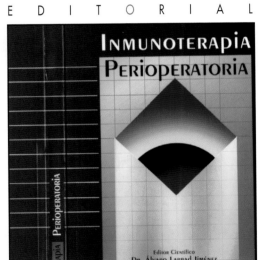

M A R K E T I N G

D I R E C T O

P U B L I C I D A D

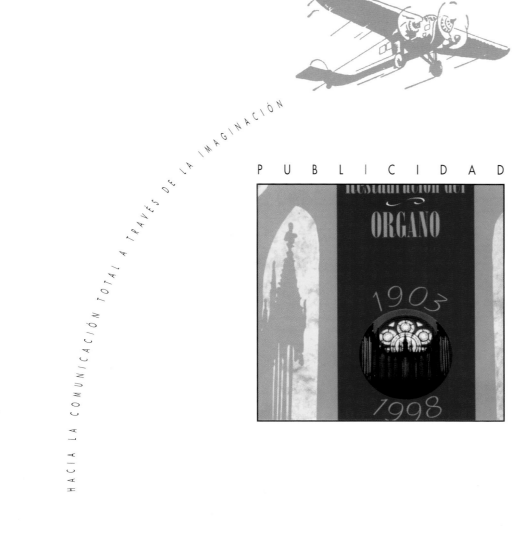

G E N E R A L

I D E N T I D A D   C O R P O R A T I V A

Ilustración

campaña

Packaging

Nuñez de Balboa 49, 6. pta 63. 28001 Madrid
Teléfono: (91) 578 30 47 **Fax:** (91) 578 28 32
Internet: www./readysoft.es/home/customgraphics
E-mail: customgr@readysoft.es

Custom Graphics es una Agencia de Publicidad vanguardista e innovadora, que apuesta por la utilización de los últimos avances tecnológicos y las nuevas tendencias comunicativas.

Su mayor potencial reside en su equipo técnico y creativo formado por profesionales de distintos medios, donde la actualización de conocimientos y la aplicación de estos al servicio del cliente refuerza nuestra competitividad.

Esta apuesta se refleja en la creación de cuatro departamentos interconectados entre sí.

Departamento de Diseño

Departamento de Multimedia

Departamento de Audiovisuales

Departamento de Telemática

La creación de estos departamentos permite a **Custom Graphics** desarrollar en todos los niveles una producción audiovisual y comunicativa, cubriendo internamente cualquier necesidad publicitaria requerida por nuestros clientes.

DIRECTORES Y GERENTES

JOSE CARLOS CEPERO GONZÁLEZ
Director de Arte

VICENTE DELFA MENÉNDEZ
Director Creativo

PERSONA DE CONTACTO

ISABEL HIGUERA. ARROGANTE

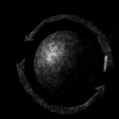

Telemática

Audiovisuales

Multimedia

Diseño

www.readysoft.es/home/customgraphics

DIGRAF

25 años creando

Costa Rica 13. 1°A3
E-28016 Madrid
Tel. (91) 345 15 76
Fax (91) 345 10 44

Personas de contacto: José M. Sáenz Almeida & Santiago Bermejo García

ERIC MILET GRAPHIC DESIGN

Gran Vía, 68 - 3ºG

28013 MADRID / Spain

Tél.: + 34 1-559 72 77 / + 34 08 204 558

Fax.: + 34 1-548 01 17

e-mail: 101622.2444 @ compuserve.com

STRUCTURE

Eric Milet is a free lance graphic designer
who works with a team of designers, sharing
creative ideas, a powerful computer equipment
and an office in the center of Madrid.

SERVICES

Eric Milet offers to his clients corporate
identity design, brand identity design and
graphic design services.
He also offers production follow-up and
quality control.

Brochure cover
Madrid

Corporate identity
for a shopping mall
Barcelona
CO-DESIGNER: Leandro Lattes
AGENCY: Addison España

Visual identity for a
french car exhibition
Madrid

Corporate identity
for a horticultural
company
Madrid

las jaras

Logotype
for a design book
sales company
Madrid

OPEN BOOK

neomoción

Brand identity
for a farmaceutical
laboratory
Mexico
CO-DESIGNER: Jean-François Ricbour
AGENCY: Wolff Olins (Madrid)

ALTIA

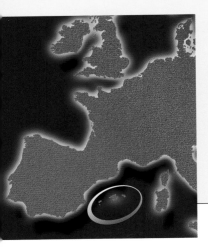

Aquí está su mercado

8 millones de turistas cada año y la renta per cápita más elevada de toda España son dos razones de peso para considerar Baleares como un mercado en el que sus productos y servicios no pueden dejar de triunfar.

Here is your market

8 million visitors every year and the highest income per capita in the whole of Spain are two weighty reasons for considering the Balearic Islands as a market in which your products and services cannot fail to triumph.

Festes des Vermar

Mancomunitat des Raiguer

Antoni Pons Ribas
Dirección Comercial
Sales Director

Alberto Ruiz Vidal
Publicidad
Advertising

Joan Rosselló Borràs
Diseño Gráfico
Graphic Design

Pep Lluís García Reus
Diseño Gráfico
Graphic Design

Raquel Saucedo Muñoz
Infografía
Infography

Cresce Molina Cerrato
Gestión de Medios
Resources Management

Embat librería

QUARS

Quars librería

Aquí, sus vendedores

Estamos convencidos de que la mejor forma de vender es hacer lo necesario para que te compren. Y en eso estamos. En Mallorca, un mercado que conocemos a fondo. Creando, diseñando, editando, planificando y persuadiendo en beneficio de nuestros clientes; optimizando sus inversiones bajo la perspectiva de la comunicación global. Fijando conceptos. Con experiencia y dedicación. Vendiendo, sin ser vendedores.

Here, your salesmen

We are convinced that the best way of selling is to do everything necessary to make them buy your product. And this is our job. In Mallorca, a market which we know in depth. Creating, designing, publishing, planning and persuasive for the benefit of our clients; optimising their investments within the perspective of overall communication. Fixing concepts. With experience and dedication. Selling without being salesmen.

FCS Preimpresión

Institut Balear d'Estadística

COMUNICACIÓ

Publicidad, diseño gráfico y edición
Publicity, graphic design and publishing

Antoni Torrandell, 17 . 07350 Binissalem . Illes Balears
Teléfono 34 71 **870348** . Fax 34 71 870591 . e-mail: di7@stnet.es

Terra Consultors

**Consorci per al Desenvolupament
Econòmic del Raiguer. CDER**

Logotipo y campaña de publicidad
Folletos, cartel, prensa, radio, TV, exterior

*Logo and publicity campaign
Brochures, poster, press, radio, TV, hoardings*

Govern Balear. CDER

Baleares from Europe
Promoción Baleares y calzado balear

*The Balearic Islands from Europe
Balearic islands and Footwear Promotion*

Fundació "la Caixa"

Exposición CUBA SIGLO XX
Folleto, cartel, banderola, indicadores

*Exhibition: CUBA XXTH CENTURY
Brochure, poster, banners, notice boards*

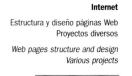

Eurocarnavales

Catálogos fotográficos
Navidad y otros

*Photographic catalogues
Christmas and others*

Internet

Estructura y diseño páginas Web
Proyectos diversos

*Web pages structure and design
Various projects*

ParcBIT

Govern Balear

ParcBit. Baleares Innovación Tecnológica

ParcBit. Balearic Innovative Technology

MIXIC
Imagen & Comunicación
Mix Technologies, S.L.

Miguel Santandreu Nº 4, 2º i
07006 Palma de Mallorca, Baleares
Tel: 971-77 07 10 Fax: 971-77 12 64
e-mail: mixtecno.@mail.sendanet.es

Salomón Serruya
Director creativo

Lourdes Torres
Servicios al cliente

Xesca Rabell
Medios

Fecha de creación
Enero 1992

Filosofía de la Compañía
Creatividad y servicio. Nuestro sistema de trabajo se fundamenta en una gran implicación con nuestros clientes, proporcionándoles un amplio soporte tanto a nivel de asesoría como de creación y producción en todo lo referente a su imagen y comunicación, actuando como lo haría un departamento propio. Trabajamos con clientes locales y a nivel nacional, utilizamos los medios más avanzados contando con un plantel de excelentes colaboradores en Madrid y Barcelona.

Orientación
Empresas exportadoras, de ámbito nacional e internacional.

Especialidad
Estrategias de comunicación
Diseño gráfico publicitario
Imagen corporativa
Decoración de stands
Asesoría de imagen

Clientes Principales
Calzados Bestard
Calzados Coll
Casino Gran Madrid
Gran Casino de Ceuta
Hoteles Fiesta
Veletto Shoes

Mercados Principales
Español y Europeo

Personas a contactar
Lourdes Torres
Salomón Serruya

Casino Gran Madrid

UNA NUEVA GENERACION COLL A NEW GENERATION

COLL

COLECCIÓN

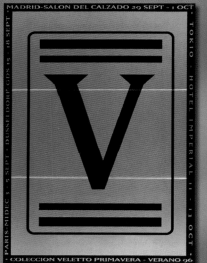

V

MADRID-SALON DEL CALZADO 29 SEPT - 1 OCT

COLECCION VELETTO PRIMAVERA - VERANO 96

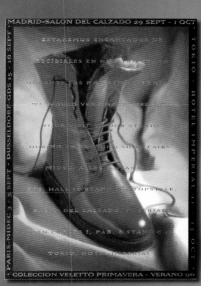

MADRID-SALON DEL CALZADO 29 SEPT - 1 OCT

COLECCION VELETTO PRIMAVERA - VERANO 96

GORE-TEX

Bestard

ALTA MONTAÑA · HIGH MOUNTAIN · HAUTE MONTAGNE

LO AGUANTA TODO.

HASTA DONDE TU QUIERAS
JUSQU'OÙ TU VOUDRAS
GO WHERE YOU WILL

Bestard
MOUNTAIN BOOTS

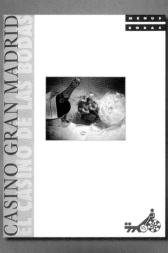

CASINO GRAN MADRID
EL CASINO DE LAS BODAS

MENUS BODAS

CASINO GRAN MADRID
EL CASINO DE LAS BODAS

BODAS Y BANQUETES

Casarse...
Sin duda
uno de los
momentos más
importantes
en la vida.

CASINO GRAN MADRID
EL CASINO DE LAS EMPRESAS

EMPRESAS

El mundo de las
empresas también
tiene su espacio en
el Casino Gran
Madrid.

CASINO GRAN MADRID
EL CASINO DE LAS EMPRESAS

MENUS TRABAJO

Jornadas Gastronómicas de la
Comunidad de Madrid

Casa José
3 DE JUNIO

Jornadas Gastronómicas
de la
Comunidad de Madrid

CHAROLES
28 DE MAYO

La Gastronomía
en el Casino

Jornadas Gastronómicas de la Comunidad de Madrid

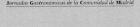

Casino Gran Madrid

CREATIVOS MERCENARIOS

XOSE TEIGA
Director de Arte/Creativo
Joaquín Costa 24-3º
36001 Pontevedra (SPAIN)
Tlf.(986) 862551

ALBERTO VIDAL
Fotógrafo Creativo
Ardán, Moledo 70-A
36912 Marín, Pontevedra (SPAIN)
Tlf.(986) 702817

Teléfono directo de contacto
para España 908/087132

Nuestra especialidad son las campañas publicitarias completas o parciales. El principal objetivo dar servicios creativos auxiliares a Agencias de Publicidad, Estudios de Diseño y Anunciantes, en cualquier lugar de España o del Extranjero.

Damos un servicio haciendo uso de nuestra capacidad creativa multidisciplinar, Campañas completas, Fotografías arriesgadas, Dirección de arte y creativa, Diseño gráfico e Identidad corporativa, son algunos de los trabajos en los que estamos especializados. Somos "Creativos Mercenarios" con el único fín de servir a cualquiera que nos lo demande, en trabajos puntuales o continuos, que necesiten de expertos en creatividad.

CAMPAÑAS

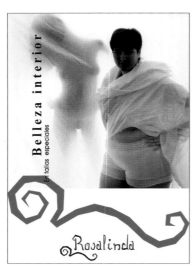 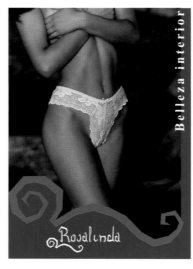 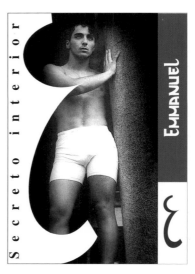

CAMPAÑA PUNTO DE VENTA PARA FIRMA DE ROPA INTERIOR. IDENTIDAD CORPORATIVA, SLOGAN, DIRECCIÓN DE ARTE Y FOTOGRAFÍAS CAMPAÑA.

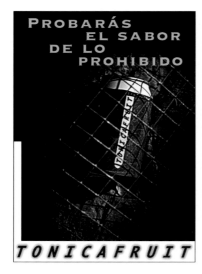 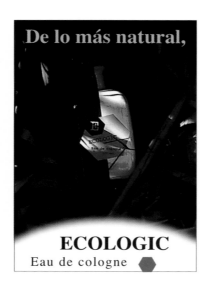 

CAMPAÑAS COMPLETAS PARA DISTINTOS SECTORES: BEBIDAS, COLONIA E INSTITUCIONAL. DIRECCIÓN DE ARTE, SLOGAN Y FOTOGRAFÍA CREATIVA.

IMAGEN CORPORATIVA

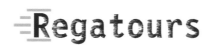  

Desde hace más de una década, ADCV integra a diseñadores gráficos y de producto que tabajamos en el ámbito de la Comunidad Valenciana y que, unidos, buscamos la promoción, la representación y la defensa de nuestros intereses profesionales. Clarificar el concepto de diseño, mejorar y actualizar

ASOCIACIÓN DE DISEÑADORES DE LA COMUNIDAD VALENCIANA

A D C V

nuestra formación y facilitar el contacto entre diseñadores y -como no- entre la profesión y la empresa son algunos de nuestros objetivos. Y en su consecución nos hemos empeñado, hoy por hoy, más de 150 asociados inscritos en ADCV como profesionales, noveles, empresas o colaboradores.

S.VICENTE 35, 4 A - 46002 VALENCIA - TEL. 96/351 00 28 - FAX 96/394 08 42 - E. MAIL: adcv@iglobal.es

NACHO LAVERNIA Y ASOCIADOS
DISEÑO INDUSTRIAL Y GRÁFICO

Del Justicia,1, Entresuelo 2º
46003 Valencia. España.
Tfno. 96- 352 24 22   Fax 96- 352 48 55

DISEÑO DE PRODUCTO

PROGRAMAS DE IDENTIDAD CORPORATIVA

SISTEMAS DE SEÑALIZACIÓN

DISEÑO EDITORIAL

DESARROLLO DEL SISTEMA DE SEÑALIZACIÓN IMACO Y LÍNEA GRÁFICA DE LA EMPRESA. CLIENTE: **LOGOPOST.**

DISEÑO DE BOTELLA Y ETIQUETAS. CLIENTE: **D'ESPERITS.**

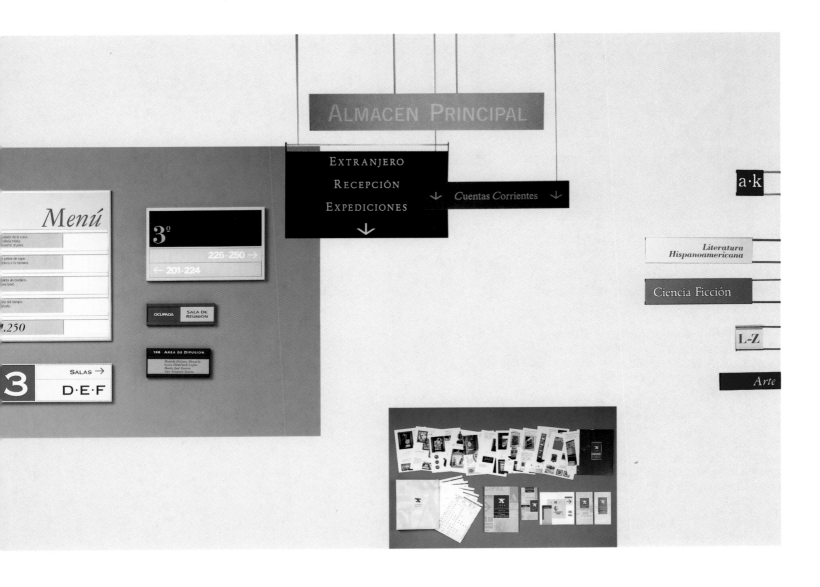

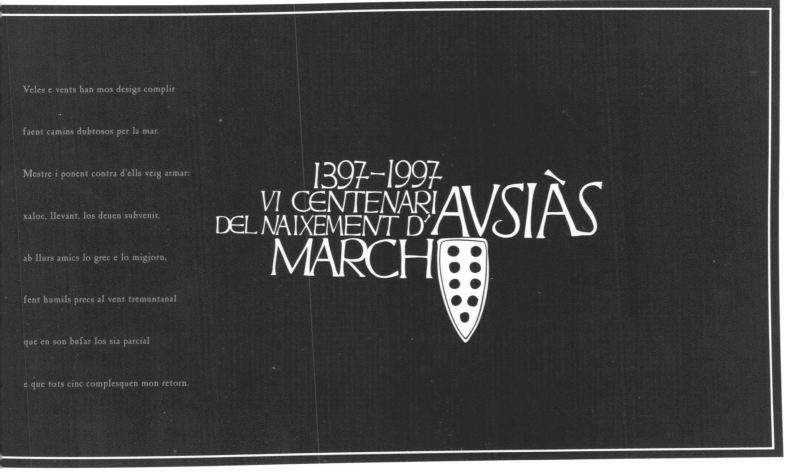

PROGRAMA DE IDENTIDAD GRÁFICA DEL "AÑO AUSIÀS MARCH". CLIENTE: **GENERALITAT VALENCIANA.**

CONCEPTE
&FORMA sl

Plaza del angel, 2 pta. 6
46450 Benifaió
Valencia Spain
TEL. 96 / 178 16 71
FAX 96 / 179 47 13

CONCEPTE & FORMA es un estudio de diseño, con más de quince años de experiencia.

A lo largo de este tiempo ha desarrollado criterios y metodología propia para llevar a cabo proyectos que principalmente se sitúan en el ámbito de las necesidades empresariales y relacionados con la comunicación: Imagen Corporativa, Packaging, Naming, Catálogos, Sales Folders, Product Design, etc., buscando reforzar los valores del producto, sus cuotas de compra y los factores de diferenciación.

Tenemos como norma el **ANÁLISIS** en profundidad, del producto, sus objetivos, estrategias de posicionamiento e impulsión en el mercado. Nuestro trabajo se desarrolla en estrecha colaboración con la empresa hasta alcanzar, conjuntamente, un amplio desarrollo de los conceptos que la empresa desea trasmitir.

Consideramos la **CREATIVIDAD** como la fuerza capaz de impulsar y alcanzar, a través de un exhaustivo proceso de exploración / maquetación, la imagen y expresión innovadora y diferencial, con estilo propio, capaz de estimular la compra de los bienes y servicios de su empresa.

Y por fin, nos valemos de la **EXPERIENCIA** en las técnicas de estampación / reproducción para poder llevar a cabo los proyectos con total precisión y calidad en el resultado final.

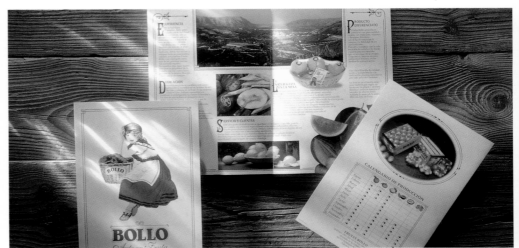

Baiocchi — Crema di Bosco — Ciocchini — Tenerezze — Gemme

Palicao

IL NUOVO PANE
Sette 7 Giorni
INTEGRALE
BUONO TUTTA LA SETTIMANA

MULINO BIANCO
Barilla
Settembrini
con Polpa di Fico

PanBauletto OLIO D'OLIVA — PanBauletto 5 CEREALI — PanBauletto INTEGRALE

MULINO BIANCO
Barilla
Palicao
Meraviglia di Cacao!*
scioglie all'istante

COTA CERO

H.G.BROKERS · Colección Frutos secos · DEPARTAMENTO DE IMAGEN · MONTHAUD LIBROS · AYUNTAMIENTO DE ALICANTE · AULA DE ECOLOGIA · K.SAALFELD

Una amplia experiencia en el diseño gráfico, introduce a Cota Cero en el mundo de la comunicación.
Más de diez años avalan ya esta trayectoria cargada de interesantes proyectos de comunicación en los que un meticuloso estudio de todos los factores que influyen en cada trabajo, convierten el diseño y la creatividad más en una ciencia que en un arte.

En los últimos años, Cota Cero se ha dotado de los más innovadores sistemas informáticos y de un importante equipo de profesionales que confieren a cada trabajo la calidad y funcionalidad máxima.

Imagen corporativa, publicidad, diseño editorial y diseño de espacios, conforman las 4 áreas principales de trabajo

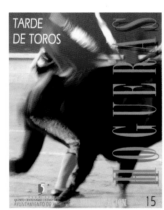

Calle San Fernando, 55 - entlo. izqda. 03001 Alicante Telf. (96) 520 72 37 Fax (96) 520 62 54 e.mail: cotacero@ctv.es

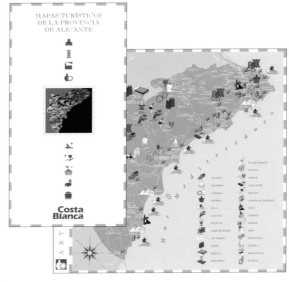

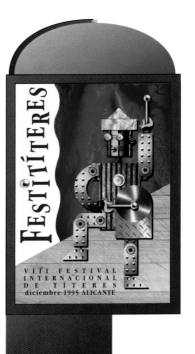

equipo guía s.l.

Avda. de Alcoy, Nº 3
Tel.: 96 • 563 46 25 • 563 42 84
Fax: 96 • 563 63 73
03560 Campello (Alicante)

Si Ud. es de los que aparte de

trabajar con gente buena, le gusta

formar equipo con buena gente.

Esta es su agencia.

Ante niveles de calidad profesional,

oficio y experiencia similares. La

única diferencia que existe entre

un equipo y otro está en las

personas que lo integran.

"Su forma de ser y hacer".

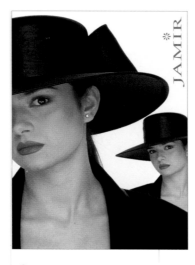

● Publicidad Gráfica. Campañas Revistas Gran Público.

● Catalogo Forlasa

● Catalogo Pompadour

● Ilustraciones Técnicas: Aplicadas a un Poster de Promoción.
Jardinerias Huerto del Cura.

● Packaging Forlasa:
Presentación Nuevo Producto
"Tiramisú"

● Packaging Forlasa:
Lanzamiento Queso Fresco
"Forlafres"

● Expositor Hi-Tec.

TE QUIERO VIDA

PATROCINADORES
FUNDACION OSO DE ASTURIAS

● Publicidad Exterior. Vallas Hi-Tec.

ACCION

COMPAÑIA DE SERVICIOS DE PUBLICIDAD, S.L.

Asociación de Galerias y Salas de Arte
de la Comunidad Valenciana

ASOCIACION DE EMPRESARIOS DE CERAMICA Y REGALO DE VALENCIA

En activo desde 1989

Somos partidarios de la teoría del
posicionamiento y buscamos la calidad
objetivo de producto o servicios, incorporando
en su planificación las características que
gustan al cliente.

Servicios

Desarrollamos todo el ámbito que envuelve el diseño gráfico.

◆ Imagen corporativa.
◆ Packaging.
◆ Edición gráfica (Catálogos, folletos, etc.)
◆ Comunicación de empresas y productos.

Staff

Dirección: Juan Carlos Romero Perez.
Dirección de arte: Juan Ramón Medina Tapia.
Estudio: Ana Pastor Cantizano.
          Conchita Pilar Sánchez Sultan.
Administración y medios: Lola Menosi.

C/ Doctor Domack 3, 2º Pta.8
46006 Valencia
Tel.: (96) 334 10 77 / 82.
Fax: (96) 334 10 91

TINTES Y ACABADOS
MEDITERRANEO, S.L.

Juan Carlos Romero Juan Ramón Medina

Desarrollo promocional.
CLIENTE: SWAROVSKI ILUMINACIÓN.

Envío de presentación de marca
CLIENTE: PULL'S TRAFFIC

Desarrollo Corporativo.
CLIENTE: ANTARES/PORSCHE

Muestrario CLIENTE: YARNS CORPORACIÓN S.A.

Envase y presentación CLIENTE: MUNDITIENDA

 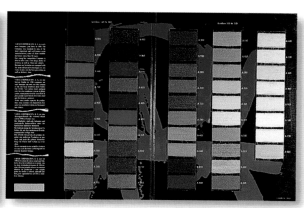

ALCOGRAF

FORM/PLAST

■ ALMANSEÑA COMERCIAL GRAFICA,S.L.
AVDA. DE AYORA, 26
02640 ALMANSA-ALBACETE
TEL:967-340611
FAX:967-340344

■ DISEÑO Y PRODUCCION DE ELEMENTOS
PARA LA PRESENTACION DEL PRODUCTO
EN EL PUNTO DE VENTA.

■ PERSONA DE CONTACTO:
        SOLEDAD CUESTA AVILA

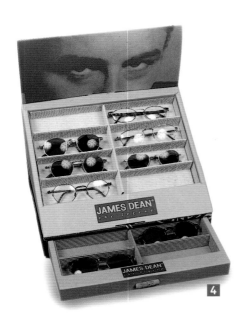

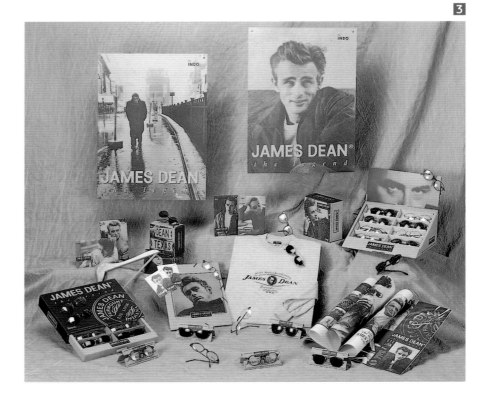

PACKAGING Y PLV EN **1**
CARTON ONDULADO

PACKAGING Y PLV EN **2**
CARTON Y RAFIA

DESARROLLO DE PLV EN **3**
CARTON RECICLADO

EXPOSITOR EN CARTON **4**
RECICLADO

ESTUCHES Y BOLSA EN **5**
CARTON Y PAPEL

KJ PACKAGING, S. L.

Packaging de diseño
Pl. Ramón Contreras Mongrell, 8 bajos
Tel.: (96) 365 56 78
Fax: (96) 365 57 01
46019 VALENCIA

Jorge Fco. Albors Gisbert
Gerente

Javier Ferragut Aguilar
Comercialización de producto

Salvador Just Cifres
Producción

Carlos Calero Trimiño
Creatividad y desarrollo

Emilio Bernáldez Ramos
Fotógrafo

PERSONAL
Número de empleados 12

FECHA DE CREACIÓN
Abril 1993

FILOSOFÍA DE LA EMPRESA
Hemos creado KJ PACKAGING, S. L.,
poniendo a su disposición una serie
de servicios auxiliares en la elaboración
de productos relacionados con el campo del
packaging: elaboración, creación y diseño,
para la presentación y promoción en sectores
diversos.

Nuestra línea está centrada en la utilización
de materiales tan novedosos como
polipropileno (laminado y microcanal),
axpet, vivak, etc., complementando
los diversos soportes papeleros y plásticos
existentes en el mercado, (papeles y cartones
especiales, PVC, vinilos, etc.).

ESPECIALIDAD Y SERVICIOS
Creatividad y diseño
I+D (Investigación y desarrollo)
Serigrafía convencional y UVI
Termoestampación
Troquelado
Soldadura por ultrasonidos
Acabados especiales
Logística

EQUIPAMIENTO
Entorno PC
Entorno Macintosh

PERSONAS A CONTACTAR
Javier Ferragut Aguilar
Jorge Fco. Albors Gisbert

E de P

imagen y producción gráfica

Folgueroles, 15 bajos 2ª
08022 Barcelona
Tel. 212 45 63
Fax 418 26 48
e-mail: edep@seker.es
web:http://bbs.seker/~edep.es

Estudio de diseño gráfico-publicitario creado en 1990 para dar servicios creativos, abarcando todas las etapas que van desde la creación y desarrollo gráfico de elementos promocionales, hasta la producción final de cada uno de ellos.

PRINCIPALES CLIENTES

Ander's, Blanco y Negro, Dasler, Chefaro Española, EBA España, El Mundo, Greenflex, Grimani, Hugo Dax, Inver Money, Lafuente, Mattel, Massís Quer, Max Music, Nani Marquina, RACC, Ramondin, Sodexho, TCP, UPC, Valira...

Eduardo de Pfaff
Dirección Creativa

Max Altés
Diseño Gráfico

Juan Francisco Martorell
Dirección de Arte

Elena de Pfaff
Departamento Comercial

César Martínez
Diseño Gráfico

Angels Alum
Departamento Comercial

CR@ZY

www.adv.es/crazy

La Segunda Guerra Mundial	
Catálogo Merlin Gerin	
Demo Montytronic	
Presentación Hotel Estela	
Ara Lleida	
Woman de Margaret Astor	

MULTIMEDIA
- **Catalogos Digitales**
- **Presentaciones de Productos**
- **Puntos de Información Interactivos en el punto de venta**
- **Convenciones**

WEB
- **Creación de Páginas**
- **Conexiones**
- **Asesoramiento**

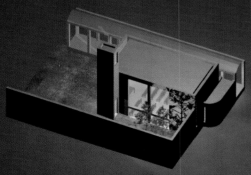

2D/3D
- **Modelado y Rendering de Proyectos Arquitectónicos**
- **Infografía**
- **Animación**

Rambla Catalunya, 120. ent. Tel. (93) 415 67 25 Fax (93) 237 82 65 - 08008 Barcelona

SERVICIOS MULTIMEDIA

ESTUDIO FEELING. S.L.

Troneta, 20 2º
03203 ELCHE (Alicante) SPAIN
Tel. (96) 542 48 26
Fax. (96) 545 90 44

ACTIVIDADES:

Diseño Gráfico
Packaging
Imagen Corporativa
Diseño de Producto
Publicidad

PRINCIPALES CLIENTES:

Gorila   Le Freak
Worker's   Agbar

PERSONA DE CONTACTO:

Antonio Mora

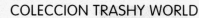

COLECCION TRASHY WORLD

Catalogo

Serie Recycle

Proyecto La Caixa

PACKAGING SLUP'S

STATIONERY PARA EL GRUPO AGBAR

CAMPAÑA ESCOLAR AGBAR

Feel iNG

ESTUDIO FACHADAS

STAND ECOMED

PARA EL GRUPO ABGAR

PACKAGING Y DISPLAYS
PARA GORILA

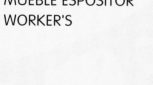

DISPLAYS WORKER'S

ESTUDIO PARA
MUEBLE ESPOSITOR
WORKER'S

IMAGEN GLOBAL PARA LE FREAK

Zona de Comunicació

▌Creatividad en sus objetivos de comunicación.

El producto o la empresa es lo que comunican, lo que

transmiten. Por eso, transmitir una buena imagen es el

principio de la venta y, por tanto, la demostración de una

creatividad eficaz

Publicidad

D D i s se ñ e o ñ o

Marketing Directo   Marketing Directo

Multimedia
Multimedia

Personas de contacto

Jacint Lluch

Màrius Sala

Joan Cardosa

Gran Via 640 1er 1a
08007 BARCELONA
TEL: 34 - 3 - 4 123 567
FAX: 34 - 3 - 412 71 06

@
E-mail: zona.com@bcn.servicom.es

TV

Publicidad

Hermes Editorial

Lanzamiento "Guías de Salud"

Creative Index

Campaña para inserción de obras
en la guía de la creatividad española

Marketing Directo

CAMPAÑA GLOBAL

Grupo Cirsa

Presentación del centro de hidroterapia Azalea

Coissa - Grupo Volkswagen

Lanzamiento seguro "TodoHogar"

Comunicación Integral

MAILING

CTC, Cable i Televisió de Catalunya

Diseño de la imagen corporativa
y lanzamiento de los servicios de TV por cable

Multimedia

CD-ROM

INTERNET

CTC

Diseño y creación de la Web corporativa
para difusión de los servicios
avanzados de cable.

SENSILIS

Demo en CD-Rom para presentación de la empresa
y su gama de productos cosméticos.

Ilustración

DAVID RUIZ + COMPANY
Enric Granados 135, 2ª 1ª
Tel. 2181119 / 4160183
Fax. 4160183. 08008 BCN

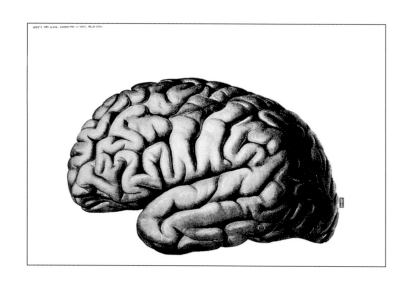

Campaña de
revistas para
Levi's, realizada
con Bassat
Ogilvy & Mather
Barcelona.

Premios
obtenidos:
Grand Clio de
Gráfica y 4 Clios
de oro en San
Francisco, oro en
el Art directors
club de Nueva
York, medalla de
plata en el
festival de Nueva
York, Gran Premio
de gráfica en San
Sebastián, Award
of excellence
Comunication
Arts, león de
bronce en el
festival de
Cannes, selección
The One Show,
finalista Epica,
finalista
Eurobest.

Línea de Packaging
para La Bella Easo,
con Enric Aguilera

Serie de cortinillas para TV Canal Plus

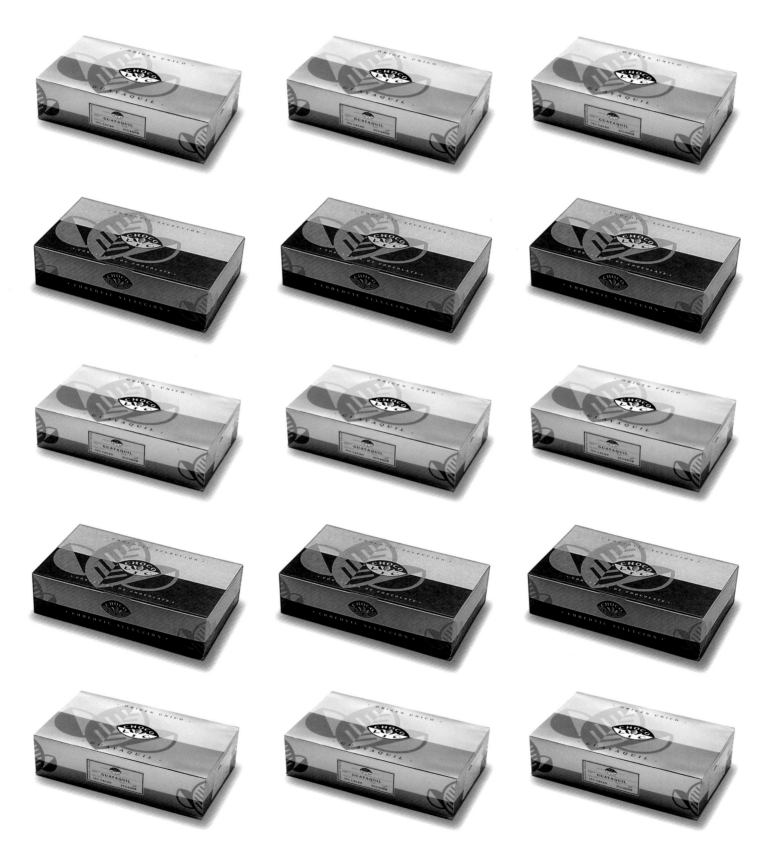

IMAGEN CORPORATIVA - IMAGEN DE PRODUCTO - PACKAGING - COMUNICACIÓN

David Espluga. Dirección de arte, diseño gráfico.
Enric Granados, 135 Ático 1ª. 08008 Barcelona. Tel. (93) 218 74 08 Fax (93) 218 99 71.

Campaña Marketing Directo
Llibreta JOVE TOTAL de Caixa de Catalunya.
Cliente: Cano & Asociados Direct
Dirección creativa: Marc Ros

Turisme d'Andorra. Hivern 95-96.
Cliente: Slogan
Dirección creativa: Rosa Martín / Pablo Burgos-Bosch
Directora de cuentas: Cristina Más de Xaxás
Ejecutiva de cuentas: Vicky García-Nieto

Felicitación Navidad I.G.
Cliente: Iniciativas Gráficas
Laus Bronce 1995

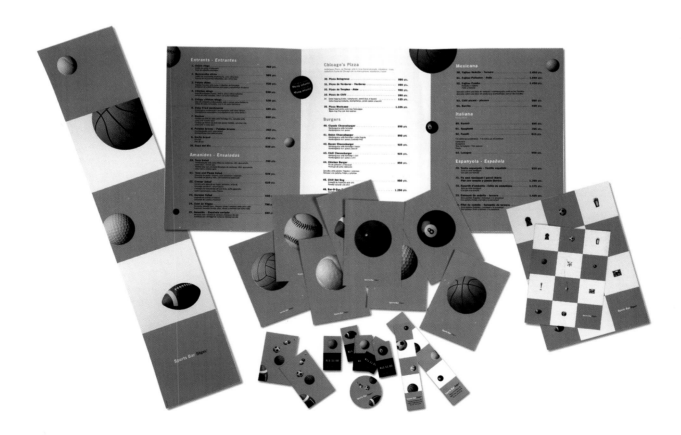

Imágen Gráfica franquicia SPORTS BAR
Cliente: Grup Matas Arnalot
Fotografía: Carlos Suarez

NEXT

Dirección de Arte
Comunicación Publicitaria

DIRECTOR DE ARTE
Norberto Thomas

*Queremos demostrarle de lo
que somos capaces. De hacer
trabajos como éstos, por ejemplo.
Y de tener la confianza de
clientes como éstos, por ejemplo.*
NEXT *es un estudio de
Dirección de Arte que le ofrece
servicios de agencia, eficaces y
creativos, para satisfacer todas
sus necesidades de comunicación
publicitaria, y asegurarle
propuestas ágiles y adecuadas
a su producto, sea cual sea.*

*Tenemos muchos más ejemplos,
llámenos al (93) 487 22 69
y verá de lo que somos capaces.*

Passeig de Gràcia, 62, 3er 2a

08007 Barcelona

Tel. (93) 487 22 69

Fax. (93) 487 21 84

CAMPEONATO DEL MUNDO ATLETISMO
Desarrollo de Imagen Global

PIM & PAM
Imagen y Diseño de Locales

IBERCONSEIL
Desarrollo de Imagen y Aplicaciones

SONY
Diseño Campaña Corporativa

GENERALITAT DE CATALUNYA
Campaña Seguretat Vial

PLAZA & JANES
Diseño Lineas Editoriales e Ilustraciones

SOLSONA & FILLOY • WARNER LAMBERT
Diseño Campaña Relaciones Públicas

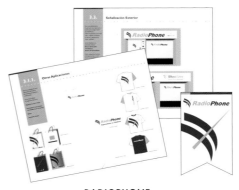

RADIOPHONE
Imagen y Manual Corporativo

C R E A T I V I D A D   •   P U B L I C I D A D   •   D I S E Ñ O

CAIXA DE CATALUNYA

Carteles Oficinas y Campañas Gráficas

OBC

Creatividad y Desarrollo de Campaña

LEVI'S ESPAÑA

Catalogos Generales y Producción Gráfica

CIRSA • BIG FUN, GAS STATION

Desarrollo de Imagen y Comunicación

MUSEO EGIPCIO DE BARCELONA

Desarrollo de Imagen y Aplicaciones

MY KINDA TOWN INGLATERRA

Elementos de Comunicación y Promociones

Dr. MUSIC FESTIVAL

Diseño de Imagen y Merchandising

TELEFÓNICA • MASTER TENNIS

Desarrollo de Imagen Global

INSTITUT DE CULTURA • GREC'96

Creatividad y Desarrollo de Campaña

TIRANT LO BLANC • BALLET

Imagen, Cartel y Comunicación

HEWLETT-PACKARD

Desarrollo de Imagen Interna

FESTIVAL DE SALSA

Carteles y Promoción

G R Á F I C O   •   P R O D U C C I Ó N   •   M U L T I M E D I A   •   I N T E R N E T

22

EIDOLOGIC
COMUNICACIO VISUAL
Av. República Argentina 28
Pral.2ª Esc.Izq.
Tels. 4183289 4182950 Barcelona 08023
Fax. 4340974

SOMOS LOS QUE SOMOS

Xavi Comas, Jordi Comas, Josep Llechà,
Rafa Andrés, Juanjo Avila, David Cabrera,
Caterina Puig, Quim Cuscó.

VENIMOS DE DONDE VENIMOS

Los distintos profesionales que desde 1994
constituimos el equipo de Eidologic, procedemos
del mundo de la comunicación visual. Sin
embargo, cada uno de nosotros posee una
especialidad diferente: Identidad corporativa,
Packaging, Ilustración, Imagen de síntesis 3D,
Tratamiento digital de imagen... De esta forma
podemos ofrecer respuestas globales a nuestros
clientes. Para nosotros, es fundamental el trabajo
en equipo y el seguimiento de todo el proceso
de creación para ofrecer un producto final
innovador y eficaz.

HACEMOS LO QUE HACEMOS

La gran diversidad de disciplinas que se dan cita
en Eidologic, sumada a todos nuestros medios
tecnológicos, nos permite ofrecer la producción
global de un producto gráfico, desde la creación
de un concepto al arte final.

TRABAJAMOS PARA QUIEN TRABAJAMOS

Chupa Chups, De Jongh, Max Music, Banc
Sabadell, Roca, Shell, Repsol, Ofita, Seat,
Aeronáutica y Automoción, Internacional de
Composites, Ajuntament de Barcelona, Ola,
Astilleros, FCC, Cubiertas y Mzov, Scacs de
Publicitat, A.B.M. ...

PERSONAS DE CONTACTO

David Cabrera, Xavi Comas.

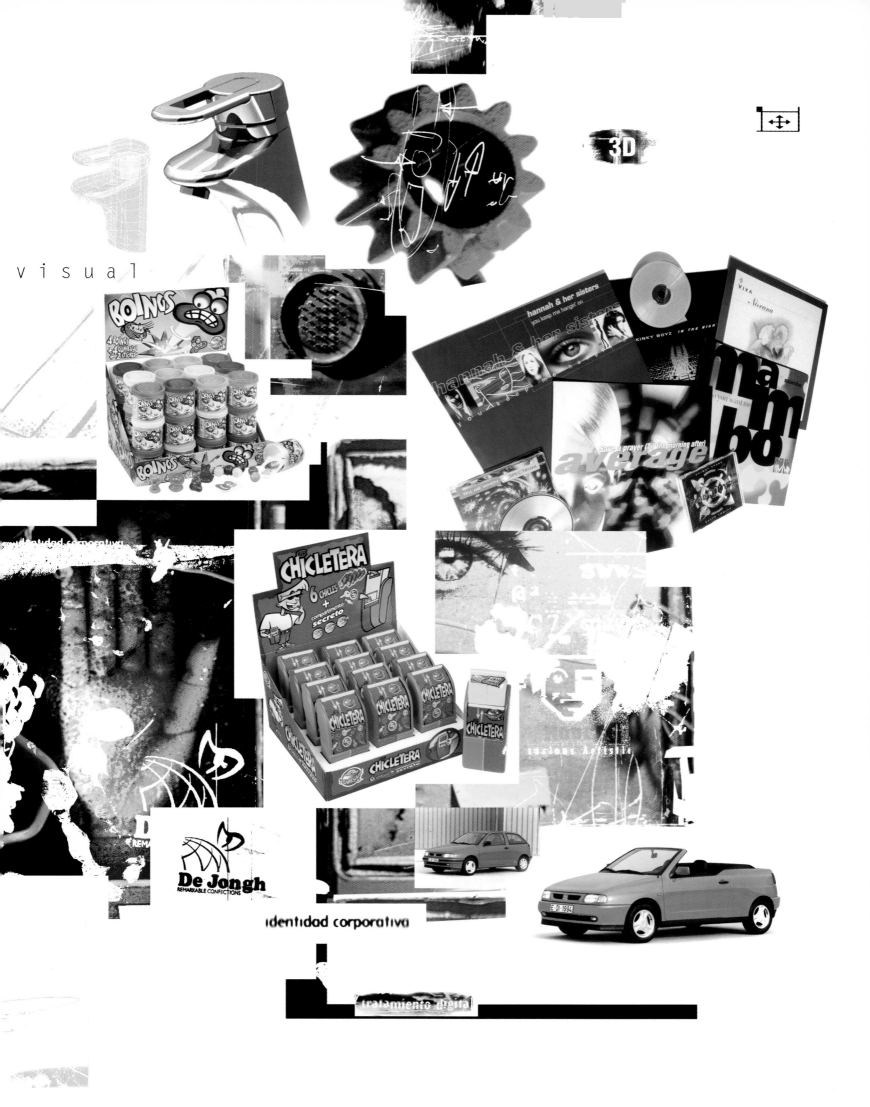

COMPAÑIA de
ACTOS SINGULARES

1.

Frankie 2.

3.

4.

Móbile

AUTOMÓVILES CON CONDUCTOR

5.

1. Imagen Integral para una empresa especializada en la organización de eventos.

2. **FRANKIE.** Diseño de alfabeto, realizado con el grupo tipográfico Type-Ø-Tones para FontShop International. *Premio Laus de Plata'92.*

3. **SAT Centre Urbà.** Línea de carteles para la temporada de danza 94-95. *Premi Barcelona 1995 de Grafisme i Comunicació Municipal a Catalunya.*

4. Ilustraciones para opis. Campaña de Navidad 93-94, "Transports Metropolitans de Barcelona" y "Ajuntament de Barcelona". Agencia: *Imagina.*

5. **MÓBILE.** Imagen integral para una empresa de alquiler de automóviles con conductor (Madrid).

6. **MEDIA CULTURE.** Libro que recopila ensayos sobre arte electrónico, editado por Claudia Giannetti (ACC L'Angelot).

7. Cartel "III Curso Internacional de Cerámica Contemporánea", para la Diputación de Pontevedra. *Merit Award CA Communication Arts 94.*

8. **FRANCAR.** Imagen Integral para una ferretería que se caracteriza por el sistema de venta por autoservicio.

9. **GUIA "UNIVERS".** Guía de las actividades que el "Servei d'Activitats Socials de la UPC" ofrece a los estudiantes. Agencia: *Bassat, Ogilvy & Mather.*

Ferreteiros desde 1954

7.

8.

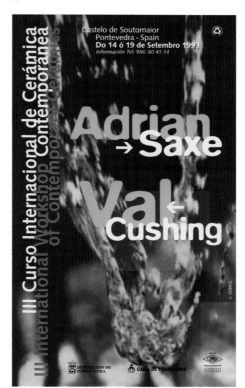

6.

9.

Cosmic se fundó en 1994, a raíz de la asociación de **Juan Dávila** y **Laura Meseguer**; dos profesionales que, actualmente, ya cuentan con diez años de experiencia adquirida como grafistas free-lance y en otras empresas dentro del campo del diseño gráfico y la publicidad. Desde entonces, Cosmic ha realizado numerosos proyectos gráficos en muy diferentes ámbitos: imagen corporativa, carteles, ilustración, publicaciones, catálogos, tipografía, packaging, dirección de arte,... Algunos de ellos han sido premiados, y otros publicados en revistas y anuarios del sector.

COSMIC

Diseño Gráfico
Aribau, 153, 5º A
Teléfono: (93) 410 99 88
Fax: (93) 410 66 02
08036 Barcelona

SIDE-ART

DISSENY GRÀFIC

COMUNICACIÓN VISUAL

DISEÑO GRÁFICO

ILUSTRACIÓN 2D/3D

RETOQUE DIGITAL

CREACIÓN MULTIMEDIA

SIDE-ART, S.L.
Sant Antoni Maria Claret, 24 2n
08037 Barcelona
TEL: 457 20 29
FAX: 459 35 08
E-MAIL: sideart@lix.intercom.es

Camiseta promocional

*Cartel para la serie
"The Smoking Collection"
Foto: Claudio Gibert*

THE SMOKING COLLECTION

At home.   On the road.   On the beach.

In flight.   In the country.   At a concert.

At work.   On the sea.   With friends.

Anywhere.

SMOKING   KING SIZE

The Largest Range on the Market

*Anuncio para
la revista
"High Life"
Holanda*

KING SIZE

GREEN

*Doble página interior de
la revista "Smoking News"
Foto: Francesc Camí*

vídeo
multimedia
sonido

CREATIVE
CREATIVE LABS

SI TE DICEN QUE SIEMPRE ESTÁS
EN OTRA GALAXIA...

CREATIVE
CREATIVE LABS

...CON LA NUEVA 3D BLASTER PCI
LLEGARÁS MÁS LEJOS.

3D BLASTER — **Descubre la última experiencia en juegos en 3D**
• Impulsa el juego en 3 dimensiones a las máximas cotas de emoción y realidad • Permite alta resolución, texturas realistas y sensación de acción en tiempo real • Acelera títulos CGL, Direct-3D, DirectDraw y Speedy 3D • Ofrece prestaciones Super VGA de clase superior.

Mayoristas autorizados: Computernet, Compusel 2000, Ingram Micro, Simmimo, UMD.
Para recibir más información rellenar y enviar este cupón a:
Creative Labs España. Apartado de Correos 38 - 08960 Sant Just Desvern
Nombre ___ Apellidos ___
Dirección ___
Código Postal ___ Población ___

*Campaña de prensa
"Creative Labs" para
revistas de informática*

*Izquierda: Tríptico información
técnica para distribuidores
de "Creative Labs"*

onno comunicación

Sant Antoni Maria Claret, 24, 2º
08037 Barcelona
Tel. 459 35 38 - Fax 459 33 41

Servicios Generales de Comunicación.

Logotipos,
Identidad Corporativa,
Packaging,
Diseño Gràfico,
Diseño Editorial,
Promociones.

Ilustración
Ilustración Digital,
Fotografía y
Retoque Digital.
Animación,
3D.

Libro de Arquitectura. Gerson Castelo Branco (Brasil)

Colección toallas para Disney

Mascotas Purina

A L A I N   B A Ñ O N

Grupo de
Rehabilitación
Cardíaca

(+) Human Care

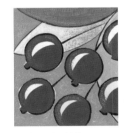 

Ilustraciones Sabores Packs. Laboratorios Fresenius-Mein

Ilustracion digital. Laboratorios Fresenius-Mein

N A D Y A

CLAUDIO
GIBERT
Fotógrafo

Promociones. Laboratorios Fresenius-Mein

Spot Hallo Pizza (Alemania)

ORBYCE

SERVICIOS Y SISTEMAS GRAFICOS, S.A.

Ballester, 27- 29 entlº 1ª
08023 Barcelona
Teléfono 418 74 62
Fax 418 27 97

SSG
SERVICIOS Y
SISTEMAS
GRAFICOS, S.A.

Empresa creada en 1986 por un equipo de profesionales, con amplia experiencia en el sector. Concebida para dar un servicio integral a sus clientes.

Agilidad, dinamismo y seriedad ante todo son cualidades que nos esforzamos en mantener, huyendo de la improvisación y el oportunismo.

Estos planteamientos nos han llevado a crear recientemente una nueva empresa, para poder dar un mejor servicio, si cabe, dedicada en exclusiva a la industria farmacéutica.

IBERO ALEMANA
de Servicios y Contratas, S.L.

NETAC SOCIEDAD LIMITADA

UNIÓ DE
COMERCIANTS
DE LES
ROQUETES
DEL GARRAF

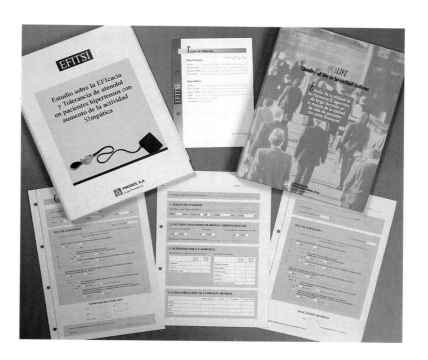

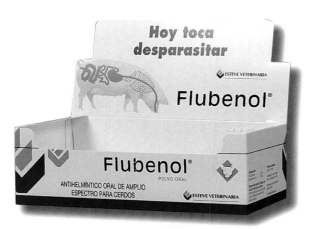

CONSTRUCTIVIST INNOVATION
MONTAGE KITS

R O T A R Y S

Movement · Weightlessness
Silece

M O B I L E

Space · Variable · Dynamic

ESCULTURAS DE VIAJE

ESCULTURAS DE SOBREMESA

REGALOS DE EMPRESA

MODELOS EN EXCLUSIVA

MODELOS SERIADOS

·

TRAVEL SCULPTURES

TABLE SCULPTURES

COMPANY GIFT

EXCLUSIVE MODELS

STANDARD MODELS

ROTARYS Modelo VELA

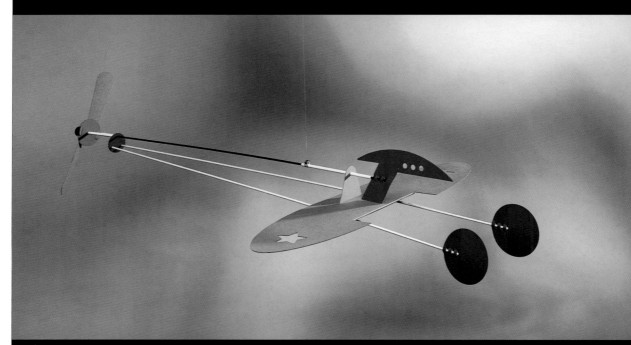

ROTARYS Modelo ASTRA

PEDRAGOSA J.

Creative Director

CARTAGENA, 245 · 3er. B
TEL. (93) 450 19 53
FAX (93) 436 05 97
08025 BARCELONA
SPAIN

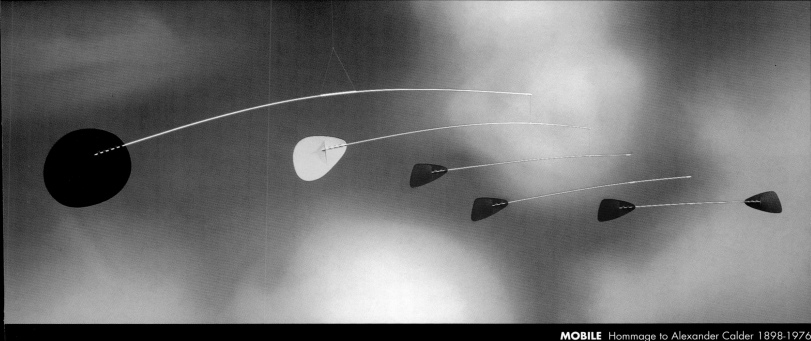

MOBILE Hommage to Alexander Calder 1898-1976

Se

Un momento dulce: el lanzamiento de un producto. Desde el packaging a la campaña. Sobrecitos individuales de Miel Viadiu.

- **Experiencia** en cuentas internacionales, nacionales y locales de muy diversos sectores: Alimentación, Electrónica de consumo, Automoción, Cosmética, Editorial, Electrodomésticos, Hostelería y Turismo, Informática, Institucional, Joyería, Juguetes, Laboratorios farmacéuticos, Maquinaria industrial, Óptica, Productos ecológicos, Textil y Moda.

- **Referencias.** A lo largo de nuestra carrera profesional hemos recibido diferentes premios nacionales e internacionales: Ampe, Euro, Fiap, Laus, Premio Mundial Matsushita, San Sebastián, ...

- **Servicios.** Imagen corporativa. Packaging. R.R.P.P. Estands Ferias. Convenciones. Audiovisuales industriales. Publicidad General: estrategia y desarrollo de campañas. Gran experiencia en creación y realización Spots TV y cine.

- **Principales clientes**
  - Ajuntament de Castellbisbal
  - Akzo
  - Estudio Legal
  - Institut Català de Seguretat Viària de la Generalitat de Catalunya
  - Nutritec
  - Pharmacia & Upjohn
  - Red de Electrodomésticos ELITE
  - Sanofi-Diagnostics Pasteur
  - Viadiu

- **Año de creación.** 1993

- **Personas de contacto.**
  Mireia Sagristà. *Directora.*
  Pilar García. *Directora creativa.*

Soluciones creativas para cualquier producto ... o suma de productos. Imagen Campaña Elitecenter. Red Elite de Electrodomésticos.

acordará de ésta

Cuando cierre este libro seguirá acordándose de esta página.

Memorabilidad y notoriedad, dos instrumentos para la venta. Y ese es nuestro objetivo: vender, aplicando la creatividad bajo la óptica del marketing. Esta sana y eficaz costumbre, adquirida a lo largo de años en multinacionales, sigue ahora acompañándonos en esta agencia de dimensiones y presupuestos a escala humana. Si busca a alguien que defienda la imagen y los objetivos de su empresa con uñas, dientes e imaginación, piense en nosotros.

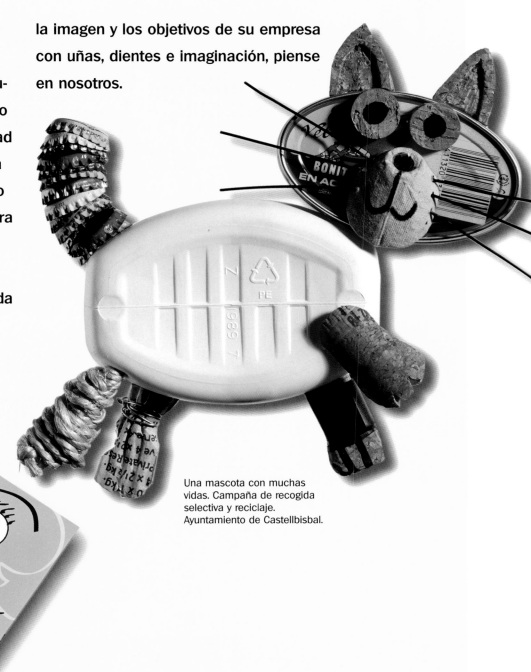

Una mascota con muchas vidas. Campaña de recogida selectiva y reciclaje. Ayuntamiento de Castellbisbal.

El trabajo, mejor con diversión. Tarjetones juego parejas para Congreso Oftalmología. Pharmacia.

sparring ✗ partners

Marketing con gancho

Congost, 21 bis 1º 2ª 08024 BCN Tel. 284 37 00 Fax 284 59 02

Pere Celma & Núria Duran

Ramon Turró, 101, 2n., 1a.
08005 Barcelona
Tel.: (93) 3009184
Fax: (93) 3003728

Equipo de dirección
Pere Celma.
Dirección de Arte y Diseño Gráfico.
Núria Duran.
Dirección de Arte y Diseño Gráfico.

Especialización
Diseño Gráfico y publicitario.
Programas de Identidad Visual Corporativa.
Programas de señalización.
Diseño de exposiciones temporales.
Diseño Editorial.
Packaging.

Filosofía
Ofrecer los mejores resultados y optimizar el diseño
gráfico globalmente. Realizamos estudios y desarrollo
de imagen empresarial, corporativa e institucional,
programas de señalización interior y exterior. Nuestra
larga experiencia en el campo del *packaging* nos
permite asumir el proceso completo de concepción,
diseño y desarrollo del mismo. Elaboramos
publicaciones y nos responsabilizamos de la
producción y control final de la edición.

Clientes Principales
Generalitat de Catalunya
Ajuntament de Barcelona
ICEX Instituto Comercio Exterior de España
Consejo Intertextil Español
IMBASA (Jardino, Bricole, Relax, Fogal)
ESPA group
Fundació Caixa de Pensions "La Caixa"
Col.legi de Periodistes de Catalunya
Col.legi d'Arquitectes de Catalunya
AITPA
Nuprosa
Universitat de Girona
Grupo Europroject
CEP (Centre d'Estudis de Planificació)
Parcs i Jardins
Mapfre
Editorial Planeta
B.J.C.
Boldú Publicitat
Bassat Ogilvy P.C.
Gas Natural, etc...